*Myxocyprinus asiatica.*
Photo by Piednoir Aqua Press.

© 1996 by T.F.H. Publications, Inc.

Distributed in the UNITED STATES to the Pet Trade by T.F.H. Publications, Inc., One T.F.H. Plaza, Neptune City, NJ 07753; distributed in the UNITED STATES to the Bookstore and Library Trade by National Book Network, Inc. 4720 Boston Way, Lanham MD 20706; in CANADA to the Pet Trade by H & L Pet Supplies Inc., 27 Kingston Crescent, Kitchener, Ontario N2B 2T6; Rolf C. Hagen Inc., 3225 Sartelon St. Laurent-Montreal Quebec H4R 1E8; in CANADA to the Book Trade by Vanwell Publishing Ltd., 1 Northrup Crescent, St. Catharines, Ontario L2M 6P5 ; in ENGLAND by T.F.H. Publications, PO Box 15, Waterlooville PO7 6BQ; in AUSTRALIA AND THE SOUTH PACIFIC by T.F.H. (Australia), Pty. Ltd., Box 149, Brookvale 2100 N.S.W., Australia; in NEW ZEALAND by Brooklands Aquarium Ltd. 5 McGiven Drive, New Plymouth, RD1 New Zealand; in Japan by T.F.H. Publications, Japan—Jiro Tsuda, 10-12-3 Ohjidai, Sakura, Chiba 285, Japan; in SOUTH AFRICA by Lopis (Pty) Ltd., P.O. Box 39127, Booysens, 2016, Johannesburg, South Africa. Published by T.F.H. Publications, Inc.

MANUFACTURED IN THE
UNITED STATES OF AMERICA
BY T.F.H. PUBLICATIONS, INC.

# HOW TO HAVE A SUCCESSFUL AQUARIUM

## The T.F.H. Book of Aquarium Science
## Fishes—Water Plants—Water Technology

by

Stephan Dreyer
and
Rainer Keppler

translated by:
U.Erich Friese
General Curator
Sydney Aquarium
Sydney, Australia

This book was originally published in German as *THE KOSMOS BOOK OF THE AQUARIUM.* It was written by Dr. Stephan Dreyer and Dr. Rainer Keppler and published by Franck-Kosmos in Stuttgart, Germany.

The English edition was published by T.F.H. Publications, Inc., 1 TFH Plaza, Neptune City, N.J. 07753

The book was completely manufactured by T.F.H. Publications, Inc. in Neptune, N.J.
The color photos were re-scanned and additional color photos were added to enhance the text. T.F.H. Publications, Inc. claims copyright for the translation and the additional photographs.

The publisher would like to express his appreciation to the photographers whose photos appeared in the original German edition. Those photos added by TFH have been credited separately with by-lines.

The following photographers and artists illustrated the original German edition:
Gerhard Brünner, Bruno Cavignaux, Dr. Stephan Dreyer, Bernd Gregor, Hambsch, Burkhard Kahl, Dr. Rainer Keppler, Horst Linke, Löbbeke-Museum and Aqua-Zoo, Düsseldorf/ Dr. H. Bosch, MP-Hetcher Aquarien, Arend van den Nieuwenhuizen, Reinhard-Tierfoto, Schubert/Uni Hohenheim, Rainer Stawikowski, Klaus Wilkerling.

**Drawings by:** Maria Bertsch/Sigrid Haag, from Engelhardt, *What lives in ponds, lakes and stream?*, Marianne Golte-Bechtle, Reinhild Hofmann, Kerstin Keppler, Dr. Rainer Keppler, Peter Löhle, Angela Paysan, from Remane/ Storch/Welsch, *Short Course in Zoology, 5th Edition*, Dr. Thomas Romig, Walter Söllner, Dieter Untergasser and Brigitte Zwickel-Noelle.
The original drawings were mostly black and white. John Quinn of T.F.H. Publications, Inc. colored them.
The cover was designed by Studio Reichert, Stuttgart. Burkhard Kahl photos: *Macropodus opercularis*, upper left; *Hemigrammus erythrozonus*, upper right. Bruno Cavignaux' *Aphyosemion gardneri* and Bernd Degen's famous *Echinodorus amazonicus.*

| CUSTOMARY U.S. MEASURES AND EQUIVALENTS | METRIC MEASURES AND EQUIVALENTS |
|---|---|

## LENGTH

| | | |
|---|---|---|
| 1 inch (in) | | = 2.54 cm |
| 1 foot (ft) | = 12 in | = .3048 m |
| 1 yard (yd) | = 3 ft | = .9144 m |
| 1 mile (mi) | = 1760 yd | = 1.6093 km |
| 1 nautical mile | = 1.152 mi | = 1.853 km |

| | | |
|---|---|---|
| 1 millimeter (mm) | | = .0394 in |
| 1 centimeter (cm) | = 10 mm | = .3937 in |
| 1 meter (m) | = 1000 mm | = 1.0936 yd |
| 1 kilometer (km) | = 1000 m | = .6214 mi |

## AREA

| | | |
|---|---|---|
| 1 square inch (in$^2$) | | = 6.4516 cm$^2$ |
| 1 square foot (ft$^2$) | = 144 in$^2$ | = .093 m$^2$ |
| 1 square yard (yd$^2$) | = 9 ft$^2$ | = .8361 m$^2$ |
| 1 acre | = 4840 yd$^2$ | = 4046.86 m$^2$ |
| 1 square mile( mi$^2$) | = 640 acre | = 2.59 km$^2$ |

| | | |
|---|---|---|
| 1 sq centimeter (cm$^2$) | = 100 mm$^2$ | = .155 in$^2$ |
| 1 sq meter (m$^2$) | = 10,000 cm$^2$ | = 1.196 yd$^2$ |
| 1 hectare (ha) | = 10,000 m$^2$ | = 2.4711 acres |
| 1 sq kilometer (km$^2$) | = 100 ha | = .3861 mi$^2$ |

## WEIGHT

| | | |
|---|---|---|
| 1 ounce (oz) | = 437.5 grains | = 28.35 g |
| 1 pound (lb) | = 16 oz | = .4536 kg |
| 1 short ton | = 2000 lb | = .9072 t |
| 1 long ton | = 2240 lb | = 1.0161 t |

| | | |
|---|---|---|
| 1 milligram (mg) | | = .0154 grain |
| 1 gram (g) | = 1000 mg | = .0353 oz |
| 1 kilogram (kg) | = 1000 g | = 2.2046 lb |
| 1 tonne (t) | = 1000 kg | = 1.1023 short tons |
| 1 tonne | | = .9842 long ton |

## VOLUME

| | | |
|---|---|---|
| 1 cubic inch (in$^3$) | | = 16.387 cm$^3$ |
| 1 cubic foot (ft$^3$) | = 1728 in$^3$ | = .028 m$^3$ |
| 1 cubic yard (yd$^3$) | = 27 ft$^3$ | = .7646 m$^3$ |
| 1 fluid ounce (fl oz) | | = 2.957 cl |
| 1 liquid pint (pt) | = 16 fl oz | = .4732 l |
| 1 liquid quart (qt) | = 2 pt | = .946 l |
| 1 gallon (gal) | = 4 qt | = 3.7853 l |
| 1 dry pint | | = .5506 l |
| 1 bushel (bu) | = 64 dry pt | = 35.2381 l |

| | | |
|---|---|---|
| 1 cubic centimeter (cm$^3$) | | = .061 in$^3$ |
| 1 cubic decimeter (dm$^3$) | = 1000 cm$^3$ | = .353 ft$^3$ |
| 1 cubic meter (m$^3$) | = 1000 dm$^3$ | = 1.3079 yd$^3$ |
| 1 liter (l) | = 1 dm$^3$ | = .2642 gal |
| 1 hectoliter (hl) | = 100 l | = 2.8378 bu |

**CELSIUS° = 5/9 (F° − 32°)   FAHRENHEIT° = 9/5 C° + 32°**
## TEMPERATURE

# CONTENTS

# FOREWORD

## AQUARIUM FEVER...

This disease is not listed in any medical dictionary, and no medical practitioner is able to treat it, principally because the patients do not want to be cured. In fact, those inflicted with this disease virtually nurture their special affliction almost with dedication; we are talking about *aquarium fever*.

Often it attacks us in our youth, but even older people are not immune to this infection. An attack is possible at any time. Apparently males are more commonly infected than females. But maybe we are being deceived, and the truth is that (grand-)fathers, uncles, sons and male grand children, etc. tend to talk more about this disease, but females carry it around with them in a more latent form. But this is something for market researchers to worry about.

One thing is certain, though: once you get the fever, it will never let go of you again. The symptoms are highly variable and do not always manifest

The authors, Drs. Dreyer (left) and Keppler.

themselves externally, but the universal characteristic is the 'watery-fishy' thinking and way of doing things. One indulges in aquarium science, in theory and in practice.

Currently, at least twenty million citizens in the U.S.A. alone are considered to be infected. This includes us, and actually we must be included in the particularly resistant category of cases. While in most of our fellow man the aquarium fever usually breaks out during their leisure time, we are actually professionally engaged in maintaining and spreading this affliction.

Together with practically all other pets, tropical fish and food fish, including of course everything relating to water, as well as food and accessories are part of our own professional involvement.

And so it is understandable that we—the authors—actually met while practicing our trade as aquarists. Soon the initial contacts led to collaborative work on tropical fish food projects. Rainer, after having completed his studies in biology and zoology, became involved initially in a tropical food fish project (breeding gouramies in Thailand); while Stephan turned to redfin perch biology and river/sea fisheries as well as to aquaculture, following his studies in agricultural biology and animal production. Yet, aquarium-related themes kept bringing us together professionally and privately.

Since then we tend to 'fever together' and when we add to this yet another close colleague and friend, the biologist Angela Wolf (our publisher's editor for pet books), it is not always idle 'shop talk' we engage in. Soon this became a joint task to produce an aquarium book. Our first reaction was: 'Another one,.... again? But to publish something that was different in content and presentation quickly challenged us.

After all, as a natural scientist one does belong—as a matter of professionalism—to the writing fraternity. In addition, the constant reviewing of relevant literature becomes a routine. The knowledge thus gained, together with practical experiences from the hobby, experiments and projects, flow on into relevant

It took two experts with aquarium fever to write this heavily researched volume.

assignments. Consequently, aquarium documentations, lectures and educational and professional seminars become pleasant duties. For both of us this has been an on-going involvement, which is never boring!

In her editorial capacity and to the point where she should almost be a co-author, Angela Wolf has continuously encouraged us to go well beyond the routine and established standards. Without her and her publisher, who has always generously supported our requests and ideas, writing this book would not have been possible.

We would like to take this opportunity to thank Angela and all her co-workers in Stuttgart, as well as our at times 'suffering' wives. Without all their (moral as well as culinary and even partially active) support, this book would not have turned out the way it did.

We sincerely hope that it will provide valuable advice not only to the beginning aquarists but also to those who have been home aquarists for a long time.

**Stephan Dreyer**
**Rainer Keppler**

# THE AQUARIUM—NATURE IN THE HOME

In American aquariums alone there are some 800 million fish in about 20 million households, so that at least that many people have let themselves become inflicted with *aquarium fever*. What do they get out of it? Do they have specific (possibly mutual) objectives and what can and should keeping an aquarium achieve? What sense or purpose can a glass box (or several of them) have, which is set up at home or even at the place of work, filled with water, plants and fishes?

Well, there is no universal answer to all these questions. There are a number of reasons why people wish to live together with fish and water plants. But—consciously or subconsciously and more or less strongly defined–one thing is common to all aquarists: *the love of nature and the joy of making particular observations on the inhabitants of their aquariums.*

If this is coupled with a certain amount of research spirit, the teaching and learning effects that arise while actively practicing 'aquariology' are then generally viewed as the principal reasons for keeping an aquarium. Especially the diverse and fascinating area of behavioral research provides a lot to be observed and analyzed even within limited space. Natural science and biology teachers in particular tend to take advantage of this through the use of aquariums in classrooms. Invariably some students will become 'hooked for life.'

The interactions between man and animal, its environment and the complexities of the relationships involved, is nowhere more obvious than in aquarium keeping. Ecology is the science of these interactions. It can be clearly depicted and conveyed by means of well-defined dependencies (fish—water—other inhabitants).

Only that which we have learned through practical experience and direct contact is appreciated and protected. Aquariology conveys an impression of what happens out there in nature, with and without interference by man. Within this concept, water—apart from its inhabitants—with its fundamental importance for all life forms, becomes the focal point of interest.

Questions and answers about habitat and landscape protection are reflected in aquariums, where the concept of environmental protection becomes reality on a small scale, within the themes of water quality and water management. The responsibility for living things and their environment, the pleasure which arises from successful care of the inhabitants of water, provides yet another possible motive for keeping an aquarium.

One can become involved in aquariums all by one's self, jointly with friends or as a participatory work project for the entire family. Many of those who are actively involved in this hobby quite specifically seek out a dialogue with like-minded souls, often within specifically oriented interest groups, such as working or project groups in schools, in other educational facilities or in aquarium clubs. Exchanging ideas or simply listening, jointly observing or being educated together with social aspects of such gatherings — all that can grow out of keeping an aquarium. It may also serve to motivate some to pick up this fascinating hobby or become deeper and more thoroughly involved in conservation.

Finally, we have to mention those people who do not need any of the above-mentioned reasons; they simply enjoy keeping an aquarium, either as a decorative item in an apartment or simply as an esthetic focal point in a room, where one can sit down and relax from the daily rat race simply by looking at an aquarium and its colorful occupants.

**Not like this!**

Any form of practical aquarium keeping requires a certain amount of subject knowledge in order to avoid mistakes and to be able to counteract the critics. By setting up and running an aquarium sensibly there is nothing that can be said against this hobby. It is a very sensible activity.

## PRELIMINARY CONSIDERATIONS

Whenever we take living animals or plants into our care, it goes without saying that we accept the responsibility for providing them with healthy and species-correct surroundings. More specifically in the case of an aquarium, where we must maintain these conditions not only in the short term but beyond that for prolonged periods of time, certain regular maintenance work is required. This in turn incurs certain costs as well as requiring time.

Since most mishaps with an aquarium are due to lack of (or incorrect) care, let us first of all look at the amount of time and effort involved in the 'average' aquarium. It then depends on you whether you are willing to invest the time and effort. If so, there is really nothing standing in your way to join this 'wet hobby', a move which may well lead to a life-long infection with the aquarium virus!

As time passes, you, like many aquarists before you, will have found out that the required maintenance effort is anything but a burden. Similarly, the time spent just watching the fish will not seem a burden. Quite to the contrary, in fact, sometimes you will regret not being able to observe all the interesting happenings in your tanks due to professional or other personal commitments!

A community tank featuring *Rasbora heteromorpha* and *Brachydanio albolineatus*.

## Care required

Under this heading we deal initially in general terms with some of the maintenance required, and the time and cost involved. Further details and other explanations are conveyed in later chapters on water management and technology. Feeding the fishes is no doubt the most frequently occurring aquarium maintenance task. As a general reference point it is suggested here that one or two feedings per day are the norm. The amount of food given must never be larger than is eaten by the fish within a few minutes. For further details about feeding, please refer to the appropriate chapter.

It is important to watch the fish while they are feeding: does every fish get its share, are there signs of diseases or injuries, are there incompatibilities between individual specimens or are there any other departures from the normal behavior? At the same time we also take a look at the thermometer and check the proper functioning of all other equipment. For these repetitive tasks we should allocate about 10 minutes daily.

The most important element in maintaining proper water conditions is regular, partial water changes. In order to avoid a steady accumulation of pollutants in the water, about $^1/_3$ to $^1/_4$ of the total water volume needs to be siphoned out and be replaced with conditioned water about every 2 weeks or so. For further details refer to the chapter on water. At the same time all dead or dying plant leaves and stems as well as excessive debris accumulations on the bottom are removed. If required, part of the filter medium should also be cleaned (rinsed out thor-

If there was one piece of equipment which benefited hobbyists most it would be this automatic aquarium water changer which enables you to replace old aquarium water with fresh tap water without carrying heavy buckets! Photo courtesy of Aquarium Products Co.,

oughly). For a 100 liter (25 gallon) aquarium these tasks require about 30 minutes.

In order to be quite sure that the water conditions in the aquarium are satisfactory we need to measure the pH value as well as monitor the nitrite content of the water. This can be done with reasonably-priced test kits available from all aquarium and pet shops. Time involved for one test is about three to five minutes.

As far as costs are concerned we would like to restrict ourselves to the actual operating costs, because the purchase price is a single acquisition (capital) cost, which ultimately depends on the aquarium you decided to buy. Since it is a well-known fact of life that prices keep changing, we are here referring merely to individual cost factors. Absolute values would not be valid for very long.

Generally, operating costs such as electricity, water, food and other items associated with regular aquarium care are recurring expenses. The main electricity costs are for lighting and heating. There is little room for economizing on lighting since a daily illumination period of about 12 hours is essential. Costs are dependent upon the difference between room temperature and the temperature requirements for a particular

A classic aquarium set up in a home.

tank. The smaller this difference is, the lower the heating costs. Electricity costs for filtration are minimal, since modern aquarium filters require very little electricity (often under 10 watt per filter).

Water costs for the regular partial water changes can (still) be largely disregarded: a 100 liter tank, with 30 liter water changes every two weeks, requires about 780 liter per year.

Food costs are dependent upon the number and sizes of fish that are being kept. In addition, there are expenses for items such as plant fertilizer and water conditioner. Other periodic expenses include the purchases of the test kits already mentioned. With up to 50 to 80 tests per kit (depending upon the brand), these are invariably not significant cost items.

## The correct location

If, even in view of the cost efforts just described, you are still determined to become infected by the aquarium virus, the time has come to select a proper location for the aquarium. In the past, the window was one of the

favored sites; however, with the advent of sophisticated aquarium lighting this site is no longer appropriate. The window sill or even the proximity of it—as is often suggested in some of the older literature—generates too many illumination problems. Here the natural, highly variable (seasonal), light regimen creates significant algae problems.

In fact, the darkest corner of a room, possibly without any natural (sun) light is the ideal location for an aquarium. Artificial lighting specifically selected for the requirements of particular plants assures correct and continuous illumination periods. This also provides an opportunity to improve the appearance of a part of a room that is less than popular.

Beyond that, the ideal location for a tank should also meet a few other prerequisites. Electrical outlets with a minimum of three outlets should be close by or be easily installed (by a licensed electrician!). One should be able to perform regular tank maintenance, mainly the required regular partial water changes, without having to engage in acrobatics.

Proximity to a water tap is not absolutely essential. For small tanks, water is normally carried in a bucket anyway, which can easily be done once every two weeks, even from a distantly located bathroom. For larger tanks, however, having to carry lots of buckets of water can be a nuisance, especially when there are (often unavoidable) minor water spillages. In this case it is advisable to acquire a water changer. One end of it is placed inside the tank, but not without a suction strainer for the fish. The other end is securely placed on a water outlet. Any amount of water can easily be removed from the aquarium.

For filling an aquarium the water changer is connected to the warm water mixing unit and appropriately heated water flows back into the aquarium. Never underestimate the inherent dynamics of hoses, and so the discharge end of the hose must be properly secured to the tank (suction cup, rock, etc.).

Complete instructions come with every water changer.

The weight of a full aquarium must also never be underestimated. A 100 liter (25 gallon) tank, including substrate, decorations and stand weighs about 120 to 150 kg.(264-330 pounds). The weight of tanks under 100 liters are largely unimportant for selecting a location, considering modern floor construction. For larger tanks, however, it is advisable to give some thought to the carrying capacity of a ceiling. This is, of course, highest closest to the walls and lowest in the middle of the floor space. If in doubt, a structural engineer should be consulted. In older types of buildings with wooden ceilings, the direction of major support beams should be taken into consideration. If a tank is positioned perpendicular to the directions of the beams and is also close to a wall, the carrying capacity is at its maximum.

An aquarium must also have a stand or some other (load-supporting) sub-structure in accordance with its weight. For small tanks (up to about 60 liters) this can be a table, desk, (strong) shelf or similar structure. Larger tanks need a specially designed sub-structure. The aquarium trade offers a number of different models and structural types. Building one yourself presupposes appropriate tradesman skills, and is really only worthwhile for a custom-made tank of non-standard dimensions.

It is, of course, understood that such sub-structure must be perfectly level. The actual area of direct contact between tank and stand must also be perfectly level and be free of any foreign particles (pebbles, rock particles, sand grains). This direct contact area (between tank and stand) must be covered with a thin sheet of styrofoam (hardware stores, building material suppliers, etc.), or a poly-soft mat specially made for aquarium use (from most aquarium suppliers).

# THE AQUARIUM

## Size

Beginning aquarists are often plagued by the question: a small tank first and a larger one later, or to start out with a larger tank? To look at this objectively, there are advantages as well as disadvantages for both. Therefore, let us first have a look at what is happing in nature.

In their natural environment fishes swim in a vast volume of water, with a chemical composition characterized by a well-defined continuity. The fish have become more or less rigidly adapted to these conditions

When selecting the tank location make sure you know where the floor support beams are located. The ideal location (1) is perpendicular to the beam. It is more stable in the corner (2) than parallel to the floor support beams along the wall (3).

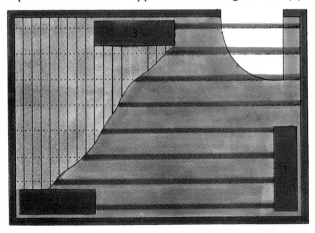

When it is impossible to place your aquarium stand directly on top of the floor support beams, a heavy wooden panel can be utilized to distribute the weight uniformly over the area under the aquarium. Keep in mind that water weighs over 8 pounds per gallon!

(more about this topic in the chapter on fishes). For that reason, one should always endeavor to offer similarly continuous environmental conditions. Any variation occurring should remain within acceptable limits.

It cannot be denied, however, that in a large aquarium any variations in environmental conditions due to occasional maintenance mistakes have a less severe impact than in a small tank. On the other hand, it is often easier to understand and appreciate the natural conformity of such a small environment than in a large one.....unless one already gives up after the very first mishap! Mistakes in tank maintenance in a small aquarium will have immediate and unequivocal consequences! As an example: a dead fish which goes unnoticed in a large tank normally does not pose a

This 1,000 gallon double bull-nose aquarium with a steel aquarium stand and complete cabinetry is available to hobbyists through the local pet shop. It is manufactured by AAMPRO of Las Vegas, Nevada.

problem. It will invariably be decomposed by bacteria and other microorganisms without unduly affecting the overall water quality. The same happens in a small tank, but the bacterial (decay) action will lead to a catastrophic oxygen deficiency. The consequences of this for the fish in such a small tank will no doubt be obvious to everyone.

Moreover, it must also be remembered that the acquisition and operating costs for a larger aquarium are correspondingly greater than for a smaller tank, especially since the aquarium trade usually offers smaller tanks of quite suitable sizes and with all essential equipment as cost-effective, complete kits. In the final analysis then, the decision whether to get a small or large tank must be your own.

In any event, the small tank requires substantially greater discipline and regularity as far as care and maintenance is concerned, than a large tank. For that reason, it can well be viewed that the better approach to starting out in the aquarium hobby is with a large tank of 200 liters (50 gallon) capacity.

If, after a while and contrary to your expectation, you feel that the aquarium hobby is not 'cut out to be what you thought it would be,' then at least the financial 'damage' is within limits if you select a 40 liter (10 gallon) aquarium. We assume, of course, that in such an event all fishes that were being kept are transferred to new, responsible ownership!

## Shape and type of construction

Nowadays the most popular type of aquarium is the all-glass tank. These are aquariums which have been glued together from precisely cut (all cuts are diamond-polished) individual glass panels. Silicon sealant is used as glue to render these tanks water-tight. Many tanks are glued with black silicon sealant. This is to prevent creeping-growth of algae into the space between silicon and glass. On the other hand, there are also tanks which have been glued with transparent silicon and where in 20 years of usage no significant algal penetration has occurred. It could then be said that the black sealant is more of a fashion statement than an essential husbandry requirement. In the final analysis the color of the sealant plays only a subordinate role. Far more important are the so-called support braces, which—at the same time—also serve as cover glass supports. You should purchase only tanks which have support braces attached along their front and back panels. In tanks longer than 1 meter (39 inches) there must also be (depending upon the actual length of the tank) one or more cross braces. In large tanks, which are equipped only with cross braces (and without support braces in the longitudinal direction) it often happens that the sealant joints of the cross braces tear apart, and the longitudinal glass panels start to bulge out significantly or even burst altogether!

Glued aquariums have fundamental advantages over the earlier-used 'frame-type' construction method. Due to the omission of the time-consuming frame structure, into which individual glass panels were cemented, it has become possible to build substantially larger tanks at smaller costs. Moreover, with this new method it is also possible to depart from the customary box-shaped tanks and build more interesting shapes, which are still cost-effective even as custom-built tanks. This has opened up vast new interior design possibilities through the use of diversely-shaped aquariums.

There is, however, a small disadvantage with all-glass tanks, which must not be hidden: especially the corners of these tanks are far more prone to transport damage than the old frame tanks. But with a bit more care while handling, this problem can be largely avoided.

When selecting a suitable type of tank the requirements of the fish should be the prime consideration and not the interior design objectives. Elongated types of fish, which are fast swimmer and need a lot of swimming space, should not be kept in short, tall tanks. On the other hand, fish with a deep (high) body are best not kept in shallow, long tanks.

If a tank must conform to a particular space avail-

**Aquariums come in all imaginable forms and sizes.**

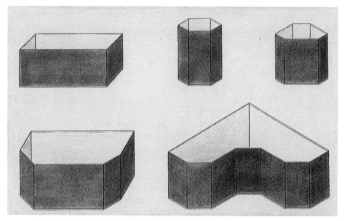

able, then select only those types of fish which would be comfortable in the available environment. For further details refer to chapters on aquarium types and fishes.

Another important criterion for selecting the tank shape is the depth. This refers to the distance between the front and back glass. The deeper a tank is, the greater are the decorative opportunities. An added point is that the distance from front to back, when viewed through water, appears substantially shorter than out of water.

Ideal tanks would be those which are deeper than high, or which are at least of equal dimensions. Unfortunately, this is a point not yet recognized by the aquarium (-making) industry. Consequently, most aquariums of standard sizes are higher than they are deep. Yet, with some skill such tanks can be structurally decorated quite effectively. Whatever shape and dimensions you select, make sure that you purchase only tanks from reputable dealers with appropriate warranties for the sealant joints.

For the sake of completeness, reference must also be made here to a few other structural aquarium types. When all-glass tanks first came out there was also a transitional type of tank where the glass panels were glued but an additional (usually plastic) frame was placed around the all-glass structure. Such a frame had no functional capacity, it only protected the edges against being damaged. This sort of tank has since then gone out of fashion. Anyone who is worried about the edges on his all-glass tank can easily assemble such a plastic profile frame from materials available from any building material supplier and glue it to the (all-glass) tank.

Plexiglass is also a material suitable for making tanks.

For reasons of economics, very large tanks can be made from a variety of materials; only for the front (viewing) panels we always select glass. For instance, it would not be the first time that an aquarist has cemented his 'dream tank' of bricks or concrete, and has then built his entire house around it!

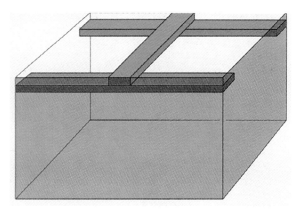

Tanks larger than a meter (39.36 inches) require a cross brace as a stabilizer.

## Insulation against heat loss

In tanks with tropical fish, the water temperature (at least during the cold season) is about 5 to 8 degrees C above room temperature. This facilitates a significant heat loss into the surrounding area. Since only very few tanks are ever positioned in such a way where all sides are viewing areas, it is advisable to insulate those sides which are not used for viewing against heat loss. This saves electricity costs. The most suitable materials for this are styrofoam sheets or so-called extruded inhibitor panels made of polystyrene. Extruded inhibitor panels are more elegant and can be cut to any size, exactly and neatly, with a cutting knife. Silicon glue or double-sided carpet tape can be used for attaching the insulation panels.

## Backgrounds

A view through an aquarium to the wall paper behind is rarely ever compatible with even the cleverest tank decoration. Before the tank is placed into its final position, all sides not used for viewing should be covered with some sort of backdrop decor, which must, of course, be in harmony with the decorative theme of the tank. Pet shops offer many backgrounds.

A school of neon tetras, *Paracheirodon innesi*, in an aquarium whose background is made up of large rocks and thick foliage. Photo by Aqua Press Piednoir.

# THE AQUARIUM HOBBY IN CHANGING TIMES

Keeping and displaying pretty fish not used for human consumption has in Asia, especially in China and Japan, a tradition which goes back hundreds of years. There, goldfish and decorative carp have been (and still are) in the center of fish breeding interests. Simple earthenware containers for the breeders, decorative and glazed pottery ware for the private hobbyist and up to the finest and most delicate porcelain container for the nobility, characterized the aquaristic practice in the Far East.

Most of these ancient practices are still in use today, and all classic goldfish and koi varieties have been selected and specifically bred on the basis of being viewed from above. Viewing fish behind glass can be considered as an essentially Western invention.

Those were the times, when our forefathers discovered the hobby of fish keeping during the last Century. Although important biological requirements were then already known (such as the temperature requirements of tropical fish), the technical possibilities to transform them effectively into practical (aquarium husbandry) terms, were limited.

### The 'steam-operated' aquarium

The very first aquarium heaters were petroleum and alcohol burners, which were placed underneath the tank; later on small gas (bunsen) burners were already considered to be progress. So-called heat domes were soldered onto the bottom (metal) panel of the tank at particular locations. There was little if any substrate around these heat domes, in order to avoid localized over-heating.

In those days most aquarists made their own tanks, and the respective working instructions used in those early days now sound almost adventurous: aquarists experimented with tar sealants, while numerous recipe changes of window putty were exchanged and tried out. After the glass panels had been installed in the frame, various sealant substances were used for additional safety reasons to prevent leakages.

In those days frames were coated with home-made insulating lacquers, usually based on various lead substances. These were often 'de-fused' through the addition of linseed oils as surface protection.

Sand and gravel were already used as bottom substrate by the early aquarists. Incidentally, modern aquarists now often go back to the observation made by early aquarists: dark substrates promote peacefulness and color intensity in many fish, which tend to frighten easily and show only pale coloration when placed in tanks with light-colored, reflective substrates. The solution in the old days: add brown pea coal!

### Air....a must!

Once water was placed in the aquarium, and the plants and fishes were added, the worries started. The fish were gasping for air, especially when the fish density was too great, especially in the absence of appropriate knowledge about filtration. Consequently, air was badly needed in the aquarium, but how? The first air reservoirs were rubber inner tubes, like those from automobile tires, which were pumped up in the morning and in the evening to provide air for the tank. This led to the development of marginally more advanced pressure vessels equipped with manometer and discharge valves. But these devices also needed to be physically re-filled after each emptying. Thick felt mats served as air 'stones' prior to the invention of little silica blocks.

### Conditions were not constant

The very first aquariums were operated without lighting and therefore were invariably positioned on window sills. Due to far too much light during the summer months, algal problems were virtually pre-programmed. During the winter it was too cold that close to a window, and so fuel consumption of the small burners rose markedly. Later, the same applied to electrical heaters. These were operated in U-shaped form, where the current was conducted through a salt solution. Size of the carbon electrodes and salt concentration in the tube provided for a certain degree of adjustment.

The seasonal transition from summer to winter was the most critical period. Among the fishes, of which paradise fish, white clouds and armored catfish of the genus *Corydoras* were the 'pioneers' in the tanks of the early aquarists, the dreaded 'autumn die off' was common. With declining light intensity and duration, oxygen production by the plants declined. And if a tank was already overcrowded, the resultant decline in water quality led to mass die-offs. As a prophylactic measure, aquarists used to give away a lot of their fish in late summer and so reduce tank populations. This then recruited a lot of new aquarists to their ranks.

For a brief period, aquarium development went off on a tangent, which now fortunately has virtually died out: the dreadful goldfish bowl was invented, which did not

**This historical aquarium drawing appeared in an article entitled (in German) *The Sea in a Glass* by E. A. Rossmaessler, which appeared in 1856.**

Goldfish bowls are the *worst* way to keep any fish, including goldfish. Fortunately, they are disappearing from the market.

utilize any of the by then available technological advancements in aquarium keeping.

## On the way to high-tech aquarium keeping

The filter canisters, incandescent tank lighting and small air pumps characterized the path to modern aquariology. Technological advancements took place, and are still taking place, accompanied by appropriate findings from different but related areas associated with aquarium keeping.

In spite of ideal conditions now, some beginning aquarists still persist with the historical principle of learning by trial and error. In the early days, there was no other way, but today with good intentions and the commitment to a single, meaningful investment, there is no need to pay such heavy dues.

## Substrate

In order to provide aquarium plants with their needed substrate and to offer the fish a "bottom under their feet," the future underwater world requires a bottom substrate. A carbonate-free, brownish gravel with a grain size of 2 to 3 mm has proven to be the most suitable. You should avoid pure white gravel, even if it looks so nice and clean. Fish feel far more comfortable with a dark substrate and will then also display more attractive coloration.

Also make sure that the individual grains are roundish. Sharp, angular material, such as crushed lava or basalt split, which may look nice and dark, can cause substantial injuries to certain bottom fish. For further details about substrate please refer to the section on water plants.

## Decorations

For properly structuring the aquarium environment, you will need water plants and certain other decorative items. So that these will do justice to the intended use and also be aesthetically appealing, here are a few fundamental thoughts about it.

The aquarium is supposed to become a small (according to biological principle) functioning, living community. The important functions fulfilled by plants in an aquarium will be explained in detail in the section on water plants. Similarly, for the other decoration materials which will be required, e.g. for caves, territorial (sight) barriers or terraces, there are also desirable materials. Natural rocks, tree roots or petrified wood are just some of the materials which are very suitable as aquarium decorations.

None of the materials placed inside an aquarium must be able to give off harmful substances into the surrounding water. Especially with wood of any kind, it is important to make sure that none of the pieces used contain

Some fishes, such as this *Botia histrionica*, keep rocks clean by constantly chewing off the algae and debris that settles on them. Photo by Aqua Press Piednoir.

decaying substances or are impregnated with humic acids from having been buried for decades in swamps. With materials purchased from specialized aquarium shops you can usually be sure that they are suitable.

Asiatic *aquarium* in which goldfish are kept. They are observed from the top.

19

Decorative items for the aquarium should be specifically designed for the aquarium out of safe materials that fit into the tank's decor. Photo courtesy of Blue Ribbon Pet Products.

The suggestion (often found in aquarium literature) to boil rocks, roots and other aquarium decor before use, you can safely forget. Not only does something like that usually proceed at the expense of family peace, but most normal households do not have pots or other containers sufficiently large for boiling large pieces of aquarium decor. Brushing all pieces individually and thoroughly under running water is usually sufficient.

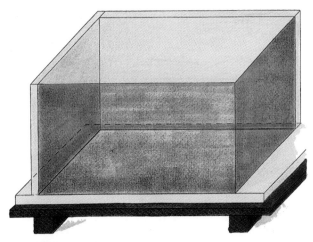
As insulation against heat loss, those sides not used for viewing should be covered with Styrofoam sheeting.

Do not overload your aquarium with pieces of decor. Here too the old saying that 'less is often more' also applies. Consequently, do not establish a rock collection under water, but use only rocks of the same type. Further details about setting up an aquarium are presented in the next chapter.

## Useful utensils

Right from the start, some useful utensils, which make servicing the aquarium easier, should always be kept at a certain place. In essence, these are: a clean bucket, which is used exclusively for the aquarium (its use for other household chores is totally taboo!!), then a siphon hose of about 2 m length and a diameter of about 15 to 22 mm. You also need a fish net in the event you have to remove fish from the aquarium. Water changers are a must.

For the removal of algal films along the inside of the front glass, a glass scraper is essential. Apart from buckets (available from super markets, household suppliers, etc.), specialized aquarium shops offer all of these implements of different quality, type and design.

A gourami aquarium can hold more than a normal amount of fishes because gouramis breathe atmospheric air and are not completely dependent upon the oxygen content in the water.

## INSURANCE

Although—thank goodness—only very rarely does one find the entire aquarium contents spread out over the expensive living room carpet, proper precautions should be taken. Just imagine what a single bucket full of water, which tips over in the living room by accident, can do and then multiply that by the entire aquarium volume! Disregarding for the moment the damage to your own property, what happens if it is a rented apartment and the damage sustained is to the property of others?

We suggest you consult an insurance expert. Liability

A glued aquarium with two types of substrata, polysoft mat, various photographic backgrounds and insulation along the back. The bottom substrata on the left is an ideal material since it is gravel of 2-3 mm (about 1/10th inch) grain size. The substrata on the right is crushed lava which, though dark in color, has sharp, dangerous edges. The polysoft mat, background and insulation are shown protruding for demonstration purposes only.

insurance covers the damage caused to third parties. If the aquarium can be included (usually for a special premium)in a household policy, your own damage will also be covered. Members of aquarium clubs, usually belonging to a national association, are sometimes covered automatically against third party damage claims.

# EXCHANGING IDEAS

Before we venture deeper into the subject of aquarium keeping in the next chapter, here is some good advice: caring for an aquarium means having to deal with a complex of mutually interactive living things. And because it involves living things, there can be no explicit directions as those available for machines and equipment, which are simply followed and everything will work out satisfactorily.

It's easy to relax in front of an aquarium.

**Utensils for regular aquarium maintenance include a bucket, net, hose and a siphon bell plus various kinds of glass cleaners. Ask your pet shop manager what he specifically recommends for your aquarium.**

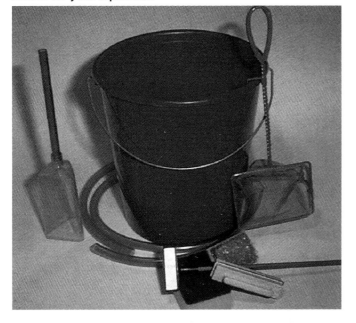

This books will attempt to steer you in the proper direction; however, sooner or later you will come across some problem for which you will not find an answer in this book. Therefore, look toward the exchanging of ideas with other aquarists.

Your first communication partner will be your aquarium shop or specialized pet shop dealer. In time you will also meet other aquarists who may belong to an aquarium club, or you will actually become a member of such a club. In often animated discussions you will discover that many ways lead to Rome, and that not everything works out just the way you initially imagined it would. But it is exactly that which makes keeping an aquarium so interesting.

***Prionobrama filigera*** **are delicate fish that should be housed in a darkened tank with fine-leafed plants. It is necessary to know about a fish's origin in order to prepare a suitable aquarium setting for them. Photo by Aqua Press Piednoir.**

## AQUARIUM DECORATION AND HOW TO SET IT UP

Before you get started on creating your very own personal aquarium interior, a word of advice: if you want to recreate the environment of your aquarium fish absolutely correctly, the result would often not be an exciting, aesthetic experience. That need not be! The decor of an aquarium can, of course, be a reflection of your own aesthetic perception. What is important is that in spite of its appearance it fulfills the functions essential for a species-correct life of the fishes. That means, fishes which require hiding places in the form of caves should have these, and fishes which must have plant thickets as sight barriers against other fishes, must not be kept in tanks resembling rocky deserts, and so on.

In the previous chapter we already learned which decorating materials can be used in an aquarium. To repeat this once more: fundamentally all natural materials can be used, which do not decompose and do not give off any harmful substances into the surrounding water. Divers, ship wrecks and other plastic articles will not disturb the fish, but they may not fit into a natural underwater landscape. Clearly, taste is something one cannot argue about!

The most frequently used items of aquarium decor have always been (and still are) rocks and various types of tree roots. All types of rocks which do not give off any hardness producing substances are suitable, for instance, granite, basalt, slate, lava, silica rocks and others. In special situations, as for instance for tanks with fish from the African rift valley lakes, carbonate rocks can also be used.

Rocks are used for building caves, territorial (sight-) barriers and to set up terraces. The latter are ideally suited to give an aquarium spatial depth if the rocks are arranged, not parallel to the longitudinal sides of the aquarium, but instead extending asymmetrically towards the back of the tank. In order to prevent the substrate from penetrating through gaps in the terrace wall, glass strips are glued with silicon sealant vertically against the bottom panel, which are then disguised with appropriately sized rocks to form the terrace wall.

Pieces of driftwood are ideal for simulating submerged sections of a tree or washed out tree roots. Moreover, they

**A beautifully laid out community aquarium featuring angelfish (*Pterophyllum*) and bleeding heart tetras.**

**Driftwood can be attached to a heavy plastic plate and secured with stainless steel screws. The plate is then covered with gravel and anchored at the bottom of the aquarium.**

offer armored catfish an essential part of their diet, that is, cellulose which these little fish extract from the roots through continuous rasping on them. Unfortunately, these roots have an annoying habit: they tend to float, sometimes even after years of submergence. The following methods have proven to be effective in keeping roots on the bottom of an aquarium: arrange them in such a way that their upper ends can be placed under one (or more) of the tank's support and/or cross braces (NOT WEDGED between the bottom and the braces); or weigh them down with suitably heavy rocks on that section of the root(s) resting on the bottom. Again, it must be emphasized here that the braces are merely to counter-act the buoyancy of the roots. If a root is firmly wedged between the bottom and one of the cross braces there is a real risk of glass breakage!

A large plastic plate can be screwed to the underside of the root with stainless steel screws. This plate is then buried under the substrate. Please do not get the idea of wanting to glue the roots to the bottom with silicon! Due to the porosity of wood, water will quickly enter between the sealant and the wood, and the root will become detached and drift to the surface. You will be lucky if the tank light is not damaged when these roots pop to the surface.

In recent times, the aquarium trade has been offering tropical woods which are suitable for use in aquariums

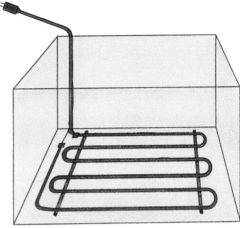

**1. Installing bottom heating coils.**

**2. Cover with gravel.**

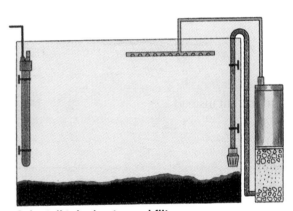

**3. Install tube heater and filter.**

and which are heavier than water! This wood must, however, be leached for some time because it tends to strongly discolor the water dark brown.

Coconut half shells or hollowed out whole coconuts with an opening make ideal brood sites for dwarf cichlids. Appropriately cut bamboo sticks placed vertically in the substrate can be used to effectively imitate submerged grass or reed areas. Coconut shells, bamboo and most roots need not be boiled before use in an aquarium.

There are certainly many other useful materials for use as aquarium decor, but listing all of these would go beyond the scope of this book. Let your imagination wander, but avoid too many different materials in the tank at the same time. This tends to give a cluttered-up appearance!

Setting up a tank is done essentially according to the following scheme:

1. Substrate heating. If you decide to use substrate heating, this will have to be installed first by positioning the heating coil in even loops over the glass bottom. For further details about substrate heating please refer to the section on aquarium technology.

2. Introducing the bottom substrate. A 4 to 6 cm (about 2-2 1/4 inch) high layer of dark-colored quartz gravel has proven to be the most satisfactory. If you buy pre-washed gravel from an aquarium or pet shop, it is not absolutely necessary to rinse it out. A slight clouding

of the water once the tank has been filled will disappear after a short time. Gravel of unknown origin must certainly be washed before it is used in an aquarium.

3. Installation of a tube heater and filter. Follow explicitly all directions and instructions provided with individual equipment items. Install the equipment in the back section of the tank, so that it can be disguised later with aquarium decor and plants.

4. Arranging the aquarium decor. If the tank is not going to contain strongly burrowing or digging fish species, rocks, roots, etc., can be placed on the bottom or be slightly buried. Heavy rock structures for digging species, such as cichlids, must be constructed BEFORE the substrate is placed on the bottom. In order to avoid damage to the bottom glass it is advisable to place a

23

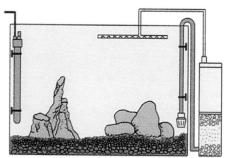

**4. Arrange tank decor.**

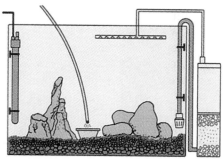

**5. Fill with water.**

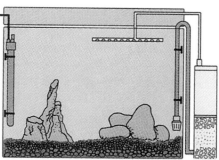

**6/7. Attach lighting and filtration.**

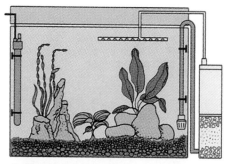

**8. Decorate and plant.**

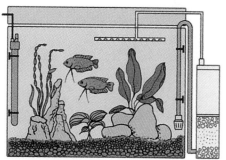

**9. Introduce fishes.**

**Selection of decorative materials: driftwood, cork and various stones; the plastic screen serves as a support for heavy stone structures (for the protection of the glass).**

styrofoam sheet or, better yet, a fine-meshed plastic grate (garden supplier) under any large rock structure.

5. Filling the tank. In order to avoid unnecessarily stirring up the bottom while filling the tank with water, a large flat object (plate, saucer, rock) is placed on the bottom and the water flow is directed onto that. The water temperature of the in-flowing water should be pre-adjusted to 25 degrees C(77° F). Any remaining adjustments are made once the tank has been filled.

6. Operation of filter and heater; installation of lighting: For details about this equipment please refer to the section on aquarium technology.

7. 'Seeding'. Now the time has come to 'seed' or 'inoculate' the aquarium with suitable bacteria. The need

for these bacteria and their specific function are discussed in the following chapters. The best way to 'seed' is as follows: acquire a small amount of some well run-in filter medium from a friend or acquaintance who also keeps an aquarium, and rinse this out in your tank. The resultant, unattractive cloudiness will quickly disappear again, and in virtually no time you have a well 'run-in' filter, and fish can be added to this tank in one or two days.

8. Introducing water plants. When all of the equipment is working correctly and the tank has been 'seeded' with bacteria, water plants can be introduced. For details please refer to the relevant section on plants.

9. Introducing the fish. A few days later the fish can be introduced. For details about that and suitable fish species in particular please refer to the relevant sections.

# THE CORRECT COMBINATION: COMMUNITY TANK

So-called community tanks are for most aquarists the start into this fascinating hobby. As indicated by the name, this sort of aquarium is used to accommodate fishes from different species. Generally applicable for keeping fishes of different species together, and this is what a community tank is all about, is an important basic rule: all animals to be kept together must be compatible with each other and they must have principally the same environmental requirements. Only this will assure a truly species-correct accommodation.

This basic rule applies, of course, also to keeping fish in home aquariums. Some 'wild mixture' of different species of fish, combined with a diverse assemblage of plants and possibly also other aquatic inhabitants, all selected on the basis of personal taste, is invariably an exercise that ends in disaster. Under such conditions the well-being of at least some, or even all, of the tank occupants is adversely affected. Vital functions can become severely impaired through the mere presence of unsuitable co-occupants. Stress, fright and pain are also known to occur in fish. If the fishes are forced to remain under totally unnatural conditions, a community tank can quickly turn into a place for pre-programmed animal torture.

Our previously mentioned basic rule about mutual compatibility with simultaneous compliance with identical habitat requirements, helps to avoid this. At the same time, those opposed to home aquarium keeping are silenced this way, and you will thoroughly enjoy such a thematic aquarium.

What is meant by the term mutual compatibility? First of all, it means that predators and their natural prey must not be kept together permanently. Predators, which constantly encounter bite-size prey, will attempt to swallow it (and with frequent success they quickly become overweight). On the other hand, even with adequate hiding places and proper cover, small prey species are placed under stress when constantly being pursued, or even when they are aware that predators are lying in wait.

**There are bad guys even among fishes.**

Compatibility can also mean self-denial: long-finned varieties, common among many commercially bred aquarium fishes, frequently have their 'veils' or fin extensions nibbled on, even by otherwise peaceful species. Consequently, these fish do not belong in a community tank.

General conduciveness to the feeding method and food offered, actually suggests the exclusive use in a community tank of omnivorous fishes or those accepting a range of food items. Otherwise, maintaining a community tank can become quite involved in terms of food and feeding.

This aspect leads to habitat requirements which must be identical for all fish in a community tank. If, first-of-all, one equates this with the preferred habitat of a fish species, it then makes sense to introduce species from the various (vertical) zones (e.g. surface, open swimming space and bottom) into a community tank. This way the available space is most effectively utilized. It is important to achieve a satisfactory balance within these areas as well as in reference to the entire tank. There must be an appropriate 'population' density. The beginner should settle for one or two species per tank zone.

In a community tank the essential water parameters have to suit all fish. Fortunately, many fish and plant species tolerate a certain species-related range with respect to temperature, pH and water hardness. One must stay within these limits in all three of these factors. Only where you find real conformity on these factors, are you dealing with fish suitable for a community tank.

Is it important to consider the geographical origin of certain species when setting up a community tank? Or can fish originating from different continents or countries be mixed together? Well, this is solely a matter of individual opinion and taste. The transition to the subse-quently discussed **thematic aquarium** types is confluent. Only on the subject of **community** is there a divergence of opinion and that is quite acceptable. We believe that everything that pleases is permitted, provided there is adequate compatibility in terms of species requirements, regardless of where the fish originates.

# LESS IS (OFTEN) MORE: AQUARIUMS WITH A THEME

Strictly speaking the tanks to be discussed in detail in this section are really nothing more than community tanks. Only the fish community in such tanks has been selected on the basis of a particular theme, which is esthetically supported by appropriately selected aquarium decor.

If, for a normal community tank only intra-specific compatibility was the critical factor, irrespective of where the fish came from, these tanks would be confined to a particular group of fish or even a single species in order to provide optimal living conditions for the tank occupants. Within this context one talks about so-called species, habitat or landscape tanks. A special case is the so-called 'Dutch' aquarium, which is more a water garden than a fish tank.

**A tankful of 3-month-old *Corydoras aeneus*. Catfishes are nice fishes for the beginner. Photo by Aqua Press Piednoir.**

# TO LIVE WITH AN AQUARIUM

There are many structural and architectural possibilities to integrate aquariums in human dwellings. Entire generations of interior architects, designers and aquarium furniture manufacturers have come up with a multitude of variants, tips and tricks in order to combine the keeping of fish and living in practical and attractive ways.

The spectrum extends from inconspicuous, almost hidden accommodation of tanks up to the development of aquariums as the eye-catching, decorative focal point of a room or even as an art object.

## FUNCTIONALITY IS MOST IMPORTANT

Irrespective of whether it is a ready-made product of an imaginative industry or whether one relies on one's own crafts skills, the esthetics and attempted effect must never interfere with flawless functionality. Even living room aquariums must be serviceable. First of all, the aquaristic requirements in regard to site selection, technic and maintenance must be considered. It is the latter (important) point that is often left unaddressed; filters and some sections of the glass are often very hard to access, so that even routine maintenance work requires considerable effort and acrobatic distortions. Many aquarists will get tired of these efforts and the tank may then well be neglected.

## ANTIQUE OR MODERN?

What is actually involved in 'pleasant living' with an aquarium? The simplest and most obvious possibility is —apart from a 'bare tank'—the established tank and built-in modules. These are available in a variety of models and designs to match any style of living. They can accommodate filter, $CO_2$ unit and other accessories in easily accessible ways.

## A TANK TO LOOK THROUGH.....

Parallel with the development of aquariums as pieces of furniture, a somewhat divergent approach was used in developing an aquarium as a special form of 'living with an aquarium': the tank as a room divider—again adapted in form and style to the other interior design elements, or as a deliberate contrast to it.

While an aquarium placed along a wall can be looked into from one to maximally three sides and its decor is arranged along the back wall, a room-divider aquarium has practically two fronts. This shifts the area for decorative structuring to a tightly restricted area around the median axis of the tank. Therefore, particularly deep aquariums are preferred as room dividers.

The room-divider aquarium offers a lot of swimming room for schooling fish of the upper and middle water zones. Fish species which need a lot of hiding places or sight barriers against other fish will be less comfortable in a room-divider aquarium.

Anyone not satisfied with the available tank sizes and shape and the assortment of built-in aquariums can build his own tank according to his very own specifications or he can get it custom-made. By the way, because of limited display space available, most pet and/ or aquarium shops are unable to show their entire range of tanks. Consult your dealer and ask for prospectuses of other tanks available, especially the larger plexi-glass tanks which are becoming very popular.

## THEME WITH VARIATIONS

Ponds are not only for your garden, but they can also enhance your apartment. This affords an opportunity to observe fish not from the side but from above instead, and to let the plants grow out of the tank so that they can actually flower. Also quite charming are landscape aquariums, which combine aquariums with plant containers (for soil, swamp or hydro-culture) or terrariums.

**The planted community aquarium can be utilized as a room divider.**

## SPECIES AQUARIUM

Most beginning aquarists will no doubt start out with a community tank. Sooner or later (as in the case of the authors) a preference develops for a particular species of fish, and the desire to find out, or experience, more about their behavior and natural history. This is the step towards the species tank, which is set up according to the specific requirements of the type or species to be kept in it.

There are, however, species and genera which, due to their special adaptations to particular habitats or because of certain types of behavior, can in fact only be kept in a specifically set-up aquarium. Successful breeding of these fishes is then the ultimate confirmation of a species-correct creation of habitats.

One group of fishes which is more popular than any other are the cichlids. There are about as many cichlid fanciers as there are aquarists keeping all other fish species. Cichlids offer a number of characteristics which virtually pre-destine them for a species tank: adaptations to particular habitats (e.g. Lakes Malawi and Tanganyika), well-defined brood behavior (extending from open brooding to highly specialized mouthbrood-

(Top):A uniquely constructed cantilevered aquarium support. (Bottom): A free-standing six-sided aquarium.

ing), with more or less strongly developed pair bonding, father-mother family and many more peculiarities. Such special types of behavior require, of course, specifically set-up and decorated tanks for these fish only.

Yet, especially for cichlids the concept of a species tank must not be too closely focused. In order for their breeding behavior to develop fully, many cichlids require different co-inhabitants in the tank, since their innate territorial behavior may be directed against the other partner. Looking at it in those terms, the species tank then once again becomes a community tank. To provide, at this point, further information about cichlid care would go beyond the scope of this book. Instead, the interested reader is referred to the comprehensive literature available on cichlids and their husbandry.

**AD KONING'S BOOK OF CICHLIDS AND ALL OTHER FISHES OF LAKE MALAWI**
By Ad Konings
**TS-157**
ISBN 0-86622-527-7
UPC 0-1821425277-1
This is the newest and most ambitious work ever undertaken on the fishes of Lake Malawi. It provides plenty of easy to absorb text.
HC, 10 x 14", 448 pages, over 1000 full color photos.

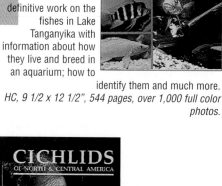

**PIERRE BRICHARD'S BOOK OF CICHLIDS & OTHER FISHES OF LAKE TANGANYIKA**
By Pierre Brichard
**TS-116**
ISBN 0-86622-667-2
UPC 0-18214-26672-3
This book is a definitive work on the fishes in Lake Tanganyika with information about how they live and breed in an aquarium; how to identify them and much more.
HC, 9 1/2 x 12 1/2", 544 pages, over 1,000 full color photos.

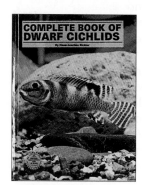

**ALL ABOUT CICHLIDS**
By Braz Walker
**PS-751**
ISBN 0-86622-038-0
UPC 0-18214-20380-3
This very practical and useful book makes a splendid first aquisition for any aquarist who would like to learn more about a fish family.
HC, 5 1/2 x 8", 96 pages.

**COMPLETE BOOK OF DWARF CICHLIDS**
By Hans- Joachim Richter
**TS-121**
ISBN 0-86622-701-6
UPC 0-18214-27016-4
Covers all the fish species popularly known as "dwarf" cichlids. Provides reader with practical, sensible, easy-to-apply tips.
HC, 8 1/2 x 11", 208 pages, over 400 full color photos.

**CICHLIDS OF NO. & CENTRAL AMERICA**
By Donald L. Conkel
**TS-184**
ISBN 0-86622-444-0
UPC 0-18214-24440-0
Don Conkel, is recognized as the world's most authoritative figure in regard to observing, collecting, and breeding North and Central American Cichlids. As a result of his efforts, people can now appreciate these fascinating fishes in illustrations with easy -to-read descriptions.
HC, 10 x 14", 192 pages, over 250 full color photos.

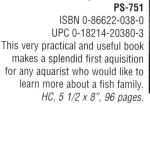

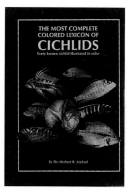

**COMPLETE INTRO. CICHLIDS (Sft cvr)**
By Dr. Robert J. Goldstein
**CO-011S**
ISBN 0-86622-279-0
UPC 0-18214-22790-8
Highly informative; perfect for beginners and experienced owners.
SC, 5 1/2 x 8 1/2", 128 pages, 120 full color photos.

**LEXICON OF CICHLIDS**
By Dr. Herbert R. Axelrod
**TS-190**
ISBN 0-86622-422-X
UPC 0-18214-80063-7
This book illustrates every scientifically described cichild species in the world.
HC, 9 x 12", 864 pages, over 2250 full color photos.

**CORYDORAS & REL. CATFISHES, COMP. INTRO. (Sft cvr)**
By Dr. Warren E. Burgess
**CO-015S**
ISBN 0-86622-287-1
UPC 0-18214-22871-4
Highly informative, perfect for beginners and experienced owners.
SC, 5 1/2 x 8 1/2", 96 pages, 154 full color photos.

**DWARF CICHLIDS**
By Dr. Jorg Vierke
**TS-118**
ISBN 0-86622-982-5
UPC 0-18214-29825-0
Provides vital information about all the dwarf cichlids, how to set up their tanks and how to breed.
HC, 5 1/2 x 8", 160 pages, 175 full color photos.

**SUCCESS WITH CICHLIDS FROM LAKES MALAWI & TANGANYIKA**
By Sabine Melke
**TT-030**
ISBN 0-86622-489-0
UPC 0-18214-24890-3
In a series of colorful books that provide readers with good information to keep their pet more enjoyably. Provides everything you need to know to get started.
HC, 7 x 10", 192 pages, over 200 full color photos.

**DISCUS**
By Tony Silva and Barbara Kotlar
**KW-097**
ISBN 0-86622-769-5
UPC 0-18214-27695-1
Presents sensible, easy-to-follow recommendations about breeding, selecting and caring for Discus fishes.It concentrates on providing readers with the information they need and want.
HC, 5 1/2 x 8", 96 pages, 43 full color photos.

# AVAILABLE AT YOUR LOCAL PET SHOP

# HABITAT OR LANDSCAPE AQUARIUMS

As part of the trend of constantly cheaper overseas travel, more and more aquarists have the opportunity to study the habitats of their charges first hand. What is more natural than to duplicate at home in the aquarium such a habitat in its elementary components and then to keep the appropriate fish species in this aquarium! Voila!!!...the birth of the habitat aquarium!

When setting up such a habitat tank it is not important to recreate a respective habitat in its original form, using original materials. Such an aquarium would most likely not be esthetically appealing.Instead the various structural elements have to fulfill the function to which the fish have become adapted in their particular habitat. For instance, a *Rasbora heteromorpha* will spawn just as readily under a leave of an Amazon sword plant as it would under a leaf of a *Cryptocoryne*. What is important, however, is that a plant with suitably broad stiff leaves is available to facilitate and accommodate spawning. The name of the plant and where it (originally) comes from is unimportant.

Similarly, when it comes to stocking the tank with fish, habitat-correctness must not be carried too far. A natural habitat always includes various representatives of the food chain, which makes sense for the real habitat. But no aquarist would place predators and their prey in the same tank, just because they come from the same habitat.

Through the use of an example, we would now like to show you exactly how to create a habitat aquarium, because it is the home of a particularly interesting group of fishes. The labyrinth fishes or climbing perches, have been selected for the habitat **'Asiatic rice paddy with adjacent standing or slowly flowing irrigation ditches.'** Maybe you too will have the opportunity to see such a flooded rice paddy and the adjacent irrigation ditches with their so typical inhabitants in Southeast Asia or Japan.

The semi-aquatic growing water spinach (*Ipomea* sp.) and numerous water lilies (*Nymphaea* sp.) form a dense

The correct aquarium for the correct fish. Tall fish, like angelfish, require a tall tank.

*Tropheus duboisi*, from Africa's Lake Tanganyika, is a rock-inhabiting species like most of the cichlids from Africa's rift lakes, therefore its aquarium should have a rocky decor.

undergrowth of stems and roots below the surface. The large floating leaves of the lilies provide shade for the underwater areas. Along the edges of the water there are a lot of reeds and other swamp plants. A bit further out we find the meter-long, narrow leaves of the hooked lily (*Crinum thaianum*) drifting on the surface. Roots from trees along the edges of the water penetrate into the water. The bottom is covered with a layer of dead and decaying plant parts and leaves which have fallen into the water.

In some areas, floating plants, like *Pistia*, water hyacinth (*Eichhornia* sp.) or water fern (*Salvinia* sp.) form nearly impenetrable floating layers. Even among the individual rice plants there are recurring patches of water lilies, water spinach and floating plants. The mostly very shallow water is heated to 28 to 33 degrees C by the tropical sun.

# LIVING ROOM PONDS, PALUDARIUMS, AQUA-TERRARIUMS

The already large and diverse area of freshwater aquarium keeping can be further enlarged and made more varied by the inclusion of specific types of tanks and decor. Even the selection of occupants plays a role.

Living room ponds provide a substantial solution for keeping cold water fish. Classical coldwater fish keeping, apart from keeping goldfish, is a nearly extinct branch of aquarium keeping.

The other side of the coin is that garden ponds are booming. A somewhat tangential development to this is the establishment of ponds indoors, in large apartments or gazebo-like facilities. Then, instead of koi, goldfish or golden orfe (cold water) tropical aquarium fish can live in warm water ponds. Important for a trouble-free operation of a living room pond are the proper dimensions of such a pool and the level of technical support equipment available for it. Such a pool opens totally new perspective for the viewer.

Paludariums (water & terrestrial [swamp] combination displays) are for those who are fans of tropical plants, and terrarium animals as well as fish. A shallow water section is dwarfed by a much higher land section, and both areas can be inhabited by typical occupants of such habitats. Paludariums can also be referred to as terrariums with a particularly large water section, which is viewed like an aquarium through a front glass panel. Technically this water section is operated like an aquarium.

Aqua-terrariums, however, go to the other extreme: the land section is minimal, usually as a pe-

**In this perfectly decorated aqua-terrarium (paludarium) there is green above and below the water line.**

ripheral attachment along the edge of the water or as a floating island. When keeping clawed dwarf frogs (*Xenopus* sp.) or an axolotl (a permanently aquatic salamander), one can do completely without a land section. On the other hand, tortoises require a land section which must be heated with an infra-red lamp, and lots of swimming and diving space under or around the floating island must be provided. Originally fish were only living food in such tanks, but aqua-terrarium fans also have possibilities of keeping terrestrial animals and fishes together.

Indoor water fountains are also sometimes misused as a place to keep fish. In view of the technical requirements this rarely ever makes sense and does not provide a species-correct habitat.

This habitat is inhabited by various species of labyrinth fishes, which, because of their special respiratory mechanism (they are air breathers), have become well adapted to the often relatively oxygen-deficient water. In the same habitat, but in less densely overgrown areas and with a slight water movement, there are various small *Cypriniformes*, for instance the red-tailed rasbora (*Rasbora borapetensis*). Along the surface there are schools of halfbeaks (*Dermogenys* sp.) and panchax (*Aplocheilus* sp.). The bottom is being scoured by various small loaches (*Botia* sp.), small spiny eels, and a multitude of almost transparent shrimp, all in search of food.

Among them, lying in wait are also some predators. Along the surface there are small schools of garfish (*Xenentodon* sp.) with their needle-sharp teeth, and along the bottom we find snakeheads (*Channa* sp.) waiting to ambush prey which pass by.

An aquarium which conforms to such a habitat could be as follows:The back and sides are taken up largely by tall water plants, such as *Vallisneria* and various stemmed plants (*Hygrophila, Heteranthera*) commonly found along

the edges of rice paddies with their tall rice plants. This impression can be further enhanced by creating a terrace in the back of the tank. Some bamboo sticks cut to size represent reed or other swamp grasses which grow well above the surface.

A bizarre-shaped root replaces tree roots protruding into the water. One or two tiger lotus plants (depending on the size of the tank) with their floating leaves provide a diffuse light below the surface. Beyond that, you can also use a few other floating plants, such as water fern (*Ceratopteris* sp.). Labyrinth fishes like to build their bubble nests among the floating leaves of these plants.

Lower plant growth in the middle of the tank and in its foreground can be provided by the undemanding *Cryptocoryne* (*C.wendtii*). Accumulating dead and decaying organic matter is easily simulated with dry autumn (fallen) leaves of beech, oak or alder trees. So that these leaves do not float, they need to be briefly immersed in boiling water.

This sort of habitat aquarium can be established in tanks as small as 60 cm (24 inches) long, using correspondingly small fish species. The principal fish for such an aquarium could, for instance, be a pair (or better yet, one male and two female) dwarf gouramies, (*Colisa lalia*), *Trichopsis vittatus*, or the honey gourami (*Colisa chuna*). Since courting males will quickly consider the entire tank as their territory, only one of the species listed should be considered. Support species could, for instance, be the dwarf rasbora (*Rasbora maculata*) or the red-tailed rasbora (*Rasbora borapetensis*), in the form of a little school of 10 to 15 specimens. The bottom of such a habitat tank can be occupied by a small school of (5 to 8) dwarf loaches (*Botia sidthimunki*). This species has been unavailable for a long time and presumedly it may have become extinct in its homeland. More recently, this fish is being bred commercially in Thailand and should be available again soon.

Larger species, such as the pearl gourami (*Trichogaster leeri*) and many others, of course, require suitably larger tanks.

One fish that must not be forgotten is the well-known Siamese fighting fish. The impression that due to their innate aggression only one male should ever be kept together with several females in the same tank, is not quite correct. Males that do not know each other will always enter into a serious fight when they encounter each other. On the other hand, things are different with fish which have grown up together. It is quite possible to keep several males which know each other together with several females in the type of habitat tank discussed here and actually breed them. This applies

**Household cleaning chemicals should NEVER be used on an aquarium as they may be poisonous to fishes and are hard to wipe away. Use only those cleaning sprays that are made especially for aquariums. Photo courtesy of Aquarium Pharmaceuticals.**

moreso to the short-finned wild form than to the commercially-produced veiltail variety. Since fighting fish tend to utilize the entire water space, from the surface down to the bottom, it is not advisable to include any other species in such a tank.

There are yet many more different ways of creating a habitat aquarium, but discussing these even briefly would well exceed the scope of this book. Instead, the interested reader is referred to the books on the subject.

**A beautiful pair of pearl gouramis, *Trichogaster leeri*. These delicate fish deserve a peaceful, delicately planted aquarium. Photo by Aqua Press Piednoir.**

The flooded rice fields of central Thailand, with an irrigation canal in the foreground, is the typical habitat of many labyrinth fishes.

## DUTCH PLANT AQUARIUM

This is a type of aquarium where the care of water plants is the principal husbandry objective. The plants are arranged according to particular esthetic considerations, with the aim of achieving a harmonious composite picture. Since this often involves plants with highly diverse requirements, maintaining such an aquarium requires considerable skill and involves an optimum of maintenance. As indicated by the name, this type of aquarium keeping was first established in Holland, where it is still very popular.

A Dutch plant aquarium (no fishes!).

Catching fishes in northern Thailand. Many aquarium fishes are also popular food fishes in their native countries.

# A 'DRY' SUBJECT: WATER

Water is 'the' environment for our fish. Because of the intimate, direct contact with water there are a multitude of reciprocal relationships between water and its occupants. The composition of water influences vital metabolic processes of animals and plants, and because of these processes substances are given off into the water, which then change its composition. Therefore, water and water quality are central topics in aquarium keeping.

## WATER IS NOT ALWAYS....WATER

Water is an ideal solvent. It can maintain a wide range of substances in solution without being perceivable by the naked eye. For instance, a liter of distilled water looks exactly the same as a liter of seawater. Only a taste sample (or direct measurement) reveals the difference. Even tap water can, depending on its origin, contain various dissolved substances.

Beyond that, the organisms in a mini-habitat aquarium exert a range of influences on the composition of the water. Various substances can react with each other in water or may become modified. Such changes

Water is not always the same: Not always can we see such clear differences as in these two streams flowing together in Costa Rica.

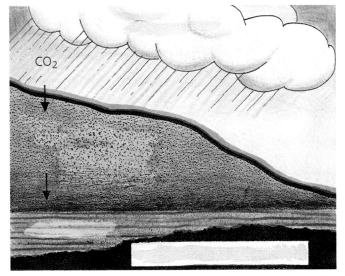

The carbon dioxide containing rainwater picks up more $CO_2$ as well as many minerals on its path through the humus and layers of rock.

in the chemistry of water all too often are not of a positive nature. They have a corresponding effect on the fishes.

In order to be able to regulate and manipulate these processes as required, we would like to introduce you to some of the significant factors which act upon water in invisible ways. In doing so we will omit explanations of some of the complex chemical interactions and concentrate, as far as possible, on that which is essential for proper aquarium maintenance.

### Water hardness

You will have noticed that when washing your hands in tap water in certain geographical regions you need a lot of soap to generate enough lather, while elsewhere it takes only very little soap. Wherever we need a lot of soap the water is hard; requiring little soap means the water is soft.

Certain mineral salts, the so-called hardness builders [calcium carbonate] determine the hardness of water. How do these get into the water? Tap water is generally ground water and water from springs and rivers. Somewhere along the line rainwater has percolated through layers of ground substrate (soil, sand, rocks, gravel, etc.). This water then accumulates above non-permeable layers as ground water and re-emerges somewhere as a spring.

On its passage through the air and through the upper humus layers of the soil, water picks up carbon dioxide and changes some of it into carbonic acid. When this acid water percolates through calcareous layers the carbon dioxide dissolves some of the mineral salts. But if the rainwater percolates through carbonate-free layers of bed rock, no minerals will be dissolved and the water remains soft.

The largest amount of substances dissolved in water consists of salts of the hardness builders calcium and magnesium. One distinguishes between total hardness, carbonate hardness and non-carbonate hardness, which, due to its main constituent, is also called sulfate hardness. Total hardness refers to the amount of alkaline ions

In this stream in central Borneo, humic acids are discoloring the water, making it tea-colored. Here various barbs and barb-like fishes, chocolate gouramis, and halfbeaks can be found.

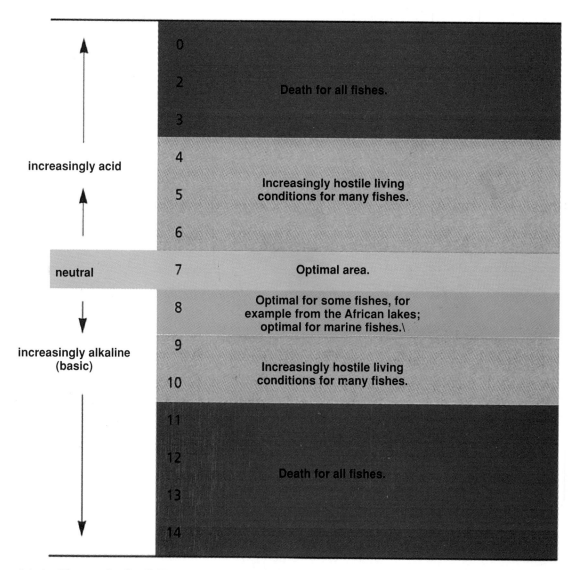

| | |
|---|---|
| increasingly acid | 0 |
| | 2 Death for all fishes. |
| | 3 |
| | 4 |
| | 5 Increasingly hostile living conditions for many fishes. |
| | 6 |
| neutral | 7 Optimal area. |
| | 8 Optimal for some fishes, for example from the African lakes; optimal for marine fishes.\ |
| increasingly alkaline (basic) | 9 |
| | 10 Increasingly hostile living conditions for many fishes. |
| | 11 |
| | 12 Death for all fishes. |
| | 13 |
| | 14 |

The pH of water is of crucial significance for the fishes.

in the water, that is, calcium and magnesium. Rarely occurring ions, as for instance potassium, sodium and others, can be ignored here.

From elementary chemistry in school we know that ions can never be present in water by themselves, since they are formed during the dissolution of salts. During this process a matching 'partner' of each ion also becomes disassociated (from the original salt). The most commonly occurring 'partners' are carbonate- and hydrocarbonate-cations, which are the builders of carbonate hardness.

In most natural waters about 80% of the calcium and magnesium ions are coupled to carbonate and hydrocarbonate cations, which then give rise to a carbonate component of about 80% of the total hardness present. The remaining 20% of calcium and magnesium ions have sulphate, chloride or nitrate ions as partners and represent the so-called non-carbonate hardness.

In some waters (e.g., in the tropics) apart from calcium and magnesium ions there are considerable amounts of potassium (K) and sodium (Na) ions, which are also coupled to carbonate and hydrocarbonate cations, but are not measurable as part of the total hardness. In this case the carbonate hardness is larger than the total hardness. The standard unit measure for hardness in Germany is 'degrees of German hardness.' It is called DH in English-speaking areas.

For most fishes and plants, water hardness plays a subordinate role. Most soft-water fishes and plants that have been bred in captivity for generations will do equally well in medium hard to hard water. Essential for good fish and plant husbandry is not a constant slopping around of water in order to lower undesirably high hardness values (which sooner or later is forgotten anyway), but instead the CONTINUITY of conditions.

Experience has shown that medium-hard water (between 8 and 20 DH) is far more stable (i.e., less prone to variations in water values, especially that of the pH). The reason is the ability of carbonate hardness to 'buffer' acids. For instance, if we add a bit of hydrochloric acid to water with a high carbonate hardness, at first nothing happens. The carbonates have become bonded to the acid and have neutralized it. Even the pH value does not change. Only the total amount of hardness has been reduced by the acid. When the same amount of acid is added to carbonate-free water, there is an immediate, dramatic drop in the pH value, the so-called 'acid crash' and fish will die. For that reason the carbonate hardness is now referred to as acid binding capacity. Only for breeding purposes should we attempt to provide approximately natural water values, since fish eggs are not very adaptable.

## pH value or degree of acidity

The pH value is a measure of how acidic or alkaline (basic) a liquid is. The pH scale extends from 0 to 14. The 0 value corresponds to extreme acidity (e.g. hydrochloric acid) and the value 14 represents an extremely alkaline solution (e.g. sodium hydroxide). The exact mid-point (7) signifies a neutral solution, which is neither acidic nor alkaline. Consequently, the degree of acidity increases as the pH value drops below 7; similarly, the alkalinity increases as the pH value rises above 7.

In our daily life we are often confronted with the pH value. For instance, the human digestive process in our stomach takes place under extreme acidic conditions. Stomach acid has a pH from 1 to 2. Foods and drinks are perceived by us as being tasty when they are more or less acidic.

A solution of bicarbonate in tap water, a standard remedy against excess stomach acid, is alkaline and is generally considered to be less tasty. Tap water is generally in the neutral region of around pH 7.

Fish can live in water with a pH ranging from 4.5 to 9. Yet the extreme regions (e.g., the very acidic black waters of Rio Negro or the strongly alkaline lakes in eastern Africa) are inhabited only by a few specially adapted fish species. The majority of freshwater fish, including those kept in aquariums, live in water of pH values between 5.5 and 7.5. Aquarium experience has shown that species from slightly acidic water with pH values of around 6 as well as those from slightly alkaline waters of around pH 7.5 can easily be kept in the neutral range of around pH 7. Only for breeding purposes do you need the preferred pH range.

The fundamental fish husbandry principle of maintaining constant water conditions also extends to the pH value. This makes sense when one keeps in mind that with a change in pH value of one point, the acid concentration does not double but instead is multiplied by a factor of ...**ten**! That means pH 5 is ten times as acidic as pH 6, and one hundred times more acidic than pH 7. On the other hand, a pH of 9 is ten-times as alkaline as pH 8 and one hundred-times as alkaline as pH 7.

The pH value in natural waters is determined principally by two components, by the carbonate hardness and carbon dioxide, and the carbonic acid that develops. The volume ratio of carbonate hardness (as the alkaline component) and carbon dioxide (as the acid component) determines the pH level. If this ratio is equal, the pH value is 7, the level preferred for keeping fish and plants in an aquarium. Other natural, pH-influencing substances are the humic and fulvic acids which occur in black waters and roots, driftwood, etc.

In the section on carbonate hardness we mentioned that water with a higher carbonate hardness is better buffered against acids than soft water. The same holds true in the other direction, that is, sudden pH increases are just as dangerous. In order to maintain carbonate in solution as hydrogen carbonate (bicarbonate), requires a specific amount of dissolved carbon dioxide to be present in the water. Consequently, the more carbonate present in the water, the more carbon dioxide is required.

Water plants remove carbon dioxide from the water during the day by means of assimilation. This lowers the carbon dioxide concentration required to keep the carbonate that is present in solution. The consequence of this is that some of the hydrogen carbonate drops out as insoluble carbonate, which is deposited as a white layer on the leaves of water plants), and carbon dioxide, which then results in a new equilibrium which keeps the remaining carbonate in solution.

If there is an insufficient external supply of carbon dioxide (e.g. $CO_2$ fertilization) this process continues until all the hydrogen carbonate has been used up and is then found as insoluble carbonate covering the leaves of plants.

As long as hydrogen carbonate is present in water the pH is only marginally moved in the direction of pH 8. There are, however, plants, which do not stop taking up carbon dioxide, even when all the hydrogen carbonate has been used up. These plants will then also remove the carbon dioxide bound-up in the carbonate precipitate. This can, in a very short period of time, raise the pH level to 10.

As an immediate consequence the delicate gill tissue and mucous membranes of fish will become damaged. Unless there is immediate corrective action, this may well be fatal for the fish. This phenomenon occurs much easier and quicker in soft water with little carbonate matter than in hard water. Therefore, once again a word of advice: *hard water is more pH-stable than soft water!*

## Oxygen

Oxygen is THE elixir of life for almost all living things. Without oxygen there would be no animal life on earth. Consequently, oxygen is also the single most important factor for an aquarium and the well-being of all of its inhabitants depends on it. Fish need oxygen for respiration, and plants need it, at least during the night. But oxygen is even far more important for the many millions of bacteria, which decompose the organic waste products generated by the fish and plants in an aquarium. Without bacteria aquarium keeping would be impossible! More about these bacteria and their beneficial activity in the next section.

Gases (including oxygen) have the tendency to establish an equilibrium of partial pressures between air and water. This results, depending upon the temperature, in a specific oxygen content in water. The colder the water, the more oxygen it contains due to the equilibrium of partial pressures. This is then also the maximum oxygen content that can be achieved through aeration. At 25° C this is 8.11 mg/l. The oxygen levels for other temperatures are listed in the accompanying table.

**Temperature dependence of oxygen content in the water.**

| Temperature (°C) | Oxygen Content (MG $O_2$/L) |
| --- | --- |
| 10 | 10,92 |
| 11 | 10,67 |
| 12 | 10,43 |
| 13 | 10,20 |
| 14 | 9,98 |
| 15 | 9,76 |
| 16 | 9,56 |
| 17 | 9,37 |
| 18 | 9,18 |
| 19 | 9,01 |
| 20 | 8,84 |
| 21 | 8,68 |
| 22 | 8,53 |
| 23 | 8,38 |
| 24 | 8,25 |
| 25 | 8,11 |
| 26 | 7,99 |
| 27 | 7,86 |
| 28 | 7,75 |
| 29 | 7,64 |
| 30 | 7,53 |
| 31 | 7,42 |
| 32 | 7,32 |
| 33 | 7,22 |
| 34 | 7,13 |
| 35 | 7,04 |

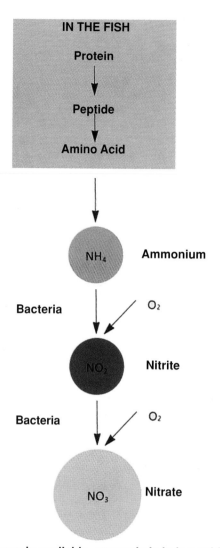

When oxygen is available, ammonia is being oxidized to nitrate via the nitrification process.

## Nitrite

In an aquarium one should attempt to generate the required oxygen by biological means, which means through the assimilation activities of plants (except aquariums with fish which are incompatible with plants). In order to be on the safe side, strive for an oxygen level (just before turning off the lights) which approximates the equilibrium for the prevailing temperature. But this is only possible with suitable illumination intensity and optimal plant care.

It is wrong to use oxygen values from the native habitat of our aquarium fish as role model, since these values are often below equilibrium level. In contrast to aquarium conditions, the oxygen values in nature are—although low—of extreme constancy, which is not influenced by animal respiration. The fishes have adapted to such (oxygen) levels.

If, on the other hand, we should be tempted to run our aquarium at only 3 or 4 mg/l oxygen, we would be courting disaster. The first night, at the latest when fishes AND plants require oxygen, there will be, in the relatively small volume of water of a home aquarium, a catastrophic oxygen deficiency, with all its fatal consequences. This problem may even be FURTHER compounded by unintentional over-feeding (left-over food in the water) or the occasional fish which has died un-

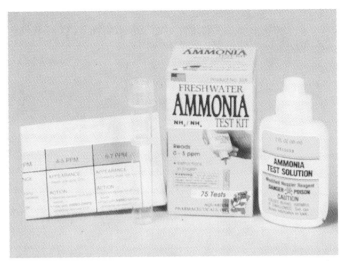

Freshwater ammonia test kit. Test kits that enable the hobbyist to monitor various factors affecting the quality of the water, such as its ammonia content, are relatively inexpensive and easy to use. Photo courtesy of Aquarium Pharmaceuticals.

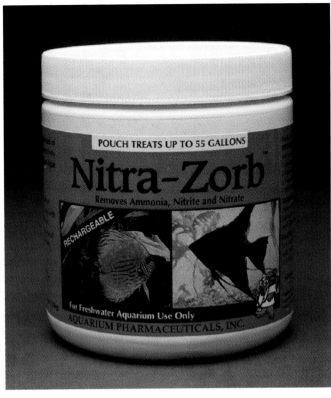

noticed, placing an additional oxygen demand on the water. The environment 'aquarium' reacts differently than a natural habitat and so a high oxygen level in the evening approximating the equilibrium is a fundamental prerequisite for the well-being of the aquarium occupants!

## Fish, too, make a 'mess'

All animals require food, from which a more or less complex digestive process extracts the nutrients required for the maintenance of bodily functions and for growth. Anything not needed or which goes un-utilized will be excreted. These excretion products are then decomposed (= mineralized) via various intermediate stages, and taken up by the plants as nutrients to be used to produce plant cell material. These plants are eventually eaten by animals, and the entire process starts all over again.

This very much over-simplified cycle occurs in properly functioning ecosystems without any significant accumulation of intermediate products. The system is in a

*Above:* A number of products have been developed to aid in removing potentially dangerous nitrogenous wastes from aquarium water. Photo courtesy of Aquarium Pharmaceuticals.
*Right:* A number of water conditioning products intended to remove chlorine and reduce or eliminate potential stress damage to fishes in a newly set up tank are available. Some contain aloe vera which helps to form a synthetic protective slime coating on the skin of fishes. Photo courtesy Aquarium Pharmaceuticals.

### Ammonia content dependence on pH values (amended as per Krause).

| $NH_4^+/NH_3$ Total Content (MG/$_L$) | Portion of the Poisonous Ammonia (M$^G$/$_L$) at pH Value | | | | | |
|---|---|---|---|---|---|---|
| | 6,5 | 7,0 | 7,5 | 8,0 | 8,5 | 9,0 |
| 0,1 | < 0,001 | 0,001 | 0,002 | 0,006 | 0,014 | 0,035 |
| 0,2 | < 0,001 | 0,001 | 0,004 | 0,011 | 0,029 | 0,069 |
| 0,3 | 0,001 | 0,002 | 0,006 | 0,017 | 0,043 | 0,104 |
| 0,5 | 0,001 | 0,003 | 0,010 | 0,029 | 0,072 | 0,173 |
| 0,8 | 0,002 | 0,005 | 0,015 | 0,046 | 0,115 | 0,277 |
| 1,0 | 0,002 | 0,006 | 0,019 | 0,057 | 0,144 | 0,346 |
| 1,2 | 0,002 | 0,007 | 0,023 | 0,069 | 0,173 | 0,415 |
| 1,5 | 0,003 | 0,009 | 0,029 | 0,086 | 0,216 | 0,519 |
| 2,0 | 0,004 | 0,012 | 0,038 | 0,114 | 0,288 | 0,692 |
| 4,0 | 0,008 | 0,024 | 0,076 | 0,229 | 0,576 | 1,384 |
| 6,0 | 0,011 | 0,036 | 0,114 | 0,342 | 0,864 | 2,076 |
| 8,0 | 0,015 | 0,048 | 0,152 | 0,458 | 1,152 | 2,70 |

The table is valid only at 24°C. Every 1°C higher/lower temperature there exists up to 4% higher/lower values.

Valuation  ☐ Harmless  ▨ Critical  ▦ Acutely Dangerous

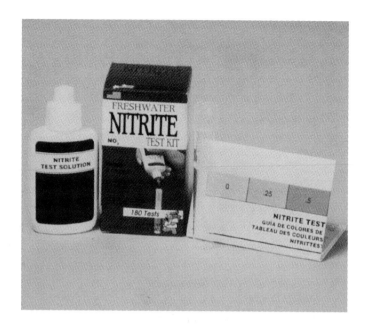

so-called *biological equilibrium*, but a fundamentally different situation exists in an aquarium. In comparison to natural systems, an aquarium usually contains a far greater animal density (number of animals per unit volume) with relatively few plants.

The fish give off substantially more metabolic waste products than can be utilized by the plants. Consequently, there is an accumulation of waste products from the digestive process of the fishes. For that reason it is important to be aware of what happens to these metabolic waste products in an aquarium.

## Ammonium, nitrite and nitrate

Of greatest importance in an aquarium are the nitrogenous compounds ammonia, nitrite and nitrate. Of these, only nitrite represents a direct danger for the fishes and ammonia only under certain conditions. These compounds originate from the digestion of proteins which are broken down to ammonia in the fish's body. This is then excreted.

The breakdown of proteins occurs via the following steps: proteins → peptides → amino acids → ammonium → nitrite → nitrate. We are particularly interested in the last steps, from ammonium to nitrate, since these take place in the aquarium and have a direct influence on the aquarium. Uneaten food is also broken down by various organisms, which, of course, also excrete ammonium.

What happens to this ammonium? In nature it serves as the principal plant nutrient and as such it is largely used up. The further breakdown from nitrite to nitrate plays only a minor role. Under aquarium conditions even the most luxuriant plant growth cannot use up as much ammonium as is being generated by the fish. Therefore, certain bacteria oxidize ammonium (by using oxygen) via the intermediate stage of nitrite to nitrate. Nitrate can also be utilized by plants as a nutrient, but ammonium is generally preferred.

In the final analysis, however, nitrate accumulates in an aquarium. This is beneficial because the bacterial breakdown of ammonium into nitrate—the so-called *nitrification*—is practically life insurance for our aquarium fish. Why? This is easy to explain.

Ammonium as such is not toxic, but depending upon the prevailing pH it can change into highly toxic ammonia. The following general rule applies: the higher the pH the greater the presence of toxic ammonia.

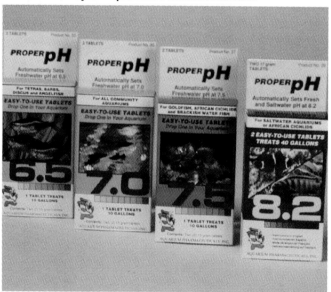

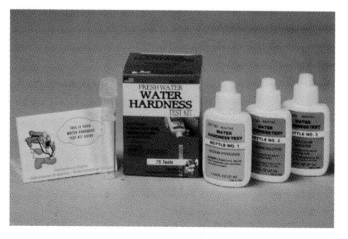

# ALGAE IN THE AQUARIUM

Is there anybody who is not familiar with what are undoubtedly the most dreaded of all living things in a freshwater aquarium: the **algae**? Unfortunately, they are only too often the main reason why an enthusiastically started aquarium hobby is given up. The worst are the blue-green algae, which can also be dirty blackish-blue. They can quickly cover everything inside an aquarium with a slimy film, and frequently give off a penetrating, musty odor which can be detected a few meters away from the aquarium. Those plants affected by it can no longer assimilate and will gradually die. Oxygen supply for the fish and the important bacteria deteriorates. Moreover, these algae also give off harmful metabolic waste products, and the catastrophe begins unless proper maintenance procedures have been implemented from the start to prevent blue-green algae from becoming established in the first place.

Apart from blue-green algae there are many other algae. The most important ones will be discussed later on.

## EFFECTIVE COUNTER MEASURES

What can an aquarist do to make life difficult for algae? First of all it is important to know that algae are plants. Even though they are primitive forms they require the same nutrients as water plants. Yet, unlike higher plants, which have moderate needs for certain nutrients, algae require enormous amounts of nitrate and phosphate. Algae are less developed life forms. They are also less demanding and more adaptable than higher plants.

As a general statement it can be said that in a well-planted aquarium algae hardly have a chance for substantial development. The maintenance requirements outlined in the section on water plants are also the preventative measures against algae. Normally growing higher plants with an adequate nutrient uptake will make sure that there is hardly anything left for the algae.

The rule of uppermost importance is continuity of all conditions. If there is any change, higher plants require longer to adapt to these changes and during this period they assimilate little or not at all. The far more adaptable algae can (and will) take advantage of this situation; nutrients not utilized by the higher plants will then be utilized for a massive development of algae.

Consequently, aquarists should not experiment with lighting, such as changing the light color, lighting intensity or duration. It is well-known that fluorescent tubes with an emphasis of red and blue in their color spectrum tend to promote algal growth. Therefore, they must not be used on their own, but only in conjunction with daylight tubes. Nitrate and phosphate levels, the principal nutrients of algae, should be kept at a minimum. This is most effectively done by dense plant growth right from the start and through regular partial water changes.

**Algae-removing wands are available for both glass and plastic aquaria; those designed for use in plastic aquaria are less abrasive than those used in glass aquaria. Photo courtesy of Aquarium Pharmaceuticals.**

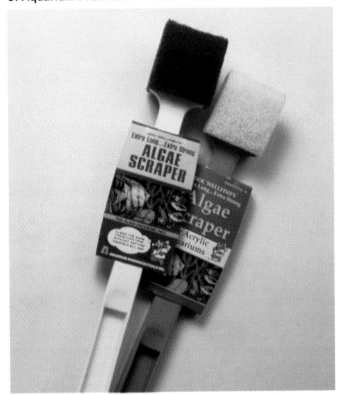

## Help for beginners

Dangers of an algal plague are particularly profound in a newly set-up aquarium, since the plants are not yet able to fully assimilate until the tank is properly conditioned. During that time period aquarists need to be extremely vigilant. The slightest algal formation must be removed immediately.

Algae-eating fish are a useful aid in the fight against undesirable algae. They should be planned into the original fish population of a tank. Those species that should be considered are all the various sucker catfish, e.g., *Otocinclus* (also suitable for small tanks), *Ancistrus* (will also feed on plants if there are not enough algae present), *Loricaria*, *Farlowella* and many others.

Young *Crossocheilus siamensis* is an eager algae eater. Live-bearers continuously pick on algal covers. Using snails to combat algae can quickly lead to a snail plague!

**Sucker catfishes, such as this *Otocinclus*, are excellent helpers in the fight against algae.**

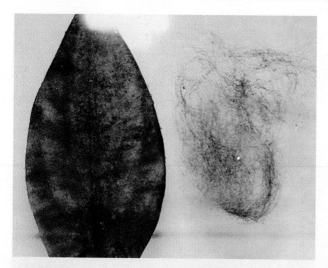

Top: Leaf of *Cryptocoryne pontederiifolia* with beginning brown algal growth; on the right threads of green algae. Bottom: (left) *Cryptocoryne* leaf with blue-green algae. (center) Leaf of *Anubias barteri* var. *glabra* with "brush" algae. (right) Vallisneria leaf with long threads of "beard" algae.

It is also possible to kill algae chemically, but this should only be contemplated in an emergency. Since algae are also plants, chemical agents used to exterminate them will also affect regular aquatic plants. It is therefore a question of dosage and how far the sensitivity of algae (to the chemical) varies from that of the other aquarium plants. Therefore, it is imperative to exactly comply with the directions of use provided by the manufacturer. Overdosage must be avoided under all circumstances.

## An algal portrait

The division of algae into green algae, brown algae, blue-green algae, as well as bearded or brush algae is scientifically not quite correct, but is being maintained here, since this grouping is probably familiar to most aquarists.

GREEN ALGAE occur as a layer on aquarium glasses or sometimes as masses of long threads on aquarium plants. They are harmless and indicate good water conditions. They are removed from the front glass using appropriate cleaning utensils. The long threads can easily be removed by hand or with a rough-surface, wooden stick.

BROWN ALGAE are actually diatoms (Diatomaceae) and have nothing at all in common with true brown algae commonly found in the ocean. They are generally a sign of light deficiency.

BLUE-GREEN ALGAE occur, as a rule, in water carrying a heavy load of organic waste products. Usually siphoning out these algae very thoroughly with a hose, combined with regular (partial) water changes, will gradually eliminate this problem.

BEARDED ALGAE (*Compsopogon*) and BRUSH ALGAE belong the red algae (Rhodophyta) and they are the most stubborn to get rid of once they are in an aquarium. Presumedly they were introduced to the aquarium hobby together with water plants during the 1960's. The bearded algae form long, blue to blackish green threads, while the brush algae grow as blackish, about 10 mm long, brush-like clumps. Both types of algae establish themselves most commonly on rough substrate such as the edges of thick-leaved water plants or pieces of aquarium decor.

Carbonate deposits, caused by $CO_2$ deficiency, offer particularly good sites of attachment. When this happens the pH is usually strongly elevated. The safest way to eliminate these types of algae is the physical removal of affected plant leaves. $CO_2$ fertilization, combined with a lowering of the pH value usually prevents a renewed outbreak of these algae.

## Nitrite

Nitrite is a very potent fish poison. Values from about 0.5 mg/l are critical and 2.0 mg/l is usually lethal. On the other hand, the end product, nitrate, is rather more fish compatible. Fishes can tolerate levels of a few hundred milligram per liter. In a properly conditioned aquarium ammonium and nitrite should be virtually absent, and only nitrate can be permitted to gradually accumulate. Such a situation is ideal for fishes. Nevertheless, a steadily increasing nitrate level also creates a somewhat different problem. Unless the nitrate concentration is being constantly diluted through regular, partial water changes,

**A water change is a useful maintenance procedure — to the delight of the fishes.**

Phosphate also gets into natural waters through human activities, such as doing the laundry in a local river.

certain undesirable 'guests' will enjoy the sudden windfall of ideal nutrients: the algae.

Which are the bacteria which effect nitrification and how do they get into the aquarium? Two vastly different groups of bacteria have specialized in nitrification, that is, the change (oxidation) of ammonium to nitrate. One group oxidizes ammonium to nitrite and the other oxidizes nitrite into nitrate. Consequently, one group cannot exist without the other, since it derives the nitrite from it.

In order to become engaged in this beneficial activity, these bacteria make certain demands on the environment around them. They need sufficient oxygen for the oxidation, a pH value around neutral to weakly alkaline and carbon dioxide for food.

Since an aquarium is not a sterile system (and that is why boiling pieces of aquarium decor is pointless), one could, of course, wait after a tank has been set up until the nitrification bacteria have become established, were it not for the extremely slow growth of these bacteria and the understandable impatience of the new aquarist.

Nitrifying bacteria require 10 to 20 hours to double their numbers, what other bacteria can do in a few minutes! Therefore, without outside intervention and help it would take about 2 to 3 weeks for a newly set-up aquarium until sufficient nitrifying bacteria have accumulated. In that time period we can monitor bacterial build-up by the progress of ammonium, nitrite and nitrate concentrations. Initially the ammonium level increases strongly and then drops again after a while. At the time the nitrite level starts to climb, the first group of bacteria has become established in sufficient numbers. Again, some time will pass until the nitrite level starts to drop. Now the second group of bacteria begins to do its task, oxidizing nitrite to nitrate. When finally the nitrite level approaches 0 and a gradual increase in nitrate is noticed, the aquarium can

be considered as being properly conditioned and fish can be introduced.

Now another problem can occur. The number of bacteria is dependent upon the substrate. When a tank has been conditioned only with plants present and without any metabolic waste products accumulating, the initial problem (lack of nitrification) can re-emerge, because the bacterial colony has yet to grow in order to adjust to increased amounts of waste products created by fish.

All that may not concern you at all if you have inoculated your new tanks properly. The principal area of activity of these bacteria is, apart from the substrate and everything else inside the tank, the filter, where suitable media offer appropriate settling sites for the bacteria. For that reason, rinsing out well-conditioned filter media (which must not have been permitted to dry out) in the new tank is absolutely the best inoculation method. The cloudiness thus caused in the new tank will disappear quickly, and you have instantly a conditioned aquarium, ready to accept fish.

Aquarium clubs have been using this method for decades to set up tanks for their regular shows. It should be remembered that nitrifying bacteria are extremely sensitive and cannot be easily preserved!

So far the impression may have arisen that only nitrifying bacteria live in an aquarium. That is, of course, incorrect. Many different species of bacteria live in an aquarium. They are all involved in the recycling of organic materials; only, these bacteria occur naturally without our help.

## DANGER OUT OF THE TAP

Nowadays in all new buildings (as well as in older ones which are being extensively renovated) it is common practice to use water pipes made of copper. These copper pipes can present a serious danger to all aquarium inhabitants.

Newly installed copper pipes do not yet have an insulating layer of carbonate deposits coating their insides. If particular pipes are not being used and water is held in them, substantial amounts of copper can be leached out into the water. Since dissolved copper is highly toxic, it can lead to the poisoning of fish as well as inhibiting plant growth.

A similar danger exists in newly installed hot water boilers or flow-through heaters, or in those where the carbonate coating has recently been removed. Here the water should be permitted to run off for a few minutes before it is used in an aquarium. Usually within a year a layer of carbonate deposit will form, which prevents any further dissolution of copper in a pipe network.

through water changes. Consequently, phosphate is often not recognized as the real culprit in such a situation.

## Organic substances in the water

All natural waters contain large amounts of dissolved, large-molecular organic compounds. These substances come partly from the metabolic waste products of fish and also from plant decay. Hygienically speaking, these are pollutant indicators and must not be present in drinking water.

Yet, these substances have quite a positive effect on fishes. As so-called protective colloids they protect the mucous membranes against harmful influences. Humic substances, which occur mainly in black waters, have a bactericidal effect and repair mucous membranes. But water plants also benefit from dissolved organic sub-

A hose (with suction protection) leading to the nearest drain saves a lot of bucket carrying!

## Phosphate

Phosphate compounds perform important functions for fishes as well as plants. Energy-rich phosphates are needed as energy suppliers for muscle activities or in plants to build sugar. Phosphates are also needed for the development of bone. It gets into the water from the digestive processes of fishes and from left-over (uneaten) food. The level and effect of phosphates are concentrations in an aquarium are often underestimated. Plants in the wild have adjusted to the fact that phosphates are scarce, so they have appropriate mechanisms which enable them to get by on even the smallest amounts of phosphate.

What happens now when there is suddenly phosphate in quantities which exceed the requirements of water plants more than a hundredfold? Our special friends, the algae, will be overjoyed and virtually devour the phosphate. When there are also suitable amounts of nitrate present, an algae plague is virtually pre-programmed! The disturbing fact here is that algae can store phosphate if there is more than they need at the moment. Therefore, algae can continue to thrive even long after the phosphate content in aquarium water has been lowered

stances, since many of them act as natural chelating agents (nutrient carriers) and so keep important nutrients available.

It has been shown that fresh tapwater acts aggressively on gill and mucous membranes of fishes. Only supplements of organic substances makes the water suitable for fish. The addition of such water conditioning substances, available from pet and aquarium shops, eliminates this problem.

## WATER CONDITIONING

In this section we would like to give you hints on how to modify undesirable water chemistry values of tap water. Furthermore, we will show you how to keep water values which have changed while the aquarium is in operation, within certain limits. Remember, continuity is the most important 'commandment'!

However, before you start changing the composition of tap water which you are about to add to your tank, you have to carefully consider whether it is really necessary for the fish you intend to keep. As mentioned before, most commonly kept tropical fish will do well in tap water, provided the continuity of conditions is maintained. This is easier done with straight tap water than by continuously tampering with the water.

Things are different when it comes to breeding. For that purpose we need water chemistry values which are as close as possible to natural values, since fish eggs have little capacity to adjust.

## Changing water hardness

**Increasing hardness:** Elevating the level of water hardness is really only ever necessary when hard water species are kept in areas which have soft water. Cases in point are cichlids from the East African rift valley lakes, or Australian rainbow fish.

Filtration over crushed marble or pulverized calcium carbonate increases total hardness and carbonate hardness evenly. This, however, requires a simultaneous carbon dioxide supplement in order to bring the carbonate material properly into solution and then keep it dissolved. Total hardness without carbonate hardness can be achieved with calcium sulfate. More convenient carbonate and total hardness builders are available from pet and aquarium shops.

**Lowering hardness:** Softening hard water is far more complicated than increasing the hardness. Generally, there are only three methods which are practical from an aquarist's point of view. Which method you eventually use depends ultimately on your local situation. The methods presented here are discussed only in principle, since there is comprehensive literature available for those who are interested in greater details.

Two procedures are based on the principle of ion exchange. These are PARTIAL DESALINIZATION or decarbonization and TOTAL DESALINIZATION. As is indicated by their names these procedures rely on the exchange of certain ions with those that cause the water hardness to disappear. The central component of such equipment is certain artificial resins with ion exchange characteristics. Water to be softened is simply filtered over these resins, just as if it were a filter.

Decarbonization is really only practical if the carbonate hardness in the water makes up at least 80% of the total hardness. Decarbonization displaces the ion distribution in the water. An extremely low total salt content (as required for breeding certain soft water fishes) is not achievable, so this method is really only suitable for less sensitive fish species.

With total desalinization one obtains virtually distilled water which is used for mixing with regular water to obtain the desired hardness.

All ion exchangers have a limited capacity (= 'working life'), which depends on the hardness of the original water and the amount of resin used. Once exhausted the resins need to be re-charged, either with hydrochloric acid (decarbonization) or with hydrochloric acid and sodium hydroxide (total desalinization). CAUTION IS OF PARAMOUNT IMPORTANCE WHEN THESE CHEMICALS ARE BEING USED. In most industrialized countries the regeneration liquid is considered to be special waste material and must not be poured into the kitchen sink! There are also commercial regeneration services, which may be slightly more expensive but save effort, time and the problems of waste disposal.

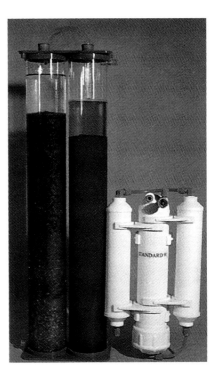

Water softening: On the left is an ion-exchanger (full desalinator) with indicator resin, which indicates the need for regeneration through a color change (red); on the right is a reverse osmosis unit.

As the third method we have to list REVERSE OSMOSIS. Equipment that uses this method is now more commonly available. These machines use the line pressure from the municipal water supply pushing against a membrane, which, like a micro-fine sieve, retains everything that is larger than pure water molecules. But a small remnant amount of salt always remains in the water.

The effectiveness of reverse osmosis units depends on the water pressure and the temperature. At normal line pressure this is about 20%. This means that from every one hundred liters of tap water one obtains 20 liters of desalinated water (permeate) and 80% of remnant water with an elevated salt content (concentrate), that is being discharged as waste. Whenever possible reverse osmosis units should be kept permanently in operation in order to obtain maximum longevity of the membrane. Consequently, investing in such equipment is only cost-effective if there is a continuous demand for such water. There are no regeneration costs, but the membrane needs to be replaced periodically. This is expensive and there are also higher water costs, particularly with a continuous operation.

Do not contemplate any other methods, as for instance those used in household appliances that make water softer. This equipment works on the basis of neutral exchangers, recognizable by the fact that salt is used for regeneration.

In effect, the hardness builders are changed into salts, which in terms of cleaning technology makes sense but is useless for aquarium purposes since the total salt content remains unchanged.

## Changing the pH value

**Lowering the pH:** As you already know, in nature the pH value is principally derived from the interaction between carbonate hardness and dissolved carbon dioxide. Since the pH in an aquarium usually increases (due to $CO_2$ deficiency, which is being used up by water plants), it should be lowered again by equally natural means,

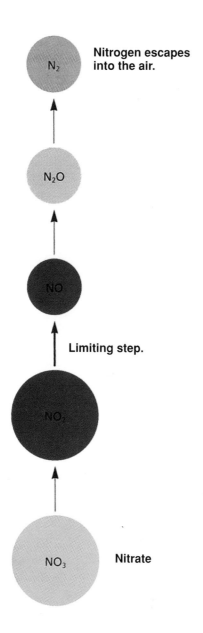

**N₂** Nitrogen escapes into the air.

**N₂O**

When there is no oxygen present, various bacteria can utilize the oxygen present in nitrate and so reduce the nitrate back to nitrogen.

**NO**

Limiting step.

**NO₂**

**NO₃** Nitrate

that is, the addition of $CO_2$, and adjusted to around neutral. Simultaneously, the plants get the essential carbon dioxide. In water with a carbonate hardness in excess of 15 DH it makes sense to lower it to a carbonate hardness of 10 DH, otherwise too much $CO_2$ is used unnecessarily, in order to lower the pH to 7.

In special cases, for instance for breeding, the pH values can also be lowered through peat filtration. However, this can only be done in soft water, since in hard water the acids released by the peat moss would be buffered by the carbonate hardness. When filtering over peat moss the pH must be monitored constantly. It must be added here, that filtration via activated carbon eliminates the effect of peat moss.

**Increasing the pH:** This is rarely ever required. However, this can be achieved through increasing the carbonate hardness. The aquarium fish trade also offers preparations for adjusting the pH values.

## Changing the carbon dioxide content

Due to $CO_2$ usage by water plants there is a frequent

carbon dioxide deficiency in well-planted aquariums. This problem can be alleviated by the installation of a $CO_2$ fertilizer unit. Further details are discussed in the next chapter. Lowering of the $CO_2$ content would really only ever become necessary in the event of an incorrectly set fertilizer unit. This can be quickly corrected with strong water movement or equally strong aeration which drives out any excess $CO_2$.

## Removal of ammonium and nitrite

The removal of ammonium and nitrite should really no longer be a topic since this is, as already discussed, accomplished by bacteria. Only if bacterial development has been disturbed (e.g. during the treatment of fish diseases, massive over-crowding or overfeeding), the ammonium and nitrite levels can increase.

In such a case, a partial water change will probably resolve the problem. Subsequently, efforts must be made to restore normal water conditions in the aquarium, that is, by filtering out the remnants of medication over charcoal, give less food, and, if need be, reduce the aquarium population.

## Removal of nitrate

The cheapest and simplest method to get rid of nitrate is regular partial water changes which, as discussed before, should be part of the regular aquarium maintenance program. This does become somewhat problematic though in areas where the tap water already contains nitrate. About 50 mg/l are permitted maximally under most municipal water supply regulations, but under certain conditions this can still cause an algal bloom.

There is, however, yet another way to remove nitrate, which is also used by nature and as a more or less technically elaborate process in municipal waste water treatment plants: the so-called *de-nitrification*. This is the capability of various bacteria to utilize the oxygen bound in nitrate for respiration instead of the oxygen dissolved in water.

In principle this may sound very good, but there is a problem! As long as there is dissolved oxygen, the bacteria concerned rather prefer this more easily accessible oxygen than the oxygen bound to nitrate molecules. Here it must be pointed out that these bacteria are not the same which produce the nitrate and now utilize the same process in reverse. Denitrifying bacteria occur in various groups of bacteria, which are all capable of 'breathing' nitrate under certain conditions. Potential denitrifying bacteria occur in all aquariums.

Only after there is no more free oxygen available in water and if organic food (e.g. sugar) is available, will these bacteria change over to using nitrate as their oxygen source. Similar conditions occur in accumulated debris on the bottom of each tank, as well as in the actual substrate, unless all debris is meticulously removed and the substrate constantly cleaned with a gravel siphon. Therefore, aquariums with a little bit of dirt are often healthier than those which are constantly scrubbed clean.

These sorts of conditions can also be created artificially, in specially constructed filters with an extremely slow flow rate and a long filter path. What is also important for such a filter is a regular food supply for the bacteria. Etha-

# UNDESIRABLE GUESTS

In spite of all precautions, a number of undesirable guests can appear in an aquarium. Principally, these are various snail species. Usually they come into an aquarium as eggs attached to water plants or as juveniles with certain live foods, etc. On one hand, snails can have certain benefits since they will eat left-over fish foods and algae. Moreover, cork-screw snails (*Melanoides tuberculata*) are burrowing snails, which will loosen up the substrate. In fact, they are often referred to as the earthworms of the aquarium. Most aquarists, however, are not strict enough with their feeding procedures, so that there is all too often a lot of food for snails left over, which then sets the stage for a massive development of snails. When their food supply runs out, some snails will actually attack plants!

Should it happen that the substrate harbors too many of these burrowing snails or there are masses of ramshorn snails and other small snails, a remedy is called for. The trade offers substances that will get rid of snails, but these should only be used in an emer-

Ramshorn snail with eggs.

gency. It would be impossible to find all the dead snails scattered all over the tank after such a treatment. These would then quickly pollute the water. Moreover, certain kinds of snails seem to be largely immune against these substances. The alternatives are manual removal of the snails (which can be extremely laborious) or the keeping of fish (pufferfish) which feed on snails. We advise against freshwater pufferfish. More suitable are the loaches (*Botia* spec.), because they are easier to keep and they also devour burrowing snails.

Freshwater polyps (*Hydra*) and glass worms (*Planaria*) are usually introduced into the aquarium with live foods. Very careful and deliberate feeding usually causes these undesirable guests to disappear by themselves. Certain undemanding fish species (*Macropodus* and others) will actually eat them. Apart from that, Hydra make highly interesting objects, especially when kept in a separate small tank.

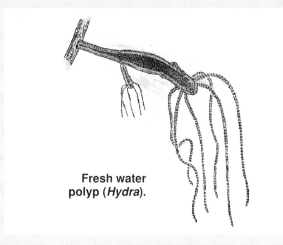

Fresh water polyp (*Hydra*).

nol is used for that purpose in waste treatment plants. But this cannot be done under aquarium conditions since ethanol would lead to a population explosion of bacteria, producing a severe oxygen deficiency. More suitable bacterial food for use in aquaria has yet to be found.

Since nitrate respiration is via the nitrite stage, there is the danger of secondary nitrite enrichment in the presence of a high nitrate content. That is, the step from nitrate to nitrite occurs much quicker than the successive steps from nitrite via the various intermediate steps to nitrogen. Therefore, a denitrifying filter must never be hooked up directly to the aquarium, but instead must be used as a filter on a filter.

The nitrate removal by means of exchange resins is not a method of choice, since this would enrich the water with other ions, usually chloride. This has a detrimental effect on the ion distribution in the water.

## Removal of phosphate

An excess of phosphate in the water can really only be removed by changing the water. An unnecessary in-

crease in phosphate level can be prevented through deliberate, careful feeding (and not on the 'generous' side) and by avoiding phosphate-containing maintenance products. Moreover, luxuriant, healthy plant growth also contributes to the reduction of phosphate levels.

Unfortunately, some water plant fertilizers contain phosphate and nitrates. By the way, fertilizers developed for house plants must never find their way into a home aquarium! Also some of the water conditioners still utilize polyphosphates as complex builders for heavy metal ions. *Avoid aquarium care products which contain phosphates!* If, after a water change and the addition of fertilizer or water conditioner, the phosphate level increases again within a short period of time to the previous level, at least one of the products must contain phosphate.

You should also check your tap water for phosphate. Often home installations include phosphate dosing units which are to prevent the formation of carbonate deposits in the water pipes. In such a case you must try to take your aquarium water from a point in front of the location of such a dosing unit.

Some test kits allow for the measurement of just one water quality condition, such as pH or water hardness, but kits are available also to make a number of other measurements, such as chlorine and ammonia content, as well. Photo courtesy Aquarium Pharmaceuticals.

## Changing the oxygen content

Situations of acute oxygen deficiency can be alleviated through aeration and strong water movements. In well-planted tanks and with proper care of the water plants (nutrients, illumination) there should not be any oxygen deficiencies, at least not during the day. Possible substantial declines in oxygen level during the night can be prevented with slight aeration (time switch set for after dark activation). Oxygen deficiency in fishes can be recognized by an increase in respiratory movements (gill cover activity). In acute cases the fish will be hanging, mouth up, on the surface, accompanied by very strong respiratory movements.

## EVERYTHING UNDER CONTROL – MONITORING THE AQUARIUM WATER

In order to be able to initiate specific adjustments to the water condition in an aquarium or simply to find out whether everything is satisfactory, the respective water quality parameters must be checked with appropriate methods. Specialized aquarium or pet shops offer easy-to-use test kits, which are sufficiently precise and cost-effective. Electronic measuring units are also available for particular parameters, but this sort of equipment is expensive and becomes worthwhile only when used frequently.

The test kits are based essentially on two methods. One method (titration) measures particular substances by adding the test solution to a water sample until the indicator (in the test solution) changes color. The number of drops of test solution required to cause a color change in the water sample gives the concentration of the substance tested for.

The other method is based on the principle that certain substances react with particular chemicals, creating a specific color. The intensity of that color is then proportional to the concentration of the substance tested for. By comparing this color with a calibrated color chart (colorimetry) the concentration can be determined. Make it a habit to record all test results, including the time of day it was taken (some test results vary with time of day). This will enable you to quickly recognize changes and tendencies, and, if required, immediately implement the necessary corrective action.

## Measuring hardness and total salt content

Measuring total hardness and carbonate hardness does not vary in terms of methodology. A reagent is added to a 5 ml water sample until, for total hardness, there is a color change from red to green and for carbonate hardness from blue to yellow. One drop of reagent used equals 1 DH total or carbonate hardness, respectively. The preciseness of this method can be enhanced by increasing the sample size from 5 ml to 10 ml. One drop of reagent then equals .5 DH. In order to be able to compare the values obtained with other commonly used units of measure (e.g., municipal water supplies) a conversion table is useful.

Measuring the total salt content of water requires a so-called *conductivity meter*. This technique takes advantage of the ability of water, depending on the content of dissolved salts, to more or less conduct eletricity. The unit of measure is micro-Siemens, abbreviated µS. Starting out with the fact that one degree DH conforms to a conductivity of about 30 µS, such a measurement then also determines whether there are other dissolved salts apart from hardness builders. The type of salt, however, cannot be determined. For that reason using the hardness to determine the total salt content is not possible.

## Measuring the pH value

Measuring the pH with liquid indicator solutions is the most common method used by aquarists today. An indicator solution is given drop-by-drop to a water sample (usually 5 ml) and the color obtained is compared with a calibrated color scale. Depending upon the specific application, one can select between different pH scales and graduations. Wide-range test (e.g pH 4 to 10) are generally measured in .5 pH increments. Intermediate values can be estimated.

Anyone who wants more precise details has to use tests with a narrower (measuring) range (e.g. pH 6 to 7.6), which give results in increments of pH .2 or .3. Aquarists who want to keep their fish and plants at the most favorable pH of around 7 (often in conjunction with $CO_2$ fertilization), are best advised to go for a test kit with a narrower range with higher precision.

Liquid pH test kits available from aquarium and pet shops usually contain sufficient indicator solution for 50 to 80 tests per package. Some manufacturers also offer inexpensive refills (reagents only, without sample vial, color scale, etc.). Occasional pH strips are still avail-

**It is easy to monitor water values with test kits.**

able, but these are not precise enough for aquarium purposes; they have some use for pH orientation purposes only.

Anyone who has to rely on frequent and precise pH measurements (breeders), will probably want to contemplate the acquisition of an electronic pH meter. In order to avoid incorrect measurements there must be strict adherence to the directions provided with each meter. Regular and meticulous calibration of these units is of fundamental importance for correct measurements. Incorrectly calibrated units or those which have not been re-calibrated for a long time will give telephone numbers as readings!

The calibration liquids provided must be carefully protected against contamination, especially against dilution by aquarium water. In fact, they should be replaced every year. Water temperature also influences pH measurements. For meters with automatic temperature compensation this is, of course, unimportant. On others, the temperature scale needs to be adjusted to the prevailing tank temperature before each measurement.

The pH value in an aquarium varies with the time of day, depending upon the assimilation activities of plants. In tanks without $CO_2$ fertilization the pH in the evening should not be higher than 8 to 8.5. If need be, lighting period and intensity should be adjusted correspondingly. In such a case one should do without fast-growing plants, because their rapid rate of assimilation can quickly drive the pH above 8.5. When using $CO_2$ fertilization it is advisable to strive for a more or less constant setting between 6.8 and 7.4.

For some time after a tank has been newly set up, it is advisable to take frequent pH readings and at different times of the day (always record the time!). Later on, when the tank is properly conditioned, it is normally sufficient to test the pH once or twice a week (always at the same time of day!).

## Measuring the carbon dioxide content

You have read above that the pH value is largely determined by the interaction between carbonate hardness and $CO_2$. Because of that the $CO_2$ content can be calculated if the carbonate hardness and the pH are known—provided, of course, there are no other pH-lowering substances (humic acids) in the water. In order to spare you such calculations, there is a table on page 55 that lists the $CO_2$ content. However, it is also possible to determine the $CO_2$ content directly with a test kit.

An indicator is added to a water sample and then a test solution is added drop-by-drop until a recurring slight pink coloration no longer disappears. Usually one drop of test solution used corresponds to 2 mg $CO_2$/l.

If there are, however, other pH-lowering substances present (apart from $CO_2$) you will obtain values that are higher than those listed in the table. To exclude the possibility of such false measurements, you proceed as follows: take two water samples simultaneously, of which the first one is tested immediately. The second sample is aerated for about an hour to drive out all $CO_2$. The second measurement then records the $CO_2$ content simulated by other substances then records the $CO_2$ content simulated by other substances. The result of the second test is subtracted from the first one, and the result is the actual $CO_2$ content present in the water.

## Measuring the oxygen content

Measuring the oxygen content by chemical means is rather complicated. Test kits developed for aquarium purposes usually contain 4 reagents. Their application requires meticulous work according to the directions supplied, if one wants to obtain reliable results. Far easier, but expensive, is using an oxygen meter. This unit also requires proper care if it is to give accurate results.

Just like the pH value, oxygen levels (at least in planted

tanks) are also subject to variations according to time-of-day because of the photosynthetic activities of the plants. At a water temperature of 25 degrees C (77°F.), there should be an oxygen concentration of about 8 mg/l in the evening and at least 4 mg/l remaining in the morning. Under normal conditions one measurement per week is sufficient.

## Measuring ammonium, nitrite and nitrate

These three measurements provide an overview of the complete waste reduction pathway in an aquarium. In general, these tests consist of two to three reagents (depending upon the manufacturer) and are quite easy to handle. In a well-planted, thoroughly conditioned tank, ammonium and nitrite should not be measurable! But up to .5 mg/l ammonium and .2 mg/l nitrite can, however, be considered as normal, whereby regular monitoring must be used to determine whether these values are stable or whether they are on the increase.

Especially after disease treatment it is advisable to check whether the medication used has also had a detrimental effect on the nitrifying bacteria. Here it may be relevant to point out the pH-dependant toxicity of ammonium. Nitrate levels in excess of 20 mg/l can facilitate algal growth and should therefore be avoided, although fish can tolerate substantially higher levels without adverse effects.

Usually the test kits available have sufficient reagents for about 50 tests (ammonium and nitrite) and about 25 to 50 tests for nitrate. Under normal conditions one test per week is normally sufficient. The time of day is not important. As far as the test range of these kits is concerned a level of .2 mg/l for ammonium can still be clearly measurable. The upper limit of the test range should be between 5 mg/l and 10 mg/l. For nitrite a lower limit of .05 mg/l is easily recognizable, whereby the upper limit can be about 1 to 1.5 mg/l.

Nitrate tests come in a relatively narrow test range from .1 mg/l to about 10 mg/l as well as in a wide test range from about 10 mg/l to a few 100's mg/l. Test kits with a narrow range are more precise, but require a specific dilution of the sample with distilled water if higher nitrate values are to be determined. This is not necessary for test kits with a wide testing range, but this is at the expense of accuracy at the lower end of the range. Consequently, a decision needs to be made based upon the test objective.

## Measuring phosphate

Unfortunately phosphate test kits for aquarium purposes are still somewhat scarce. Should your aquarium or pet shop dealer not be in a position to sell you such a kit, we suggest you approach a laboratory or chemical supply company. Large chemical companies have had test kits available for a long time for fisheries scientists. These kits are also ideally suited for aquarium use. Although most kits contain enough reagents for a large number of tests (up to about 100), they are relatively expensive, and can only be justified for particular cases, e.g. for phosphate determination.

In nature phosphate values in excess of .1 mg/l are considered to be high and indicate the onset of eutrophication (excess fertilization) of a particular body of water. In an aquarium we can consider values of .5 to 1.0 mg/l as being normal; however, the phosphate content should not be permanently higher than that. We measured phosphate values as high as 10 mg/l in some aquariums!

## Measuring the iron content

So far we have not yet discussed the significance of iron in the aquarium; we will make up for that in the chapter

Conversion of total hardness.

| | Earth Alkali Ions | Earth Alkali Ions | German Degrees | CaCo$_3$ | English Degrees | French Degrees |
|---|---|---|---|---|---|---|
| | (mmol/l) | (mval/l) | (°d) | (ppm) | (°e) | (°f) |
| 1 mmol/l Earch Alkali Ions | | 2,00 | 5,60 | 100,0 | 7,02 | 10,00 |
| 1 mval/l Earth Alkali Ions | 0,50 | | 2,80 | 50,0 | 3,51 | 5,00 |
| 1 German Degree | 0,18 | 0,357 | | 17,8 | 1,25 | 1,78 |
| 1 ppm CaCo$_3$ | 0,01 | 0,020 | 0,056 | | 0,0702 | 0,100 |
| 1 English Degree | 0,14 | 0,285 | 0,798 | 14,3 | | 1,43 |
| 1 French Degree | 0,10 | 0,200 | 0,560 | 10,0 | 0,702 | |

Conversion of carbonate hardness (after Krause).

| | Acid Capacity | German Degrees | French Degrees | Hydrogen Carbonate |
|---|---|---|---|---|
| | (mmol/l) | (°d) | (°TAC) | (mg/l) |
| Acid Capacity Immol/l | – | 2,78 | 4,94 | 61,0 |
| German Degrees I°d | 0,36 | – | 1,78 | 21,8 |
| French Degrees I°TAC | 0,20 | 0,56 | – | 12,3 |
| Hydrogen Carbonate Img/l | 0,016 | 0,046 | 0,08 | – |

on plants. Iron test kits are utilized in order to monitor the dosing of iron-based fertilizers. Here it is important that the test also includes all chelate-bound iron. You can check this by adding some iron test reagent to a water sample and let it stand for a few hours. If the color intensity of this sample increases gradually during this time interval, the test kit is unsuitable for aquarium purposes.

Guide values for aquarium conditions are around .1 mg/l . The test kit should be able to show levels as low as .05 mg/l. The number of tests per pack are about 50 measurements.

## HANDLING CHEMICALS

We do not want to close this chapter without a word or two about handling the chemicals involved in the various tests discussed above. All test kits consist of chemicals which are more or less toxic and can cause injuries if handled incorrectly. Therefore, these kits do not belong in the hands of children or in the close proximity of food.

Avoid skin contact with the test solutions as well as with the water sample treated with them; not only because various test solutions can possibly cause caustic burns but also because through skin contact the test results can be distorted.

For conducting these tests select a site which does not come into contact with food items. Moreover, do not pour water samples which have been tested and are no longer required down the kitchen sink, but into the toilet or the wash basin in the bathroom and flush thoroughly.

The shelf-life of these test kits varies depending upon the type of chemicals used. As a rule, one can assume a minimum shelf-life of two years; however, since the aquarist at the time of purchase of each test kit did not know how long it has been stored (at the manufacturer, wholesaler, retailer), it would desirable if the manufacturer would print a 'use-by' date on the packages.

For people with touch or contact phobias about chemical things many specialized aquarium shops do water analysis for a nominal fee.

"Water conditioning."

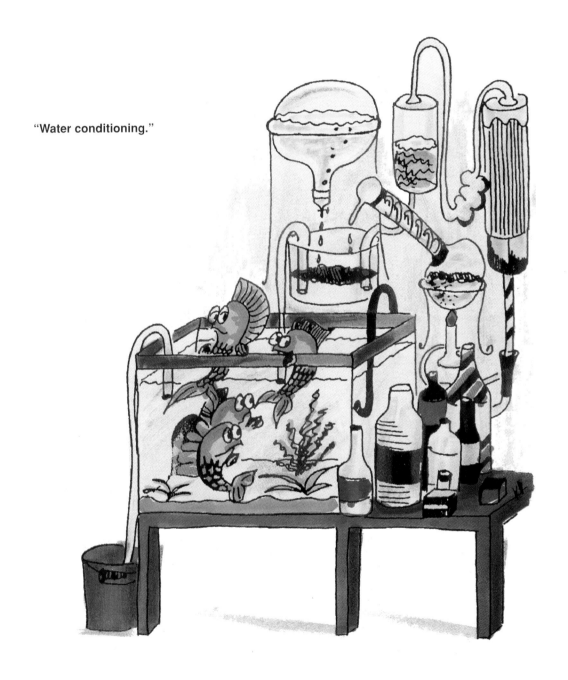

# TECHNOLOGY: TO HELP NATURE ALONG

Advancements in modern aquarium keeping have made tank maintenance much simpler and safer. If we remember how our forefathers had to struggle along with all sorts of 'home-made inventions' to keep their fish alive, we tend to shake our heads in disbelief.

In spite of that, technology is not the is-all-end-all. A certain affinity for biological processes in the aquarium can not be replaced by even the most sophisticated technological efforts. Therefore, consider technology as a beneficial support, which, when applied with proper judgment, essentially helps nature along.

Within the course of this chapter we would like to attempt to give you a feeling for the correct judgment. But first of all an important pointer: The majority of the equipment items discussed below are operated with the standard electrical current of 110 volts. It is this combination of water and electricity which carries considerable inherent dangers. Therefore, you should only use equipment which complies with relevant statutory regulations and guidelines and carries the appropriate test symbol.

Do not fiddle with any electrical work around the aquarium! If home-building is really necessary, for instance, to fit tank lighting to a custom-built tank, use only certified parts and appliances, and when finished have the result checked by an expert (tradesman) before you put it into operation. To be totally safe, it is advisable to plug all aquarium electrics into a so-called circuit breaker. This will turn off the power in the event of danger (tank lighting falls into water, etc.) and before an accident can happen. In modern buildings appropriate circuit breakers are standard.

## THE INVISIBLE HELPERS...FILTERS

You may perhaps ask why 'invisible' helpers? Because of design and function, filters must have certain sizes and at best they can only be invisible with some clever positioning or appropriate camouflage or disguise. The actual invisible helpers are not the actual plastic structures which we buy from an aquarium or pet shop, but instead they are located on the inside of the filter, following a certain running-in period. But more about that later.

## WHAT DOES A FILTER HAVE TO DO?

As suggested by the name, a filter must filter something. In our case it must filter aquarium water, with the aim to keep it 'clean', whatever that means. Beyond that, it must create a certain water current in the aquarium, which must fulfil several tasks simultaneously: provide an even heat distribution in the aquarium, assure that nutrient-rich water is transported to the aquarium plants, carry away metabolic waste products (growth inhibiting substances, etc.) and, in sparsely planted tanks, enrich the water with oxygen.

The circulation capacity of the filter depends on the specific requirements of fishes and plants to be kept. Species which prefer (slight) currents, the hourly (circulating) capacity of a filter should be about equal to two or three tank volumes. For species which do not need a current, about one-half or one tank volume per hour is sufficient. When selecting the filter, keep in mind that the hourly capacity indicated always refers to the pump operating without a head (load); under actual operating conditions this may well drop down by as much as 50%!

### Mechanical or biological filtration?

Nothing is debated more hotly and persistently among aquarists than types of filters and filtration methods. One group is of the opinion that a filter cannot be cleaned often enough and so virtually deny that it has any biological function. The dirt which accumulates in a filter has only been moved and is still within the tank where it rots in the filter with all the possible bad consequences for the tank.

Those opposed to this view equate filter cleaning with killing a holy cow in India! They swear by the biological cleansing ability of a filter. The valuable nitrifying bacteria should be able to continue their beneficial activities of detoxifying, which would be unnecessarily disturbed by cleaning the filter.

We have presented here the two opposing viewpoints in somewhat extreme terms. As so often in life, there is some truth in both opinions and the golden middle is

**The working principle of a closed outside filter.**

1. Prefilter medium.
2. Main filter medium.
3. Pump head (power head).

once again the right compromise. Every filter will sooner or later also work biologically, that is, its filter medium will sooner or later be settled with nitrifying bacteria; there is no question about that, only their 'work place' should be as optimal as possible. That means that they should be left in peace (holy cow), and all unnecessary dirt should be kept away from them.

In other words, a filter should be built up in such a way that the water is forced to run firstly over an easily accessible pre-filter medium, which is cleaned regularly. Then the water to be filtered should flow through a coarser filter medium with the largest possible internal surface area which is rarely ever cleaned and so offers an optimal environment for the bacteria. Unfortunately, this operating principle is not easy to realize in many of the commercially available filters. Numerous discussions with customers in aquarium shops always keep coming up with the same problems. Aquarists which keep cleaning their filters meticulously or who add new filter medium once a week, always seem to have problems with high nitrite and ammonium levels, because nitrification cannot get started properly. On the other hand, those aquarists who never clean their filters have continuous problems with rapidly increasing nitrate levels, since all the dirt is being left for the bacteria to break down.

## Filter types

The type of filter you decide to get depends on how you can implement the filter principles, the availability of space and finally how to prevent a possible accidental flooding of your apartment.

Firstly we need to distinguish between outside and inside filters. INSIDE FILTERS have the decided advantage that they are located inside an aquarium, and so water-carrying pipes and tubes do not need to be installed outside of the aquarium. A disadvantage is the relatively small filter volume and the additional 'foreign body' in the aquarium which needs to be suitably camouflaged. When it is being taken out of the tank for cleaning one usually gets wet (which should not be a deterrent for the aquarist) and possibly the fish may become stressed. Tightly fitting, motor-driven corner filters are very popular for small tanks. Since it is not possible to separate pre-filter medium and permanent medium, some middle

**Pumps come in different sizes and should be selected according to the task they are set to do. Photo courtesy Eheim.**

**There are many differnt filter media that can be used, each with its own particular advantages. Some are used in combination with others to produce the desired effect. Here is a sample of different media. Photo courtesy Eheim.**

ground needs to be found for this sort of filter in terms of cleaning intervals.

OUTSIDE FILTERS come as an open and a closed type. CLOSED OUTSIDE FILTERS can easily be installed virtually invisibly underneath, next to or behind the aquarium. Disadvantage: Water-carrying hoses lead from the tank to the filter and back. Most manufacturers have recognized this as a source of danger and supply their filter models with (more or less easily servicable) threaded hose fittings. Highly recommended for these filters are double shut-off valves, separating a quick-release coupling, which facilitates easy removal and re-installation of the filter without any significant loss of water.

The flow-through in most of these canister outside filters is from the bottom to the top, so that the pre-filter medium can only be cleaned after the entire filter medium has been removed from the canister. This is awkward. There are already a few reasonably useful pre-filters on the market, which are attached to the filter intake line, but cleaning these is also not quite as easy as it may seem; they usually end up in a fairly inaccessible part of the tank, since the suction pipe with attached pre-filter needs to be camouflaged.

OPEN OUTSIDE FILTERS are containers which are open at the top, which are attached like backpacks to smaller tanks or as separate units for large tanks. The latter arrangement necessitates that filter and aquarium are positioned so that the water level in both are the same. Then a large diameter siphon tube transfers water, using the lift principle, from the aquarium to the filter. The water then flows through the filter, and is ultimately returned to the aquarium by means of a pump (submersible or circulating pump). Apart from the disadvantage of no

Selection of filter media: charcoal, various plastic filter media, peat granulate, various plastic fibers, fine and coarse filter wool, lava and ceramic rings.

real choice in regard to positioning such a filter, the decisive advantage of it is the extreme ease of access to the filter medium for cleaning purposes.

## Filter media

As pre-filter media to keep out large dirt particles such materials as fine synthetic fiber (nylon or perlon wool) or medium to low density styrofoam is available from most aquarium and pet shops. Do not use plastic foam from packing material of unknown origin; this could give off undesirable substances into the water or be decomposed ('eaten') by bacteria.

Virtually any open-porous, inert material can be used as long-term filter media and as substrates for the developing nitrifying bacteria. Attention must be paid to certain pore or grain sizes of the material used. Classic, and in our opinion an optimal, material is foam rubber with a pore size of 1 to 2 mm. Equally suitable are crushed lava rock, clay granulate and certain ceramic rings which have a distinctly reduced surface area when compared to other substances.

## Special filter media

Peat moss and activated charcoal, two important filter media with special functions, must also be mentioned. To say it up front: the simultaneous filtration over peat moss and activated charcoal is pure nonsense; it is about the same as if you attempt to drive your car forward and in reverse at the same time. That is, activated charcoal will remove those particles which we are trying to get into the water by filtering over peat moss.

ACTIVATED CHARCOAL is a special filter medium, which because of its peculiar characteristics and special manufacture, is capable of removing large-molecular organic compounds from the water by means of adsorption. Such large molecular compounds include, for instance, remnants of medication, which needs to be removed from the water following treatment, but also such desirable substances as humic acids, protective colloids and nutrient carriers (natural as well as

artificial) including bound nutrients which have been added with considerable efforts through water conditioners and specially adapted fertilizers.

For those reasons permanent filtration over high-quality activated charcoal has no place in a freshwater aquarium, but is highly effective in special cases (removal of medication remnants, etc.). The best adsorption characteristics occur in so-called formed or compressed charcoal, which are granules pressed into different sizes from coal dust. By comparison, crushed coal, which displays wood granulation is ineffective.

Peat moss is the filter medium of choice for breeding soft water fishes and to acidify the water in the breeding tank the natural way. At the same time peat moss gives off valuable humic substances into the water, which because of their bactericidal effect provides for a bacteria-poor environment for fishes. The pH value must be monitored closely in order too avoid to strong a drop in the soft water. The aquarium fish trade offers a variety of peat mosses, but one can also use normal bale peat provided no fertilizers have been added. If in doubt, soak a sample of the peat moss in water and check it a few days later for ammonium, nitrate and phosphate.

*No matter what a filter looks like, it can never replace regular, partial water changes.*

# AND THEN THERE WAS LIGHT ...TANK LIGHTING

Tank lighting is one of the most important technical aids in modern aquarium keeping. This makes the aquarium independent of difficult to control daylight on the window sill! Moreover, such lighting can be adapted to the actual requirements of the aquarium inhabitants, which makes the overall tank maintenance much easier.

Light controls all vital processes in fishes, for instance the day and night activities of various species, time of spawning and much more.

The most important function of light, however, is the supply of energy for that process in plants referred

**Correct lighting is important.**

52

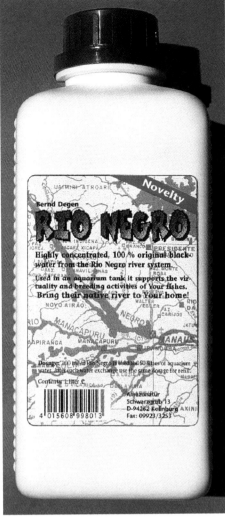

The black waters of the Rio Negro in Brazil look like coffee. Bernd Degen took the Rio Negro waters, evaporated them and bottled the concentrate. This product is now available to add to your aquarium when needed for maintaining such acid-loving fishes as Discus and Cardinal Tetras.

which consists of several lamps, it is advisable to adjust the time switch setting in such a way that only half of the lamps or, if possible, only a third operate for 10 to 12 hours, and the full capacity (all lamps) only for a peak periods of about 8 to 9 hours.

As far as light intensity is concerned, the more the better. Especially the highly desired lawn-forming foreground plants are usually very light-hungry and have most of the light-absorbing water between them and the light source. Most plants can adjust well to stronger light, but rarely ever to insufficient light. In addition, incoming light is often shaded by floating plants or the floating leaves of stemmed plants.

## Light color

The topic of light color continues to be debated hotly among aquarists. For a long time lamps with an emphasis on red and blue tones were considered to be the state-of-the-art in aquarium lighting. It gave the underwater world an unnatural, candy-colored light. A realization that maximum photosynthesis takes place in the blue and red spectral region led to this light color.

Since then we have learned not to necessarily rely on the emphasis of red and blue spectral components, but rather on a more even spectrum. If possible with daylight characteristics, but of sufficient intensity. Besides, red and blue lamps have the reputation of promoting algal growth. Since it has been shown that plants can adapt to virtually any light color if given enough time, selecting a particular light color is, in the final analysis, a matter of personal choice and how natural an aquarium is to appear.

## Types of lamps

Nowadays, the most commonly used aquarium lighting is provided by fluorescent tubes. They have a far greater light efficiency than incandescent bulbs, they last longer and give off less heat. Hardly a year goes by without some sensational new fluorescent tube coming on the (aquarium) market, with totally new light characteristics, never seen before.

to as assimilation or photosynthesis. The waste product of this process is oxygen, which facilitates animal life on our planet. It is exactly that function, i.e. the supply of energy for assimilation by the water plants, that needs to be catered to through proper selection of the correct type of lighting.

## How much light do water plants need?

Here we have to resolve first of all the question of lighting duration or lighting period. For that purpose let us look at the situation existing in the natural environment of our tropical fish; there the 'light day' is approximately even throughout the entire year. Variable lengths of daylight periods, as occur in our latitudes, do not exist. Year after year there are 12 hours of daylight and 12 hours of night. Moreover, the light (breaking) angle at the air/water interface assures that hardly any light extends below the surface at a low (rising or setting) sun during the early morning or late afternoon hours. The end effect is that below water there are really only 10 hours of 'day' and 14 hours of 'darkness'. Consequently, an aquarium should be illuminated for maximally 12 hours per day only.

The use of time switches assures not only regular turning on and off, but with an appropriate setting so that the fish are still awake when we sit down in front of the aquarium in the evening. The switching sequence could, for instance, look like this: 11:30/12:00 hours on and 23:00/23:30 hours off. If you use tank lighting

**Tank lighting: aquarium cover on the left (lid removed) with safe installation of two fluorescent tubes; on right an HQL lamp.**

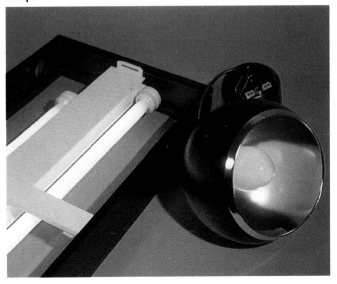

**Tanks with fishes that tend to jump must have a suitable cover, otherwise there can be dangerous "excursions."**

Apart from the fact that light color is merely a matter of taste, be selective! Different brands vary quite substantially in the amount of light provided for identical electricity consumption. After all, it is the light intensity we are principally after. This can easily be calculated from the lumens per watt. Lumens for a particular type of tube is usually listed in circulars issued by the manufacturer. Divide this value by the power input. If this gives you a value of around 90, you can proceed with the purchase without worries. You will then quickly notice that under these conditions daylight tubes are way ahead.

As a rule of thumb, for acceptable light intensity you can use the following: for a tank height of 45 to 50 cm (20 inches) and a depth of 40 cm (16 inches) use two tubes of about the same length as the tank; add one tube for each additional 10 cm (4 inches) in depth. Suitable reflectors are supposed to prevent light from penetrating above the tank. The trade offers reflector sheets which are clipped to the tubes. The light intensity of fluorescent tubes tends to diminish with time, consequently they should be replaced once a year (even if they are still working!). Record the latest date of change-over somewhere. If several tubes are used, exchange them in turn (not all at once), so that the plants are not stressed.

In order to get sufficient light into the aquarium, the light source should be positioned as close to the water surface as possible. It is, of course, understood that all light fittings must be of the outdoor (waterproof) type, and for safety's sake do not build your own! Waterproof fluorescent fittings are commercially available for any standard tank size, as well as those which can be fitted to custom-built light hoods. In spite of the fact that fluorescent tubes give off little heat, it still can get rather warm in a totally closed light hood, especially on hot summer days. For that reason, enclosed aquarium lights (hoods, etc.) should have appropriate ventilation slots or holes.

The introduction of mercury vapor, high-pressure lamps opened up totally new lighting perspectives for the aquarium hobby. While fluorescent tubes needed to be installed in more or less closed boxes, positioned on top of the aquarium, mercury vapor (HQL) lamps installed well above an aquarium provide an unimpeded view onto the surface of the tank. Plants can grow above the surface and develop blossoms. Working around the tank becomes easier. Because the light is projected largely as a beam, tanks can be effectively illuminated from a height of more than 50 cm (20 inches), which was hardly ever possible with fluorescent tubes.

The number of lamps is dependent upon the length of the tank. One lamp is required per 50 cm (20 inches) length of the tank and a depth of 40 to 50 cm. Most HQL lamps can be switched from 80 W to 125 W, so that the light intensity can be adapted to different heights. HQL lamps should also be replaced once a year, since their intensity tends to diminish with time.

The use of metal halide vapor lamps has really only been established for marine aquariums or for very large freshwater tanks, where enormous light intensities are required.

# PLANTS NEED FOOD TOO...$CO_2$

Until not very long ago $CO_2$ was considered to be fish enemy number one in aquariums, and everything conceivable was being done in order to drive $CO_2$ out of the water. One would install strongly bubbling airstones, air injection jets were placed on the intake side of filter pump, and with spray bars and other imaginative constructions waterfall-like structures were built which would create noises which made sensitive people look for the shortest way to a toilet!

Now we know that $CO_2$ is quantitatively the most important principal plant nutrient, and even without such 'water games' it is likely to be in short supply. Consequently, the trend has been reversed and one tries to keep the $CO_2$ created by the respiration of fish and

**A densely planted aquarium. When positioning the plants, consideration was given to the effect of contrast, various leaf colors, and leaf shapes.**

## Is $CO_2$ dangerous for fishes?

To provide the answer up front: under normal aquarium conditions, with a carbonate hardness between 5 and 15 degrees DH and a pH value around the neutral mark, $CO_2$ is definitely not dangerous to fish. Here it does not matter whether the $CO_2$ content is 20 or 60 mg/l, as long as the amount required to keep the carbonate hardness in solution is not being exceeded.

Dangerous levels of $CO_2$ can only be obtained when there is more $CO_2$ being added and the pH drops sharply. Since a certain minimal amount of $CO_2$ is required for adequate plant growth, there can be, at carbonate hardness levels below 4 or 5 degrees DH, too little carbonate available. On the other hand, very high carbonate hardness values would require uneconomically large amounts of $CO_2$ to be added to adjust the pH to about 7. The interaction between carbonate hardness, pH and $CO_2$ content is depicted in the accompanying table.

**$CO_2$ content (mg/l) determined from pH values and hardness (modified after Krause).**

| Carbonate Hardness (°d) | pH 6,6 | 6,8 | 7,0 | 7,2 | 7,4 | 7,6 |
|---|---|---|---|---|---|---|
| 2 | 16 | 10 | 7 | 4 | 3 | 2 |
| 4 | 32 | 20 | 13 | 8 | 5 | 3 |
| 6 | 50 | 30 | 20 | 12 | 8 | 5 |
| 8 | 65 | 40 | 25 | 16 | 10 | 6 |
| 10 | 80 | 50 | 32 | 20 | 13 | 8 |
| 12 | 100 | 60 | 40 | 24 | 15 | 10 |
| 14 | 115 | 70 | 45 | 28 | 18 | 11 |
| 16 | 130 | 80 | 50 | 32 | 20 | 12 |
| 18 | 145 | 90 | 58 | 36 | 23 | 14 |
| 20 | 160 | 100 | 65 | 40 | 25 | 16 |

Recommended Hardness

Recommended pH

Area of optimal $CO_2$ content

the activity of bacteria in the aquarium. In fact, often major efforts are made to get more $CO_2$ into the water in order to provide the water plants with their required food. And so we have difficulties in comprehending the marketing strategy of some filter manufacturers who continue to drive out the last remaining $CO_2$, and so make the life of plants difficult with all sorts of 'water games'. Consequently, plants cannot generate enough oxygen, which needs to be compensated for with the installation of $O_2$ diffusers and spray bars in order to increase the oxygen level. This is a bit like the cat biting its own tail! It is, of course, possible to operate an aquarium successfully without a $CO_2$ supplement if one specifically and meticulously selects only those plants which grow slowly enough and so can get by on the $CO_2$ generated in the tank, without driving the pH value to dizzying heights in the evening.

In doing that we must avoid many of the popular plants available. If we were to add fast-growing plants, they would quickly use up all available $CO_2$ and there would be nothing left for the slow growers. Moreover, since fast-growing plants could also attack the carbonate bound in $CO_2$ and make pH values increase dramatically, we then would make the water environment hostile for fishes and plants.

This is also the reason for the often stated opinion that certain plants are 'incompatible'. The simple explanation is: one type of plant will deny another plant access to $CO_2$. In tanks where the water is supplemented with $CO_2$ from the outside, these competitors usually grow peacefully side-by-side. From what has been said it is obvious that if there is a sufficient $CO_2$ supply, plants with different requirements can be kept together in the same aquarium. This affords us a plant diversity in an aquarium which would not be possible without an external $CO_2$ supply.

## Methods for adding $CO_2$ to aquarium water

There are a number of more or less effective methods of enriching aquarium water with $CO_2$. Right from the start you should forget about mineral water and so-called $CO_2$ fertilizer tablets as $CO_2$ sources. Both of these would be little more than the proverbial 'drop in

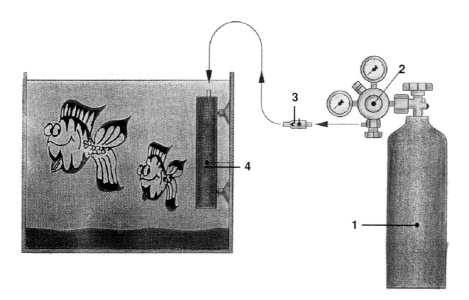

Working principle of a $CO_2$ fertilizer unit:
(1) $CO_2$ pressure bottle;
(2) pressure reducer with manometer for working pressure and bottle pressure;
(3) non-return valve with flow indicator;
(4) diffuser unit.

a bucket'. To generate $CO_2$ in a container by means of chemical reaction between hydrochloric acid and marble is possible but dangerous because of the necessity to handle hydrochloric acid. Small tanks can be supplied reasonably well with $CO_2$ for a while by means of alcoholic fermentation of yeast in a sugar solution.

The most widely used methods, and also the most effective, is the use of $CO_2$ which is stored in liquid form in pressurized bottles. A small but even flow is put into the aquarium via a pressure reducing device (regulator), and using various types of diffusers, brought into contact with the water for as long a time as possible. During this process the gas diffuses totally in the aquarium water. By utilizing pressure bottles it is possible to keep a large amount of $CO_2$ available in a small space, so that this procedure is the most cost-effective. Pet shops sell this equipment.

## Handling pressurized bottles

As all pressure vessels, $CO_2$ bottles are also subject to stringent pressure vessel regulations. Usually the bottle can be used for ten years and must then be pressure tested again. At a normal room temperature the internal pressure is about 60 bar. With rising temperatures, the internal pressure increases rapidly. In order to avoid accidents, all bottles are equipped with a so-called burst disc, which bursts when the internal pressure exceeds a certain value, letting out the gas with a controlled flow (e.g. a forgotten bottle in an overheated car). Defective burst discs can only be replaced by authorized specialists!

In your own interest, do not attempt to re-fill empty $CO_2$ bottles yourself, or even to fill other containers (not registered as $CO_2$ bottles)! Pressure bottles may only be filled by authorized dealers (manufacturers or $CO_2$ services).

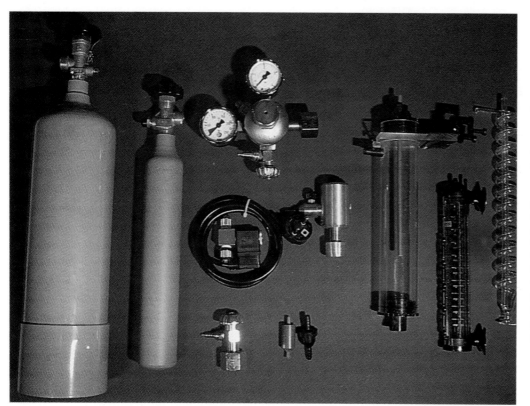

Equipment selection for $CO_2$ fertilization: (left) pressure bottles of different sizes; (center, from top to bottom) pressure reducer (regulator) with manometers and variably adjustable working pressure, pressure reducer without manometer and preset (fixed) working pressure, magnetic valve, needle valve and non-return valve, which prevent water from flowing into the equipment; (right) diffuser unit for operation without pump (far outside) and with pump (remainder).

# MAINTENANCE PLAN

Especially the beginning aquarist, who tries particularly hard to do all the right things, has a tendency to fiddle with his tank far too much. Therefore, we have summarized once again all essential maintenance tasks. Beyond that the aquarium should be left alone!

## Daily

Feed once or twice a day, always just enough to be eaten in two to three minutes. Occasionally there needs to be a fasting day. Juvenile fish need to be fed more frequently, of course without fasting periods.

Monitor the fish: are all of them feeding, are there any incompatibilities or signs of disease? Dead fish must be removed immediately. Check: temperature, and proper operation of all equipment.

## Weekly

Weekly, at the latest once every two weeks, partial water change of about 1/4 to 1/3 of tank volume, combined with filter cleaning and pruning the water plants.
1. Prune plants as required.
2. Clean front glass.

"And what do you do with your fishes during your vacation?"

3. Turn off heater and filter.
4. Siphon (drain) water, including removal of all visible accumulations of dirt and debris.
5. Rinse out pre-filter medium under running (cold!) water. If required, clean pump housing of the filter.
6. If present, clean cover glass. Calcium deposits can be removed with vinegar, followed by a thorough rinse.
7. Re-fill tank with water of appropriate temperature.
8. Turn on heater and filter.

## Vacation preparations

1. Water changes as usual prior to departure.
2. Fish do not need to be fed if absence does not exceed two weeks (but juvenile fish must be fed as usual).
3. For longer absences sparse feeding with automatic feeder preferred over feeding by an outside person (friend, relative, etc.), unless that person is also an aquarist. In any event, leave the telephone number of an aquarist acquaintance or your aquarium pet shop dealer.

**Happy is the one who has an automatic feeder.**

How full or how empty a bottle is can only be determined by weighing it. The tare weight of each bottle is stamped on it, as well as the maximum permissible weight. Both weights added equal the weight of a full bottle.

As long as there is a single drop of liquid $CO_2$ left in the bottle, the internal pressure is 60 bar. Only when there is no longer any liquid $CO_2$ left, that is, the bottle is practically empty, does the pressure start to fall.

## Diffusion devices

The market offers a variety of diffusion devices, each conforming to the philosophy of the respective manufacturer. There are diffusers that need to be operated by pumps, and those which can do it without; those that need to be installed inside the aquarium and those which are attached to the outside of an aquarium. Seek the advice of a specialist dealer and select the unit most appropriate for your needs.

For an optimal supply to the plants, you should set a pH value between 6.8 and 7.4, at a carbonate hard-

ness which is not below 5 degrees DH and not above 15 DH degrees. Here the lower pH applies to the lower carbonate hardness value and the higher pH to the higher hardness.

## THE PROPERLY-ADJUSTED AQUARIUM TEMPERATURE

Aquarium fishes need a certain temperature range for their well-being. The temperature requirements for breeding, however, are usually somewhat higher. Details are incorporated in the individual species listing later on in this book.

At this point we would like to introduce and discuss the technical possibilities available to modern aquarium keeping for providing and maintaining the necessary temperature regimens. Since most tropical fish require a temperature which is higher than the prevailing, ambient room temperature, an aquarium for tropical fish needs a heater and thermostat to maintain the required temperature. A wonderful selection of heaters in variable wattages is available at most pet shops.

**Labyrinthfishes, like this female Siamese fighting fish, can utilize atmospheric oxygen. Photo by Aqua Press Piednoir.**

# VISIT TO A PUBLIC AQUARIUM

Comfortable warmth, relaxing semi-darkness, quietness, maybe a pleasant place to sit down and be surrounded by walls of windows into a fascinating underwater world. Coral reef fishes in bright, almost unreal colors and bizarre shapes swarm through the water and sea anemones gently move their graceful tentacles. The small polyps, clams and sea stars reveal their real beauty only upon close examination.

A few meters further down we find gruesome looking predator fishes in a giant tank almost 2 meters high, and the sharp teeth of piranhas send shivers down our spine, in spite of the thick glass separating us from the predators behind it.

Sticklebacks and minnows have a rightful place here just as the old favorites out of our aquariums, such as guppies, swordtails, cardinal tetras and rasboras.

Looking at all this underwater life in amazement, discovering new things, identifying familiar fishes, dreaming of foreign places and exotic seas...we can do all that and much more in a public aquarium. Even when there is no total silence and when it is not empty, because we are not the only visitors, who would not like to be carried away into this fascinating underwater world?

## Efforts are rewarded

Only in zoological gardens and parks, museums and similar institutions with management trained and experienced in looking after living natural history collections can public aquariums be maintained, because the efforts required in human and financial resources is enormous. Thousands of fish, plants and invertebrates with a vast range of specific husbandry requirements (food and maintenance) need to be catered to. The technical equipment must be monitored and maintained.

The pure showmanship aspects of such facilities, often associated with the exhibition of curiosity objects and simple sensationalism, has become somewhat subdued in recent decades. Of course, popular favorites are still being exhibited, but there are now also educational tasks: the re-creation of natural environments and specific habitats with their typical inhabitants, explanatory panels and graphics, conducted tours and special exhibitions and displays, go far beyond the simple display of fishes.

In more recent years public aquariums have also become involved in species protection and nature conservation. Zoos are often the only place where species can survive when their natural habitat has been destroyed. Animals which—under relevant laws and regulations—can no longer be kept by private individuals (e.g. certain groups of marine fish) can at least still be admired in public aquariums. By the way, zoos and aquariums often exchange captive-bred animals, so that the need for a re-supply with wild-caught animals is gradually diminishing.

Research has traditionally been part of the activities of zoos and aquariums, as has the gathering and exchange of animal husbandry information for the purpose of improving the care and breeding of fishes, aspects from which the aquarium hobby has also benefited. Unfortunately most public aquariums do not publish (in hobbyist magazines) the results of their experiences.

## Behind the scenes

If the large display tanks are already impressive, even moreso for those who are interested is a view behind the scenes of a public aquarium. Such conducted tours with expert commentaries are periodically or regularly available, upon request and/or appointment, at many institutions.

And the things to see and learn on such behind-the-scene tours are amazing: the dimensions and numbers of all sorts of pipes and valves. The entire scene is reminiscent of a large municipal water supply station.

Large filtration units keep the water mechanically and biologically clean. Carefully conditioned fresh water is kept available for partial water changes or for top-ups due to evaporation. All water parameters are constantly being monitored so that optimal conditions for the vast array of animals are being assured. Demands in regard to water requirements vary greatly: seawater, brackish water, fresh water with different pH values, hardnesses, etc.

Apart from the display tanks there are more aquariums behind the scenes, used for breeding and rearing, for research purposes, treating sick fishes and for quarantining new arrivals.

**Service passage behind the freshwater section.**

## Views within a Public Aquarium

**(Top)** Five pumps service the giant tank with a volume of 230,000 liters. **(Bottom)** Supersized outside filter: Trickle towers.

When filling a newly set-up aquarium and for water changes you should use properly acclimated (warm) water. It would take far too long for the aquarium heater to achieve the correct temperature. Moreover, aquarium inhabitants do not tolerate temperature variations very well.

What possibilities are there now to heat an aquarium? Depending upon the (tank) region to be heated one distinguishes between substrate heaters and water heaters.

### Substrate heaters

There are heating mats which can be placed underneath the tank; however, this type of heating is nowadays less commonly used, since relatively too much heat is lost. Even without exact data being available, it appears obvious that the substrate, the bottom of the tank and possibly also the frame tend to swallow some of the heat before it can reach the inhabitants. More effective are heating cables or cable-like elements INSIDE the tank. These are placed directly over the tank bottom when the tank is first set up, and is then secured with some of the tank decor items. There are also heating systems which are placed directly on the tank floor below artificial lattice bricks.

Substrate heaters effect the desired water movement within the bottom material, which distributes the nutrients and prevents the accumulation of waste products. Moreover, they provide warmth for the roots of the plants, which is good for their growth.

Bottom heaters are not very practical for heating the entire aquarium water to the required temperature: this will make it too warm for the plant roots. We recommend that only about 1/3 of the required heat capacity be provided by a substrate heater, and the rest by way of direct heating. Again, there are two ways to accomplish that: rod heaters and thermo-filters.

### Rod heaters

These will heat the water directly, also creating warmwater currents. This, in conjunction with any currents created by filters, assures an even heat distribution throughout the aquarium.

Rod heaters are glass tubes which contain heat elements. They must always be emersed in water, and must never be turned on when not in water because they can easily burst! When installing a rod heater in an aquarium please comply with the position markings and the manufacturer's instructions! These are the most common heaters used in aquaria. They are usually controlled by built-in thermostats.

### Thermo-filters

A comfortable and technically-refined heating method is the use of thermo-filters. The heating element is located inside the filter canister, so that filtered water returns heated to the aquarium. The temperature adjustment (thermostat) is accessible from the outside.

How much heating capacity is required? This can

be estimated with the following rule-of-thumb: about .5 to 1 watt per liter volume of the tank(about 5 watts per U.S. gallon). About .5 watt/liter should be sufficient in normally (centrally) heated rooms; in colder rooms (e.g., a hobby basement) we would probably need more like $1^{1}/_{2}$ watts/liter.

Except in very cold rooms, it is generally advisable to couple the heater together with the time switch for the lighting so that both are turned off at night (this does not work with thermo-filters which are to operate continuously). This leads to a nighttime temperature reduction by about 1 to 2 degrees C, which conforms to the conditions in the natural environment of most tropical fishes. This suggestion, though, is not important!

Regular cleaning and proper operating conditions according to instruction provided by the manufacturer increase their effectiveness and operating life. Pull the plug immediately when there is any suspicion of malfunction.

## OTHER USEFUL IMPLEMENTS

**Buckets, hoses** and **fish nets** are part of the basic equipment and these items should ONLY be used for aquarium purposes. If you have several tanks, it is advisable to have a separate fish net for each tank, and then use the same net for a particular tank ALL THE TIME. This way you avoid cross contamination with parasites and disease pathogens between tanks.

**Bottle brushes** are useful for cleaning hoses, pipe connections and filter parts.

**Glass/window cleaners** remove attached algae from the insides of the aquarium. Felt and various plastic materials remove the algae in a gentle way; in persistent cases, use razor blades (single-edge, replaceable). Whether you use magnet-controlled cleaners from the outside or scrapers on a long rod is a matter of individual taste and preference.

**Floating feeding** rings with a strainer-like insert are useful for feeding live tubifex or white worms. These worms are eaten as soon as they crawl through the holes in the strainer and so will not clutter up the bottom of the tank.

In order to remove excess dirt and debris off the bottom we **siphon** it up with a glass or plastic dirt bell or some other suction-like device with a siphoning hose attached. This way we can remove fecal matter and dirt particles without sucking up gravel. Plant tongs are useful for work on water plants. Handling of such an implement effectively requires a bit of practice; however, sooner or later the aquarist starts to appreciate the 'extended arm' and the entire arm need no longer be emersed in the tank to frighten the fishes.

In a well-planted tank we can easily do without aeration; in fact, it is nonsense, for instance, to bubble pressurized air into a tank which has a $CO_2$ fertilizer unit installed. The well-meant air bubbles actually drive out the valuable $CO_2$ quicker than it can dissolve and be taken up by plants! **Artificial aeration** is only justifiable for barely planted aquariums (e.g., cichlid tanks with rock and wood decor) and in bar-

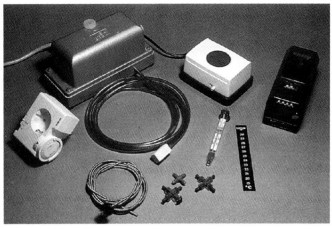

Useful equipment: timer, air pumps, automatic feeder, thermometers, air hose with air stone and valves, tube cleaning brush.

ren, hygienically set-up breeding tanks.

Appropriately powerful membrane or piston pumps compress ambient air which has been taken in and distribute it again via a thin hose and various air stones in the tank water. As far as the pump is concerned (which can of course also be used to operate a small filter), this should be a quality brand, characterized by a silent operation and a satisfactory capacity. Fresh air should actually be accessible very close to the air intake, and must not be contaminated with tobacco smoke or cooking odors. Hose clamps for reducing the air flow and T-valves to supply several air lines from the same pump, are available from pet shops.

One particular technical aid for the reduction of disease pathogens in water, which is really only required for keeping highly sensitive species or for breeding and rearing tanks, is only mentioned here as a matter of record: a UV sterilizer. The tank water is passed through a tube system, past UV radiators; the UV radiation causes a distinct reduction in the number of bacteria in the water.

Heating: Two automatic heaters (220V) and a low voltage heating cable (to be operated with a transformer).

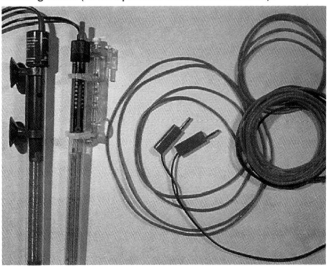

# EVERYTHING IS NICE AND GREEN...

During the last twenty years or so there has been an increasing change in our understanding of the significance of aquarium plants. Today plants in the aquarium are no longer mere decoration, which grow more or less well, but instead they are full and beneficial partners of fish and essential stabilizers of the artificial habitat aquarium.

This, however, also requires re-thinking in respect to their care and maintenance. In order for plants to develop their full beneficial potential in the aquarium, they must be able to grow normally. This requires compliance with particular prerequisites in terms of their care. Those among the readers who like to find more about water plants and their care should refer to some of the standard plant books.

## THE UNDERWATER JUNGLE...WHY?

There are many 'greens' among aquarists, who permit the "underwater jungle' to develop into an indispensable establishment for fish and the habitat aquarium. Firstly, the supply of oxygen as the most important function of plants must be pointed out. Similar to terrestrial forests on earth which provide oxygen for all animal life, the mini-habitat aquarium should also be supplied with this life elixir through the assimilation of well-kept water plants.

When light is available as an energy source together with certain nutrients, plants will produce carbohydrates (sugar, starch) from $CO_2$ and water, which they use for their own metabolism and then give off, essentially as a waste product oxygen into the water. This oxygen enrichment is done so effectively that it cannot be duplicated by artificial means (aeration, currents). Only at night do plants need oxygen for their own respiration. But the amount needed is far less than that produced during the day.

Very important under aquarium conditions is the uptake and utilization of nitrogen and phosphate compounds, which are being produced in copious amounts by the metabolism of fish. The better and faster plants grow, the more of these substances are removed from the water. With regularly required pruning, water plants remove harmful substances from the aquarium.

Plants also offer excellent surface areas for bacteria and various micro-organisms to become established on, which, on one hand, contribute to the decontamination of the water, and, on the other hand, provide newly hatched fish with their first, nutritious food. Moreover, a healthy, dense stand of plants has an inhibiting effect on disease pathogens as well as on undesirable algae. Consequently, healthy plant growth is the best insurance against excessive algal development.

A dense plant cover offers simultaneously ideal hiding places and spawning sites for fishes. Most fishes display their full behavioral repertoire only when offered the safety of adequate plant cover. Some species will only spawn in fine, bushy plants, others again prefer the broad leaves of *Cryptocoryne* and *Echinodorus* species. For juvenile fish dense plant thickets offer ideal hiding places against pursuing predators.

Apart from all these useful characteristics, healthy looking plants have a substantially higher decorative value than those showing meager growth. Consequently, luxuriant plant growth not only benefits the fish but also enhances the overall esthetic appearance of the tank.

## UNDERWATER GARDENERS

Under this slogan we are now going to attempt to familiarize you with the important fundamentals of proper and healthy plant growth. Some of the factors involved have already been discussed or at least touched on within a different context, so in these cases we will only briefly elaborate.

### Regular partial water changes

This is a recurring topic throughout most aspects of aquarium keeping. Indeed, it is the single-most important maintenance task, even for healthy plant growth. Harmful substances, which could inhibit plant growth (metabolic waste products of fishes) are diluted. Possible one-sided use of a particular nutrient, which has brought the nutrient regimen out of balance, can be corrected with partial water changes combined with re-fertilization.

**During the day the oxygen concentration in the water rises, but it sinks during the night because both fishes and plants utilize oxygen.**

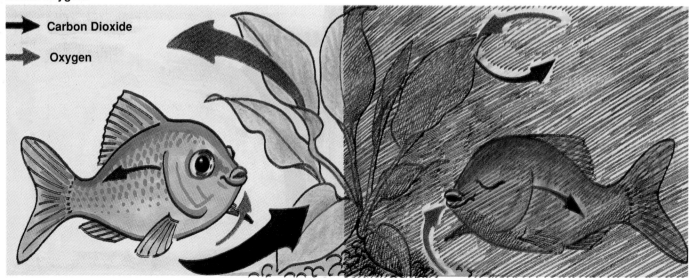

Carbon Dioxide

Oxygen

# PLANTS FOR THE AQUARIUM

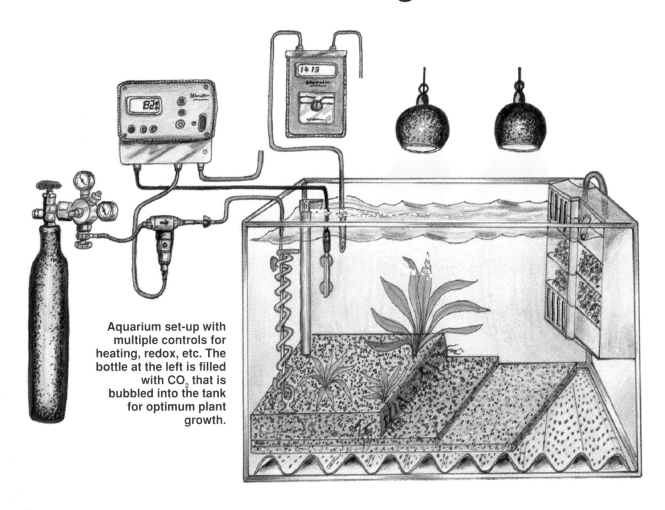

**Aquarium set-up with multiple controls for heating, redox, etc. The bottle at the left is filled with CO$_2$ that is bubbled into the tank for optimum plant growth.**

## Nutrients

To achieve healthy growth, plants need certain 'foods', which are divided into principal nutrients and trace elements. For most terrestrial plants, the nutritional requirements have been determined, because of the importance of these plants for human nutrition. The results are clearly reflected in a broad scale of fertilizers.

Generally, waterplants require the same nutrients, but in an aquarium the overall situation is fundamentally different. Some nutrients are produced in an aquarium and therefore they do not need to be supplemented, but others occur only in minimal quantities or not all, and so produce deficiency syndromes unless they are added.

Carbon is quantitatively the most important nutrient in general. Terrestrial as well as water plants obtain this from CO$_2$. The significance of CO$_2$ in the aquarium and how to correct deficiency situations has already been discussed in detail.

## Nitrate and phosphate

The principal constituents in fertilizers for terrestrial plants are produced in excess by fishes in the aquarium. Therefore, they must definitely not be contained in waterplant fertilizers.

## Calcium, magnesium and sulphate (sulphur)

These occur in sufficient quantities in tap water, unless extremely soft water is being used, which, for reasons of stability of the water values, is not recommended. Potassium occurs in variable quantities in tap water, however, it can also become a deficiency factor. Therefore, aquarium plant fertilizers contain potassium.

## Iron

This is not a trace element but indeed a principal nutrient, which has a key role in plant care. Iron plays an important part in the development of the chlorophyll in leaves. If there is an iron deficiency, the plants cannot develop chlorophyll and consequently are unable to assimilate. Glossy, yellowish young leaves are distinct signs of iron deficiency.

Iron is not desirable in tap water and is usually removed by special iron removal filters by municipal water suppliers.

For successful and effective plant maintenance nutrient-iron in a form which can be accessed by plants must be added to the water.

What does 'a form accessible by plants' mean? Many fast-growing plants take nutrients, including iron, via their leaves. But the plants can only utilize reduced, dipolar iron ions. In aquarium water which contains oxygen any dipolar iron will quickly be oxidized into tripolar ions, which cannot be used by plants. In order to avoid that, modern aquarium fertilizers use a little trick, that is, by bonding the iron to nutrient carriers. These are so-called *chelating* agents which prevent oxidation and so keep iron available for the plants.

In an earlier chapter you have been advised that natural waters always carry a certain amount of organic substances, including chelating agents which keep iron accessible for the plants. These natural chelating agents also develop to a limited degree in the aquarium during the organic decay process and in (organic) debris. Various algae can also give off chelating agents. Apparently this is the reason why plants often grow better in less than meticulously clean aquariums.

But the natural chelating agents which develop in an aquarium are not enough to assure an optimal supply of nutrient iron. This then requires a reply supplement of nutrient iron which is bound to artificial chelating agents.

This concludes the principal nutrients and brings us to the TRACE ELEMENTS. The most important trace elements are manganese, molybdenum, copper, zinc and boron. Tap water does not contain any or only very small quantities of trace elements. They, too, need to be added to aquarium water, bonded to chelating agents. Modern fertilizers usually contain precisely balanced combinations of iron and trace elements.

The above-mentioned artificial chelating agents are, of course, no excuse for careless overfertilization. Chelating agents are organic compounds that display, under laboratory conditions, high stability. In the biological system aquarium there are bacteria which can 'crack' chelating agents, and with that the respective plant nutrients are lost. Instead of the often recommended procedures to add fertilizer after each water change, it may be more appropriate to fertilize more frequently but in smaller quantities, to assure a more even nutrient supply. Optimal dosing must be determined with an iron test; levels of around 0.1 mg/l are desirable.

## Substrate

The substrate serves not only as anchoring for plants, but also as a nutrient depository especially for those plants which are dependent on a nutrient supply from the substrate due to their natural mode of life as swamp plants (*Cryptocoryne, Echinodorus*).

The advantage of iron-containing substrate additives is debatable, but they are commercially available. Unfortunately though, all of them have one disadvantage: if you are ever forced to remove or replace plants, this will always be accompanied by an unpleasant cloudiness of the water. One can, of course, do without such additives, but then the growing-in phase is substantially longer. As a compromise solution use any of the many commercially available fertilizer pellets (made of clay or similar substances) only for those plants which are dependent upon fertilizer from below.

One important criterion that the substrate must fulfil is permeability. In order to assure sufficient water circulation through the substrate use gravel with a grain size of 2 to 3 mm. Water circulation through the substrate can be further optimized by placing a heating cable over the tank bottom (under the substrate). This prevents patches of decay in the substrate,

new nutrients are transported to the plants and the development of a temperature gradient between water and substrate is avoided.

## Creating with plants

The arrangement and selection of plants matters little to fish, as long as there is adequate growth and they assimilate sufficiently. Yet, since we as aquarists and even more those who are to become aquarists, place considerable value on esthetics, so that the decorative potential that exists in all those available, different plant species, should really be taken advantage of.

One thing, however, you should not do: forcing terrestrial plants to become water plants! Unfortunately, these sorts of plants are still available from aquarium and pet shops; after all, everything in life is a matter of supply and demand! You should get suspicious when a 'water plant' is particularly colorful and reminds you of something on your living room window sill! Such plants are useless for the biology in an aquarium. They will die more or less slowly and will then pollute the water. Only buy plants rooted in small pots filled with rockwool.

Aquarium plants occur in all sorts of shapes, colors and sizes. What counts is to create, from among all

the available possibilities, a diverse and yet harmonious total picture. Here are a few tips on how to do that: Tall-growing stemmed plants and rosette-plants developing lots of 'runners' (e.g. *Vallisneria*) are used for the background of a tank and to disguise equipment, such as heater, filter intake pipe, and so on.

The center section of the tank and the foreground are covered with plants of decreasing height, i.e. plants of medium height and low-growing plants. Large plants serve as eye catchers and should not be placed right in the middle of the tank. Stemmed plants and those developing runners should always be kept together in groups, never as individual plants. Create contrasts in shape and in color; bushy plants should be placed next to broad-leave plants, red ones next to green ones, dark green ones next to light green ones, and so on.

Do not start out saving at the wrong end; plant your tank densely right from the start and the faster you will get over all the initial difficulties. When you have decided to use $CO_2$ fertilization, start out with lots of fast-growing stemmed plants. With them you make it difficult right from the start for algae to establish themselves. Later on you can replace some of the fast-growing plants with slower growing ones.

For reasons discussed already in detail, a tank with-

**Press a hole into the substrate, place the plant roots in it, cautiously refill the hole again, and gently press down on the substrate (covering the hole). Do not plant too deeply. The crown of the roots must always remain visible.**

out $CO_2$ fertilization should only be planted with slow-growing plants. Watch closely for algae right from the start, and such a tank should be fertilized sparingly.

## Planting

Remove all pots, rock wool, foam rubber strips and lead wire which come with your newly purchased plants. Rock wool and foam rubber strips often contain remnants of the nutrient solution used by the nursery for rearing these plants. This solution contains nitrate and phosphate and must not be put into the aquarium. Damaged leaves and stem segments should be cut off neatly. The roots of rosette plants should be pruned back to about 3 cm length. Stemmed plants are pushed individually and cautiously into the substrate, making sure that the stems are not squashed. For rosette plants we drilled a hole into the substrate with one finger; the plant is positioned deeply in this hole, is then covered with sand or gravel, and is then gently pulled upwards where the top of the substrate is level with the neck of the root system.

Various epiphytic plants, e.g. Java fern (*Microsorium*) or Dwarf Anubias (*Anubias barteri* var. *nana*) must not be planted into substrate. Instead, they are tied to pieces of submerged wood or to rocks, using nylon threads. Floating plants are set adrift on the surface. They require sufficient air space above the surface for their well-being, so they do best in tanks with suspended lamps and without a cover glass.

Once all the plants have been put in place they need to be left in peace to commence growing. Fertilization during the first two weeks should only be done very sparingly, or not at all, because the plants need time to adjust to their new environment. Many aquarium plants are grown out of water by plant nurseries, and will have to adjust to the new situation by developing underwater leaves. And so in time, the appearance of the plants will change since underwater leaves look different than aerial leaves.

Plants should be moved as rarely as possibly (exception: stemmed plants). Moving plants causes stress, from which the plants have to recover after each move.

**By combining various leaf shapes and heights, an aquarium's esthetic appeal can be dramatically enhanced.**

**When transferring plants or planting new ones, the roots should always be shortened.**

## Breeding plants

**Runners:** This is the easiest mode of plant reproduction, because it does not require any human intervention. Once the plants have gotten over the shock of having been replanted and have started to grow again, they will eventually produce runners with small, juvenile plants at the terminal end. This makes the stand of plants denser. Once it becomes too dense or a particular plant species is starting to exceed its assigned space, the young plants can be cut off (once they have developed about 4 or 5 leaves) and are planted elsewhere.

After a certain period of time adult plants need to be replaced with younger ones in order to avoid aging of a particular stand of plants. The development of runners proceeds at different speeds, depending upon plant species. *Cryptocoryne* tend to take their time, while *Vallisneria* will produce large numbers of runners within a short period of time.

Some plants will produce numerous juvenile plants along the margins of a leaf. These can be cautiously removed and planted.

The easiest method of plant reproduction is by runners.

A special form of reproduction is shown by the Sumatra Fern (*Ceratopteris*). The older floating leaves develop small juvenile plants along their margins, which can be split off after a while. Similar juvenile plants are produced by the Java Fern (*Microsorium*), but are far less in numbers.

**Pseudo-viviparity:** Many of the Amazon sword plants will flower quite readily in an aquarium. If the blossom stems are prevented from reaching the surface (weighing them down with a rock), they will develop numerous juvenile plants, sort of as an emergency solution. When these juvenile plants are sufficiently strong they can be cautiously removed and individually planted.

## Reproduction through seeds

Reproduction by seeds occurs relatively rarely under aquarium conditions. Some of the *Aponogeton* species will regularly reproduce flower stems, which sometimes spontaneously develop seeds or can be fertilized with a very soft brush.

## Cuttings

All stemmed plants will more or less rapidly reach the water surface, and then either grow along the surface or continue to grow upwards and out of the water. There are two ways to proceed here: if a particular stand is to be enlarged, the stems are severed about halfway from the bottom, and the cut off tips are then re-planted. The remaining stem will produce two or more shoots, which can also be cut and replanted once these reach the surface. After a while the main stems will no longer produce any shoots and should then be removed. Many of the stemmed plants will also produce, spontaneously, side shoots, which can also be cut off and planted.

If the stand (of a particular species) is not to be enlarged any further, but remains esthetically pleasing, the stems must be pulled out regularly, cut off at the bottom and the top re-planted. One normally proceeds so that the height of the plants slopes upward toward the back; however, it must be noted that this procedure is fairly labor-intensive.

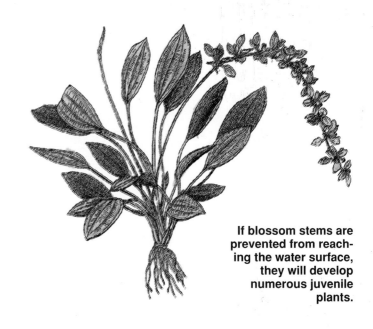

If blossom stems are prevented from reaching the water surface, they will develop numerous juvenile plants.

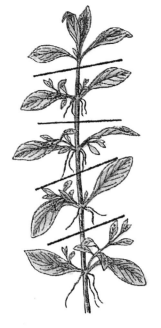

These juvenile plants can be cautiously removed and individually planted when they are sufficiently strong.

ment, in water hardness of less than 10 DH degrees growth is possible without $CO_2$ fertilization., under very intense illumination compact growth, therefore also suited for central regions of the tank; Height to 50 cm.

*Crinum thaianum*

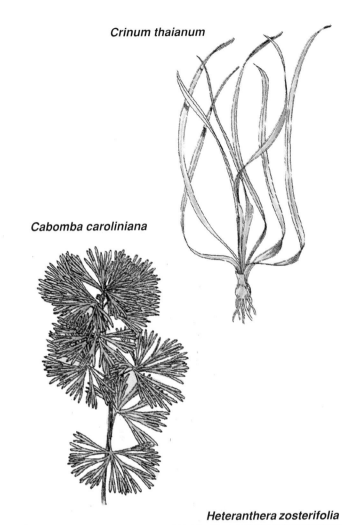

*Cabomba caroliniana*

# PARTNERS OF FISHES...SELECTED PLANT SPECIES

In this section we would like to introduce to you a selection of easily kept aquarium plants which are normally available throughout the year. There are, of course, many more species which are suitable for an aquarium. Sooner or later you will probably also find plants not mentioned here.

Please note the categorization of plants for the background, central tank region, foreground and solitary plants for particular focal points. Whether a particular plant is suitable for the back of a tank or for the middle, depends upon the intended decorative effect and the size of the tank. The plants listed below can be kept without difficulties in water with a carbonate hardness of 5 to 15 DH degrees, pH values between 6.8 and 7.4 and a temperature of around 25 degrees C (77°F). Plants with the notation '$CO_2$ fertilization recommended' will also grow without $CO_2$ fertilization. Under such circumstances though one can expect that some plants will stop growing due to $CO_2$ competition from other plants. Moreover, these plants may not show optimum development. Special characteristics are given for respective species.

## Plants for the back and sides of a tank

*Cabomba caroliniana*

Rapidly growing, high light requirement, $CO_2$ fertilization required, develops lateral shoots when surface is reached, because of bushy appearance an excellent contrast to broad-leaved plants; height 45 to 60 cm.

Thailand Hooked Lily, *Crinum thaianum*

Tall-growing plant, but very suitable for aquariums, medium to high light requirement, $CO_2$ fertilization recommended, also as solitary plant in large tanks, leaves will drift on the surface, can handle periodic pruning, bulb requires deep substrate Height to 200 cm.

*Heteranthera zosterifolia*

Moderately fast-growing plant, high light require-

*Heteranthera zosterifolia*

## Background Plants

*Hygrophila difformis*

Rapidly growing, high light requirements, $CO_2$ fertilization recommended, very decorative, at low light levels leaves less 'split'; Height 50 cm.

*Hygrophila polysperma*

Rapidly growing, medium to high light requirement, $CO_2$ fertilization recommended, light green leaves changing to reddish hues under high illumination, one of the most popular aquarium plants; Height 50 cm.

Madagascan Waterpest, *Lagarosiphon madagascariensis*

Rapidly growing, high light requirement, $CO_2$ fertilization, can be drifting freely or be anchored to the substrate, shade from other plants should be avoided; Height variable.

Swamp Friend, *Limnophila sessiliflora*

Rapidly growing, high light requirement, $CO_2$ fertilization recommended, similar type as *Cabomba*, but easier to keep; Height to 60 cm.

Creeping Ludwigia, *Ludwigia repens*

Moderately fast growing, high light requirement, $CO_2$ fertilization recommended, reddish coloration only with sufficient light, somewhat sensitive to temperatures in excess of 28 degrees C (82°F.); Height to 50 cm.

Round-leafed Rotala, *Rotala rotundifolia*

Rapidly growing, high light requirement, $CO_2$ fertilization recommended, reddish leaf tips; Height to 50 cm.

Mexican Oak leaf, *Shinnersia rivularis*

Very rapidly growing, high light requirement, heavy $CO_2$ consumption, leaf shape reminiscent of oak leaves, sensitive to temperature in excess of 25°C (77°F); Height to 60 cm.

Corkscrew Vallisneria, *Vallisneria asiatica* var. *biwaensis*

Moderately fast-growing, high light requirement, $CO_2$ fertilization recommended, in larger tanks also suitable for central areas, tightly twisted leaves, develops runners; Height 25 to 30 cm.

Common Swamp Corkscrew, *Vallisnerias spiralis*

Rapidly growing, medium high light requirement, heavy $CO_2$ consumption otherwise undemanding, develops runners; Height 40 to 60 cm.

**Lagarosiphon madagascariensis**

**Hygrophila polysperma**

**Hygrophila difformis**

**Limnophila sessiliflora**

**Rotala rotundifolia**

## Plants for the middle section

The plant species listed here are suitable for background use in smaller tanks or as solitary plants in larger tanks, small stands effective as esthetic focal point in large tank.

Parrot leaf, *Alternanthera reineckii*

Slow growing leaves with magnificent red, high light requirement, $CO_2$ fertilization, must not be shaded by other plants, growth stops upon $CO_2$ deficiency, highly decorative as a group with gradually increasing stem length towards the back of the tank; Height variable, about 50 cm.

Large Cognac Plant, *Ammania gracilis*

Moderately fast growing, high light requirement, $CO_2$ fertilization, reddish-brown leaves with excellent contrast effect, must not be shaded by other plants. *Ammania senegalensis*: similar, but smaller leaves; Height to 50 cm.

*Cryptocoryne affinis*

Undemanding, slow to moderately fast growth, moderate light requirement, coloration of leaves light-dependent and variable, develops runners; Height about 20 cm, taller under strong lighting.

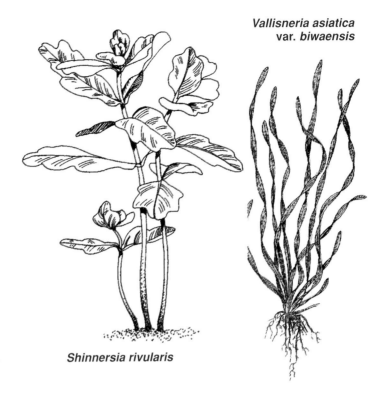

*Vallisneria asiatica var. biwaensis*

*Shinnersia rivularis*

*Vallisneria spiralis*

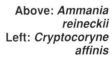

Above: *Ammania reineckii*
Left: *Cryptocoryne affinis*

## Middle tank region

*Cryptocoryne crispatula*

Slow-growing, high light requirement, $CO_2$ fertilization recommended, nobby, small dark green leaves, develops runners; Height to 40 cm.

*Cryptocoryne pontederiifolia*

Adaptable, slow-growing, moderate light requirement, with bright green (heart-shaped) leaves, develops runners; Height 20 to 30 cm.

*Cryptocoryne wendtii*

Undemanding, moderately fast growing, moderate light requirement, leaves highly variable in shape and color, develops runners, also useful as foreground plants in large tanks. Best known and most popular *Cryptocoryne* species; Height 8 to 15 cm.

Cardinal Lobelia, *Lobelia cardinalis*

Stiff, slowly growing stem plant, high light requirement, will grow tall with $CO_2$ fertilization, normally smaller, use in groups with increasing (stem) height; Height to 50 cm.

Java Fern, *Microsorium pteropus*

Slow- to moderately fast growing, moderate light requirement, adaptable, reproduction by means of adventicious plants on leaves, rhizomes must not be buried in substrate; attach to rocks or submerged wood, older leaves may get blackish spots; Height about 20 cm.

*Rotala macrandra*

Moderately fast growing, high light requirement, $CO_2$ fertilization, magnificent red, roundish leaves, excellent contrast effect, difficult to keep without $CO_2$ fertilization; Height to 50 cm.

Broad-leaf arrow-weed, *Sagittaria graminea* var. *platyphylla*

Moderately fast growing, high light requirement, $CO_2$ fertilization recommended, stiff, broad-banded leaves, which are also compatible with robust fish species, develops runners; Height to 30 cm.

Javamoss, *Vesicularia dubyana*

Moderately fast growing, moderate light requirement, undemanding, ideal for providing hiding places for juvenile fish, must be anchored/attached to rocks or submerged wood (roots); Height variable.

## Foreground plants

Dwarf Anubia, *Anubias barteri* var. *nana*

Slow-growing, high to moderate light requirement, $CO_2$ fertilisation recommended, rhizome must never be buried in substrate, grows as an epiphyte on rocks or submerged wood (roots), the stiff leaves are preferred settlement sites for certain algae; Height 10 to 15 cm

Dwarf Cyrptocoryne, *Cryptocoryne willisii*

Slow-growing, moderate light requirement, easy to keep, extensive runner development forming dense 'carpets'; Height to 10 cm.

Dwarf sword plant, *Echinodorus quadricostatus* var. *xinguensis*

Moderately fast growing, high light requirement, must not be shaded by other plants, $CO_2$ fertilization recommended, other than that quite robust; Height to 10 cm.

Tropica swordplant, *Echinodorus parviflorus* 'Tropica'

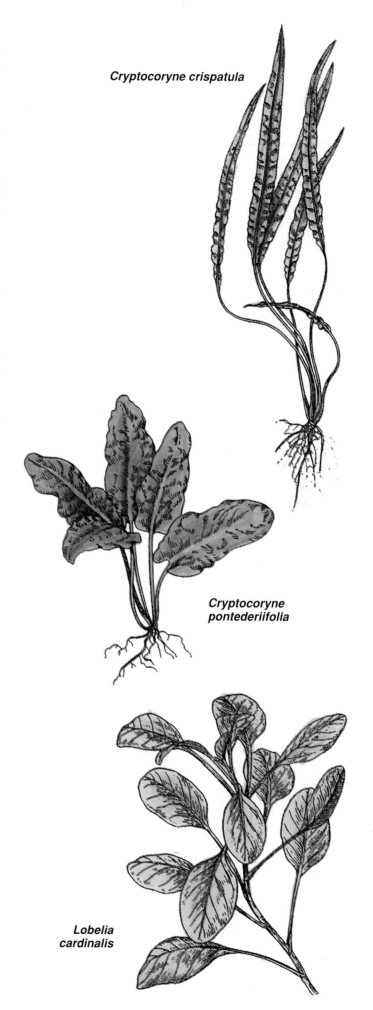

*Cryptocoryne crispatula*

*Cryptocoryne pontederiifolia*

*Lobelia cardinalis*

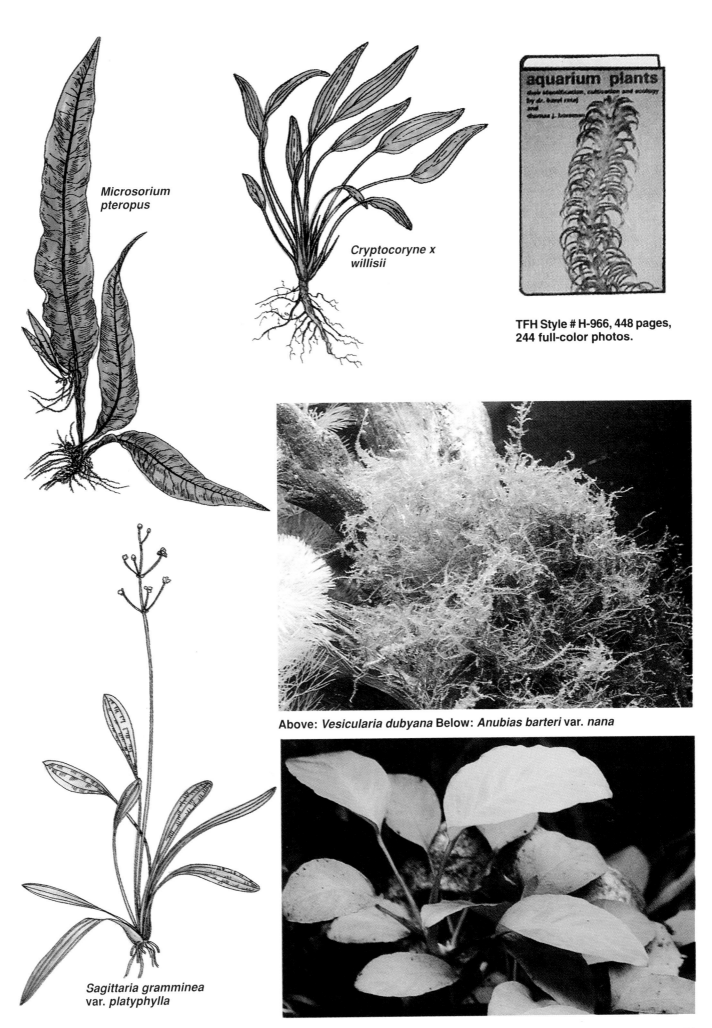

*Microsorium pteropus*

*Cryptocoryne x willisii*

aquarium plants

TFH Style # H-966, 448 pages, 244 full-color photos.

Above: *Vesicularia dubyana* Below: *Anubias barteri* var. *nana*

*Sagittaria gramminea* var. *platyphylla*

71

**Above:** *Echinodorus quadricostatus var. xinguensis*
**Below:** *Sagittaria subulata f. pusilla*

Slow growing, moderate light requirement, $CO_2$ fertilization recommended, a new decorative variety, with dense, slightly 'nobbled', dense leaf cover, adventive plants along flower stem; Height to 10 cm.

Grassy swordplant, *Echinodorus tenellus*

Moderately fast growing, high light requirement, $CO_2$ fertilization, demanding, must not be shaded, reproduces by means of runners spreading lawn-like, similar to *E.quadricostatus* but has narrower leaves; Height to 5 cm.

Dwarf arrow weed, *Sagittaria subulata* cf. *pussila*

Moderately fast growing, moderate light requirements, easy to keep, lawn-like development through runners; Height 5 to 10 cm.

## Solitary plants

The plants listed here can serve as esthetic focal points in an aquarium if planted as solitary plants. Some are also effective in small stands, when planted in a large tank.

Lettuce-leaf Aponogeton, *Aponogeton ulvaceus*

Very fast growing, moderate to high light requirement, $CO_2$ fertilization recommended, light-green decoratively waved leaves, bulb must not be completely buried, undergoes resting periods; Height to 50 cm.

Long-leaved Barclaya, *Barclaya longifolia*

Slow-growing, high light requirement, must not be shaded, $CO_2$ fertilization, one of the most attractive aquarium plants, olive-green to reddish, wavy leaves, does not like cold substrate (substrate heating!); Height to 30 cm.

Sumatra Fern, *Ceratopteris thalictroides*

Rapidly growing, undemanding, $CO_2$ fertilization recommended, floating form possible, can easily become dominant; Height to 40 cm.

*Barclaya longifolia*

*Echinodorus parviflorus* "Tropica"

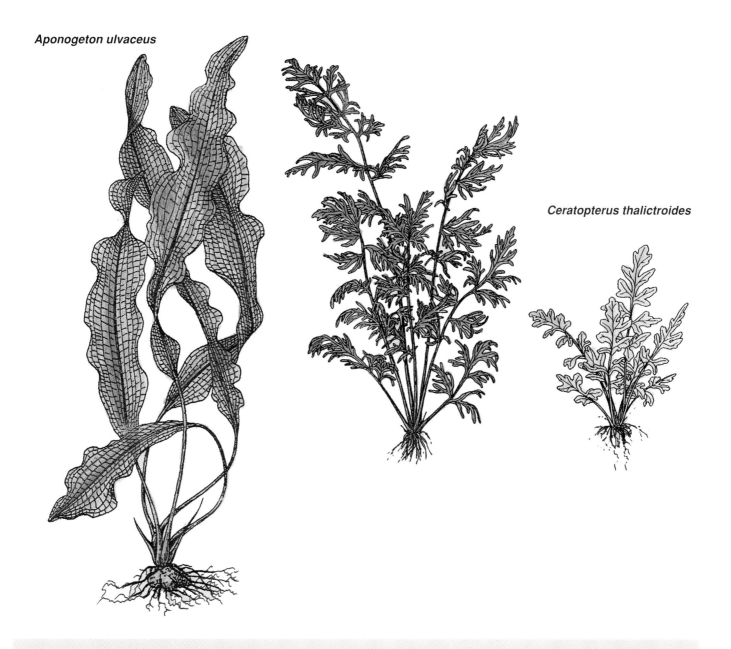

*Aponogeton ulvaceus*

*Ceratopterus thalictroides*

## THE IMPORTANT POINT IS EASY CARE...

If you do not have a green thumb and if you are simply unlucky with your underwater gardening attempts, do not despair: hygienic, colorful and as real as plastic can be, plastic plants are available. In fact, they are sprouting colorful blossoms in all imaginable shapes and forms. In due course 'nature' adds the final touch with algae covering the plastic stems.

Just as the substrate must be color-coordinated with the wall paper, the aquarium accessory industry appears to have thought of everything to fulfil any decorative wish. After all, who says that plants can only be green, yellow, red or brown? Plastic plants are easy to look after, and they do not wither under wrong illumination and spoil the view of the fish. Moreover, they do not need to be pruned, moved and fertilized. They are not

decimated by herbivorous fish: neither a hungry goldfish nor the pesky little catfish which like to chew holes in plant leaves can harm plastic plants.

But one thing plastic plants can not do: produce oxygen and turn an aquarium into a natural habitat.

*Cryptocoryne cordata blassii*

*Cryptocoryne cordata blassii*
Slow-growing, low light requirement, possible shading with floating plants, $CO_2$ fertilization, available in two different forms of variable height, large brownish-red leaves, disturb as little as possible.; Height 30 to 40 cm.

Amazon swordplant, *Echinodorus amazonicus*
Moderately fast growing, moderate to high light requirement, $CO_2$ fertilization recommended, adaptable,

best known of all swordplants, juvenile plants develop along flower stem; Height 30 to 40 cm.

Thai waterfriend, *Hygrophila stricta*
Rapid growing, $CO_2$ fertilization recommended, stemmed plant with large, light green leaves reminiscent of peach leaves, lower leaves will be lost with insufficient light or if plant grows above water surface; Height to 50 cm.

Red Tiger lotus, *Nymphaea lotus*
Moderately fast growing, high light requirement, must not be shaded, $CO_2$ fertilization, magnificent red underwater leaves with dark patches, remove floating leaves; Height 30 to 50 cm.

## Floating plants

Floating plants contribute significantly to the removal of waste products from water via their absorbent roots. The $CO_2$ fertilization demand will be met from the air (except in *Riccia*). Underwater plants with high light requirements must not be shaded by floating plants. In tanks which are covered, make sure there is sufficient air space between water and cover.

Floating water fern, *Ceratopteris pteridioides*
Very rapidly growing, reproduction by means of adventitious plants along the leaf margins, excellent hiding places for juvenile fish, labyrinth fishes like to build their bubble nest among the leaves; diameter to 40 cm.

South American Frogbit, *Limnobium laevigatum*
Moderately fast growing, dark green, spongy leaves, reproduction by means of runners, does best in open tanks.; diameter 5 to 8 cm.

*Riccia fluitans*
Rapidly growing, not a true floating plant since it drifts below water surface, forms dense, inpenetrable layer, ideal for juvenile fish.

**Living plants can flourish in an aquarium if they are provided with the proper nutrient base to get them started. Photo courtesy of Aquarium Products.**

**Nymphaea lotus**

Left: *Echinodorus amazonicus*. Right: *Hygrophila stricta*.

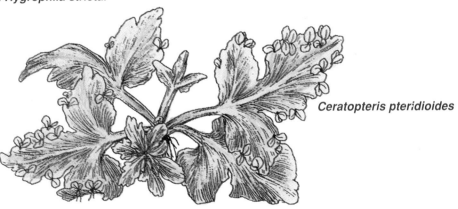

*Ceratopteris pteridioides*

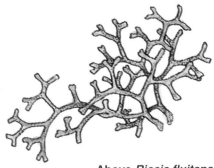

Above *Riccia fluitans*.
Left: *Limnobium laevigatum*.

# A VISIT TO THE AQUATIC PLANT BREEDER

On one of our unfortunately much too rare visits to our Thai friends, we again stayed in the ancient royal city of Ayuthaya. One day our friend told us that he had to bring some juvenile Giant Gouramis to Chachoengsao. They were needed in Germany for scientific research, and the owner of an aquatic plant farm in Chachoengsao would arrange the shipment for him.

We pricked up our ears at the mention of the aquatic plant farm, and asked our friend if he had room to bring us along and some time for us to see this farm. Naturally we were allowed to come along, and at the appointed time we set off for Chachoengsao in a pickup with bad shocks, which had seen better days.

Our friend introduced us to the owner of the farm and told him what we had in mind. The owner regretted greatly that he would be unable to show us his farm personally, because he had to attend to business, but we were welcome to look around to our heart's content. And so we did, while our friend delivered his fish and attended to the necessary formalities.

After we were led through the office building, we entered an immense area, which, as far as the eye could see, was covered with shade nets on wooden frames to ward off the scorching rays of the tropical sun. Greenhouses are not needed here, because heating is free. We strolled through the "shady kingdom" for a long time with two to three stray dogs, until our brains, which had gone completely blank in the tropical sun, finally became aware that we were on an aquatic plant farm and had yet to see any water at all.

## AQUATIC PLANTS ON DRY LAND

All the plants grew in rows in neatly laid-out beds with the, to be sure, quite moist soil that occurs here naturally, but there could be no talk about water. Our gray matter slowly started working again and our biological expertise finally came to the fore: The majority of our aquarium plants are of course marsh plants and naturally can also be cultivated without water, which is a considerably simpler and more rational technique. Furthermore, they are less delicate during shipment, as the owner of the farm later explained.

We slowly grew used to the sight, and after looking around for a while we started to recognize some aquarium plants. The rows with the beds shaded with nets were occasionally interrupted by idyllic, palm-shaded ponds. Among magnificent blooming water lilies and lotuses we spotted a few barbs and labyrinth fishes, but predatory snakeheads too.

The picture changed when we entered the next "shade gallery." Instead of the beds we had seen so far, we now found long rows of shallow concrete tanks, in part filled only with a mixture of soil and gravel. The overwhelming majority, however, were "flooded." The water was about 40 centimeters deep, and in the aforementioned soil-gravel mixture as a substrate stood rows and rows of old acquaintances in various sizes, ranging from tiny seedlings to marketable specimens. We found various *Aponogeton* species, *Cryptocoryne*, *Echinodorus*, *Hygrophila difformis*, and others.

In the middle of each of these concrete tanks, in a

**"Dry beds" shaded with nets.**

heavy concrete frame with the opening under water, stood an aquarium with a capacity of about 60 liters, the function of which was not immediately clear to us. As we continued past the rows of concrete tanks, we encountered an employee who was filling the overturned aquaria with $CO_2$ from a large steel cylinder — now everything was clear to us!

After about an hour's walk we returned to the office building dripping with sweat, where with proverbial Thai hospitality they refreshed us by turning all the available fans on us. We now had

*Hygrophila difformis* in submerged culture.

the opportunity to speak with the owner. He enumerated all the countries that he exported his plants to; Germany was one of them.

We were also interested in knowing whether all the plants were propagated here or whether they also collected plants from the wild. The owner willingly explained to us that primarily the plants not native to Thailand were propagated, whereas various native species were collected in the wild and were raised only to selling size. In the meantime our friend had completed his business, so we gave our thanks and returned to Ayuthaya.

The "turned-over aquaria" are filled with $CO_2$.

# THE PRINCIPAL PARTICIPANTS: OUR FISH

## THE FISH, AN UNKNOWN LIVING BEING?

Surely not! Since early this century natural history researchers, systematists and, of course, aquarists have gathered and accumulated an enormous store of information about fish in general and about aquarium fish in particular.

### About systematics

Fishes, as well as amphibians, reptiles, birds and mammals, belong to the vertebrates. The characteristic feature of all of these five animal groups is the presence of a backbone or vertebral column as the main load-bearing component of the skeletal system.

Fishes represent the oldest group with the largest number of species and specimens among the vertebrates. The systematics of fishes has been and still is constantly being discussed and revised. Even the total number of (recent) species is uncertain: estimates vary from 21,000 to 25,000. Since it is quite likely that there are still many species to be discovered, the ultimate total could be as high as 30,000 species.

The largest, and at the same the best-researched group among the fishes are the true bony fishes. Somewhere between 5,000 and 8,000 of these live in fresh water, and of these 4,000 could be suitable for aquarium keeping. But currently, the aquarium fish trade deals with only about 300 species and an equal number of varieties. There are color photos and vital information in *Dr. Axelrod's Atlas*.

### Body temperature

Fishes are cold-blooded. That means they are unable to regulate their own body temperature. They cannot produce any body heat and their body is as warm or as cold as the water around them (amphibians and reptiles are also cold-blooded, while birds and mammals actively regulate their body temperature).

**T.F.H. Style # H-1077, 8 ½ x 11", hardcover, 1152 pages, contains more than 7,600 full-color photos.**

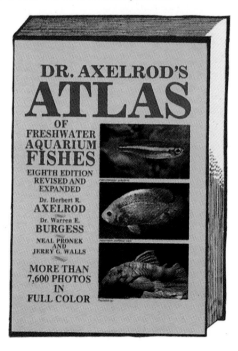

Just because fishes are cold-blooded does not mean that they can handle any temperature. Being adapted to particular environments and often very specific habitats, fish need certain temperature ranges for their well-being. A more or less wide temperature band suitable for fish invariably surrounds an optimum temperature. If it is too cold or too hot, it does not necessarily mean that a fish will die immediately; however, if not given the right temperature range the physical conditions of a fish will gradually decline. It will become susceptible to diseases and cease to reproduce.

### Fins

Fins are a typical characteristic of fishes. Fins are mainly areas of membrane supported by part of the skeleton, the so-called *fin rays*. They are moved via strands of muscle and they can be opened up (spread) or folded together ('pinched').

One distinguishes between paired and unpaired fins. Usually there are a total of seven fins: paired pectoral and abdominal fins, as well as the unpaired dorsal, anal and caudal or tail fin.

The dorsal fin can be separated into several segments; the abdominal fins can be totally regressed (externally absent) or may have become modified into organs of attachment (e.g. some catfishes). In certain labyrinth fishes they have taken on certain sensory (taste and touch) functions. The males of livebearers (toothcarps) have a reproductive organ, the so-called *gonopodium*, which has developed from a modified anal fin.

Often we distinguish between males and females on the bases of shape and color of certain fins. An atypical fin, located between the dorsal and caudal fin, is the adipose fin in many tetras. This fin does not have any supporting rays and it does not contribute to any movements; its function is still unresolved.

The fins of higher vertebrates, e.g. dolphins and whales, display the same functions as the fins of fishes (homologous), but they are built differently.

### Locomotion

Fish move through alternating the pull of lateral muscles; they practically move with sinusoidal (snake-like) motion. Dorsal, anal and caudal fins follow these wave-like body motions or actively support them (especially the caudal fin with its strong musculature). The paired pectoral and abdominal (pelvic) fins are used (in most species) for steering, braking and maintaining balance. Swimming backwards is possible with the aid of the pectoral fins.

### Skin and scales

Fish skin consists of the outer skin (epidermis) and the dermis underneath. Located in the epidermis are glands which give off the slimy protective film, that affords a certain protection to the skin of a fish against foreign bodies, parasites, bacteria and fungi. Certain diseases, poor water quality and injuries (including those due to incorrect handling) will damage this mucous layer, so that disease pathogens have easier access.

During the breeding season, males of some carp-like fishes develop white epidermal nodules, usually along the head and back. These nuptual tubercles can easily be mistaken for the white spot disease, *Ichthyophthirius*.

The scales are hornified structures, which are formed in the dermis and pushed to just below the epidermis in scale pockets. Not all fish have scales; catfish and a few loaches are 'naked'. There are a number of modifications to scale patterns, such as very small, deeply embedded scales, fish which are only partially covered by scales (mirror carp) and flat, bony plates instead of scales (armored catfish).

## Lateral line

The lateral line of fishes is a remote sensing organ, which can pick up detailed information about water movement by means of sensory cells.

## Coloration

The color in fish is caused by pigment-containing color cells located in the dermis. The entire scheme of glorious colors in fish is produced by only four types of cells, but commonly a wide range of combinations: there are red, yellow and black color cells as well as reflective cells containing special reflective crystals. The color blue is created by a mixture of black and reflective cells.

Color changes and the development of lighter or darker tones occur through changes in position and the extent of the pigments in the color cells.

## The fish skeleton

The bony skeleton of fishes functions as structural support and for the attachment of muscles. Since water essentially carries the fish, its skeleton is not exposed to such substantial structural stresses as that of terrestrial animals. Therefore, it can be relatively delicate in structure.

The central element is the vertebral column (backbone) with its projections, which extends from head to tail, and bears the ribs on the anterior section. All these structural elements are bones. Located free in the musculature are supporting elements, which are ossified tendons, and which are not connected to head, fins or the vertebral column.

## Internal organs

The digestive canal occupies most of the space in the abdominal cavity. Food enters the stomach via the mouth and esophagus. In some species it will be passed directly into the anterior part of the intestine. Carnivorous (meat-eating) fish have a short intestine. Herbivorous (plant-eating) fish have a strongly looped, long intestine. Fish do not have saliva glands, but they do have a liver, gall bladder and pancreas.

The abdominal cavity also contains a spleen, kidneys (located below the backbone) and internal sex organs, that is, testes or ovaries.

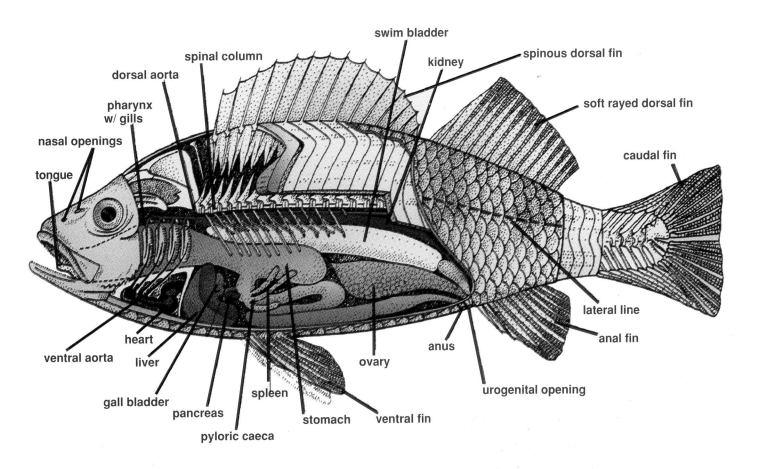

Only in fish (and not in all of them) do we find a swim bladder. This thin-skinned sac contains a gas mixture of oxygen, nitrogen and carbon dioxide; it serves as a hydrostatic organ. In many benthic (bottom-living) fishes the swim bladder regresses once they are past the larval stage.

The first filling (after the fish larvae have hatched) is facilitated by direct swallowing of air at the surface; thereafter the swim bladder content is maintained through gas exchange to compensate for changing water depth via the vascular system.

## DO FISH DRINK?

In order to answer this standard question, we have to distinguish between marine and freshwater fish, then the answer is: marine fish...YES, freshwater fish in principle...NO!

Seawater is saltier and contains more dissolved substances than the fish itself. Since there is a tendency towards a chemical equilibrium (diffusion, osmosis), a marine fish loses water across its body surface. The fish compensates for that by drinking seawater. The salt, taken in with the seawater, is excreted again, via the gills and in extremely concentrated form via urine.

In freshwater, the situation is in reverse. The fish body constituents are more concentrated than the water surrounding it. Consequently, water tends to enter the fish's body via its body surface, which must be excreted again via the kidneys. Therefore, freshwater fishes do not need to drink; only unintentionally are small volumes of water taken in.

### The gills

Gills are a typical fish characteristic. Apart from also occurring in amphibian larvae, they are not found in any other animal group. Some fish species have additional respiratory organs, which will be discussed under the respective fish groups.

**Long-finned form of the rosy barb (Puntius conchonius) developed through selective breeding from the normal (wild) form.**

Gills are delicate, strongly vascularized skin lamellae (gill filaments), which are constantly bathed in respiratory water. Located laterally on the head, they are protected by gill covers. The respiratory frequency can be noted from gill cover movements.

Blood flows from the body to the heart, and is then pumped to the gills and there into tiny capillaries, which makes it possible for the blood to remain in the gills for a brief period of time. During that period oxygen is absorbed into the blood; at the same time carbon dioxide and waste products are given off into the surrounding water. The kidneys excrete a lot of water which contains very little in terms of dissolved metabolic waste products.

### Size and age

Fish never stop growing, but once sexual maturity has been reached, growth slows down substantially. Only unfavorable environmental conditions and death due to old age terminate this potentially perpetual growth. Freshwater fishes reach sizes from little more than a few centimeters to more than 4 meters (*Arapaima*).

The longevity of fish varies from a year to several decades! Human care normally assures a greater life span for fish than conditions in the wild.

## PROGENY IN THE AQUARIUM

With appropriate care and maintenance, aquarium fishes sooner or later reach physical maturity, a point where reproductive behavior then becomes a normal expression. On the other hand, reproductive activities can also be viewed as evidence of appropriate living conditions which have been created for the fish.

For many aquarium fish, breeding takes place spontaneously, usually in a community tank; others require specific stimuli to trigger spawning. Still others may reach sexual maturity in a community tank, and they may even spawn there, but the eggs die. The reason is that hard water is often acceptable for KEEPING fish, but eggs and fish larvae require soft water for their normal development. Such fish (many tetras and barbs) have to be bred in separate breeding tanks with precisely conditioned water.

An essential prerequisite for breeding to occur in the first place is, of course, the presence of males and females. When we originally go out and buy the fish from the tanks of a dealer, we rarely ever know what will turn into males and females. Generally, we should purchase juvenile or sub-adult fish, which are better able to adapt to their new surroundings.

Consequently, when the dealer recommends you buy several fish, ideally ten or more, of one species it makes indeed a lot of sense. Statistically there is a better chance to obtain a more balanced ratio between the sexes when buying a number of fish. Moreover, many of the popular aquarium fish should not just be kept in pairs, because often they are schooling fish which do better when kept together in larger numbers.

Many species are also quite particular (e.g. cichlids) when it comes to selecting a partner. When buying a number of juveniles there is a better chance that two will find each other.

Keeping fish of the same sex, for whatever reason, is

not only unnatural, but also prevents us from experiencing the most interesting and exciting part of aquarium keeping, observing the various types of reproduction. Moreover, many fish species will really only display their true colors when both sexes are present.

## Sexual differences

Now you will want to know how to distinguish between males and females in fishes. That is not always very easy, and there is not enough space here to discuss the various aspects of sexing fish, in detail. Therefore, it is suggested you refer to the appropriate literature for further details, but the following general hints can serve as useful reference points.

The easiest fish to sex are live-bearers. The anal fin in males has become modified into the characteristic copulatory organ, the *gonopodium*, while females have a normal anal fin. Usually females are also larger than males. Furthermore, guppy males are far more colorful, and in swordtails only the males have a sword-like extension along the lower edge of the caudal fin. By the way, swordtail females can change into males, which are more robust than those fish which were males right from the start.

In many different fish families, males are often characterized by extensions of fin rays of the median fins (dorsal, anal and/or caudal fin), which are then more elongated and often terminate in a point, while those of females are generally blunter or simply rounded off.

Often males are far more colorful than females (many labyrinth fishes, cichlids, etc.). In many dwarf cichlids, the females, during the breeding season, display a typically black pattern against a yellow background, which is absent in males.

## Trigger mechanisms

As has already been explained, given the right conditions some fish breed spontaneously and there is nothing one can do about it. This includes, for instance, all of the

A breeding pair of Odessa barbs, *Puntius* sp. Photo by Aqua Press Piednoir.

"I'm in the mood for love!"

In the guppy there are clear sexual differences: The upper fish is the inconspicuous female, the lower one the colorful male, whose anal fin has become modified into the gonopodium.

Two males of the red variety of the dwarf gourami (*Colisa lalia*).

live-bearers, which gives especially the beginning aquarist a feeling of supreme accomplishment of having bred fish in his own tank.

Other fish require specific trigger factors. Generally, these are environmental stimuli which give the organism the signal to breed. For many tropical fish species the rainy season is the triggering signal. The rainy season can be simulated under aquarium conditions through frequent water changes over a short period of time. When this includes lowering the hardness slightly and the replacement water is slightly cooler, it usually works and the fish will spawn.

Many fishes, especially wild-caught specimens, are still adapted to the seasonal fluctuations in their native waters. These fish can usually only be stimulated to spawn when the rainy season occurs in their native habitat. For instance, for armored catfish, all it takes is usually a temperature reduction to stimulate breeding. Lowering the water level and increasing the temperature are the trigger for getting labyrinth fishes to breed.

In many instances, a specific food is the deciding factor for some fishes to produce eggs. Black mosquito larvae seem to promote this in some species. Beyond that there are many species, e.g. clown loaches (*Botia macracantha*) where the triggering mechanisms have not yet been worked out at all or only insufficiently. This is an area where those inclined towards scientific investigative work can still contribute much. It would not be the first time that aquarists have unmasked such a secret.

Apart from triggering mechanisms, most fishes also require a specific substrate, to which they attach their eggs. Many tetras and barbs do not need a direct substrate, but they do prefer particular plants among which they deposit their eggs.

## Juvenile fishes in a community tank

Anyone not interested in raising large numbers of juvenile fish can make sure, through cleverly setting up the community tank, that at least some of the young make it to adulthood. That does not even involve providing special rearing foods. Dense corner stands of

*Apistogramma cacatuoides* **female (with her progeny) dressed in a typical yellow and black brood care coloration.**

**"Population explosion."**

bushy plants or dense moss carpets and a section of the surface covered with floating plants can give a lot of protection to newly born fish against hungry predators, as well as provide lots of micro-organisms as food.

For many hardy tetras this is an easy avenue for recruitment of new members for the school. Similarly, enough progeny of rainbow fishes, halfbeaks and many others will survive to replenish or even increase current numbers. Live-bearers in such a tank will soon produce more young than you (or the tank) can handle. To lock up pregnant live-bearer females in spawning cages is unnatural and stresses the female.

## Breeding tanks

Any aquarist interested in numbers of young fish, has no other choice but to set up a breeding tank, whether it is for reasons of having the entire reproductive process take place in such a tank, or in order to rear young or eggs that were removed from the community tank.

All non-brood caring, egg-laying fishes (tetras, barbs and others) should actually be spawned in the breeding tank, in order to get maximum numbers of progeny.

As a breeding tank one selects an all-glass tank with a volume of 10 to 30 liters (2$^1$/$_2$ - 10 gallons), depending upon the size of the adult fish. This tank should not contain any substrate and all accessories (inside filter, rocks, etc.) must be thoroughly scrubbed and rinsed off in hot water. The basic tank set-up consists of : heater, gently bubbling airstone and a spawning substrate commensurate with the requirements of the respective species.

A bundle of wool threads (artificial fibers) tied together at one end and attached with a suction cup or simply suspended from a floating cork, is a suitable and practical spawning substrate for many species. Bottom, back, and side glass panels are darkened (dark or painted cardboard, or the glass is painted over).

Since most species which breed in this tank will also prey on their own eggs, measures must be taken to prevent that (e.g. by placing 20 mm diameter ($^3$/$_4$") glass marbles on the bottom of the tank). The eggs will fall between the marbles and are then safe against predation by the parent fish. For details about introducing the adults into the breeding tank and the choice of correct breeding water, please refer to the species descriptions later on in this book or to more comprehensive breeding literature available in pet shops.

An *Ancistrus* sp. (possibly *A. temmincki*) male and three-day-old young. Photo by Aqua Press Piednoir.

Generally, the breeding pair is introduced into this tank at night, and spawning normally occurs the next morning. Afterwards, the adult pair must be removed immediately. To transfer eggs or newly hatched larvae from the community tank, the breeding/rearing tank must first be filled with water from the community tank. The eggs, including the substrate they are attached to (rock, plant, etc.) are then transferred from the community tank to the breeding tank.

Armored catfish and related forms often spawn on the tank's sides, where the eggs can be gently removed with a razor blade and then transferred to the breeding/rearing tank. Those larvae which are already free-swimming are easily siphoned out with a hose, and are then (together with the water they are in) transferred to the breeding tank.

## Egg and larval development

Whether the fish have spawned directly in the breeding tank or whether you have siphoned the eggs out of the community tank and transferred them to the breeding tank (make sure water values are identical), in both instances this marks the first phase in the life of these fish. Within a short time span (from a few hours to several days, depending upon the species) a small larva develops inside the egg. In large and transparent eggs one can observe the embryonic development with a hand-held magnifying glass.

After a certain time the larvae will burst the egg shell. At that point in time they are not yet capable of swimming or feeding. Depending upon the species, the larvae will become attached (using a special adhesive organ) to the sides of the tank and to the solid tank decor or they remain lying on the bottom. For several days they will still feed on (absorb!) the remaining yolk, while they continue to grow until one day they start swimming freely around the tank in search of food.

*Text continues on page 87*

**Right:** Early developmental stages in the giant goramy. After hatching the larvae will feed off the yolk supply for a few days. On the sixth day they start swimming about and will be searching for food.

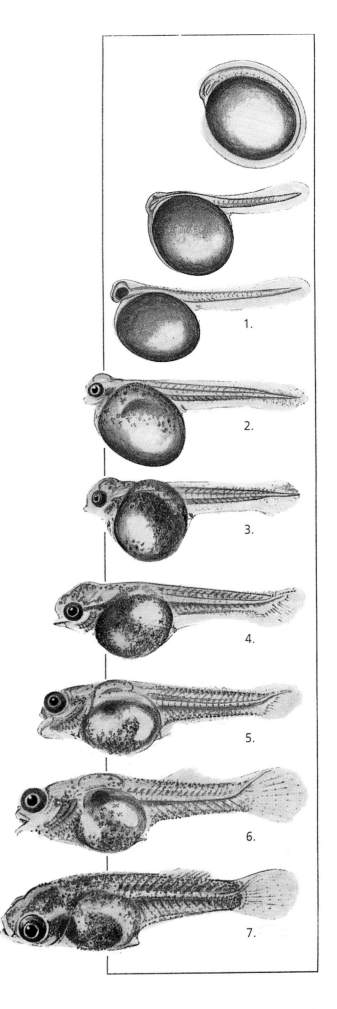

1.
2.
3.
4.
5.
6.
7.

83

# REPRODUCTION AND BROOD CARE

In the course of evolution, fish have developed diverse reproductive strategies and related brood care behavior. The scale ranges from simple shedding of reproductive products directly into the water to highly specialized brood care or even to giving birth to live young (live-bearers).

The majority of fish are egg-layers. The eggs are either discharged directly into the water or they are attached to a substrate, where they are subsequently fertilized. Fish species which do not practice brood care, usually lay large numbers of small eggs at one time, in order to compensate for high mortalities during the development and growth of the young.

Advancement in brood care goes hand-in-hand with a reduction in egg number and an increase in their size. The more specialized brood care becomes the smaller the egg numbers, with a corresponding increase in individual egg size. Brood care by the parents reduces the risk of the eggs and/or newly hatched larvae being eaten, which then requires fewer eggs in order to assure survival of the species.

A particularly advanced form of brood care occurs in live-bearing fishes, i.e. in live-bearing tooth carps. In these fishes the entire reproductive cycle—from fertilization to the development of fully formed young—occurs in the body cavity of the female. The males posses a special copulatory organ (gonopodium), derived from a modification of the anal fin.

## Fish also court...!

At the onset of reproductive activities there is courting behavior. Certain behavioral sequences, often combined with specific color and marking patterns, serve to synchronize the discharge of sex products, that is, to assure that both partners are at the same time and place, to give off eggs and sperm.

Closely related species which occur in the same habitat, often exhibit a rather different courtship behavior, which serves to avoid hybridization between the (related) species. Courtship behavior can be more or less strongly developed, depending upon the species. In many non-brood caring species (tetras, barbs, etc.) it is rather inconspicuous and usually lasts only a few hours.

Species which practice a well-defined brood care, such as cichlids, usually have a comprehensive repertoire of particular courtship activities.

The courtship behavior of brood-caring species coincides with the occupation of breeding territory, which is vigorously defended against sibling species. If this, for a particular pair, involves the entire tank, this can then lead to substantial complications, since the other fish in the tank cannot escape and often end up being severely injured.

## Spawning

Depending upon where fish spawn, one distinguishes between so-called *pelagic* spawners and *substrate* spawners. Pelagic spawners shed their eggs and sperm into the surrounding water and then no longer pay any attention to them. This can take place in open water or among plant thickets. The eggs either drop to the bottom or stick to plants. Many tetras, barbs and rainbow fishes spawn in this manner.

Substrate spawners attach their eggs to a particular surface, a substrate. This can be rocks, plant leaves,

A pair of rams (*Microgeophagus ramirezi*) guarding their spawn.

A female ram (*Microgeophagus ramirezi*) with her young.

wood or even in bubble nests. Substrate spawners usually practice a more or less strongly defined brood care. Depending upon type and duration, one distinguishes different categories of brood care.

## Care of eggs and larvae

As a rather interesting representative of this group, labyrinth fishes should be listed. They produce their own very specific type of substrate: a bubble nest. The males pick up air at the surface, surround the air with a tough mucus and then spit them out again at particular surface sites (preferably among the leaves of floating plants) along the surface, until a thick pillow of air bubbles has accumulated. The female then deposits her eggs in this nest.

After spawning has been completed the female is chased away by the male, which then defends the nest with the eggs and later on the newly hatched larvae

*(Cont'd)*

A bubblenest constructed on the surface by a dwarf gourami (*Colisa lalia*).

*Macropodus ocellatus* pair spawning. They are about to embrace prior to egg-laying.

The bubblenest of *Macropodus ocellatus*. The male is guarding his fry.

85

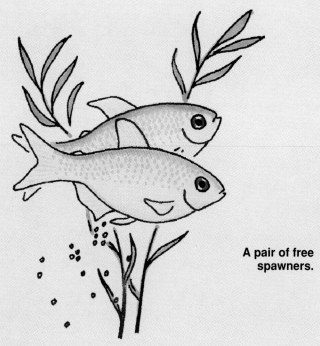

A pair of free spawners.

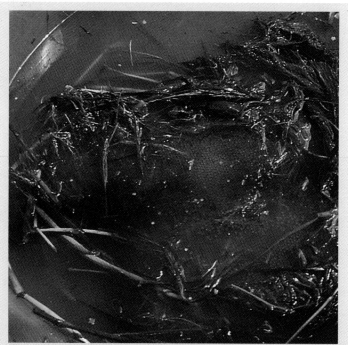

**The nest of a giant goramy removed from a brood pond and opened up. The eggs were removed for artificial rearing.**

*(Cont'd)*

(which cannot yet swim) against predators. During this period the male also repairs; the nest constantly with new air bubbles.

The largest labyrinth fish, the giant goramy (*Osphronemus gorami*) display a particular form of nest construction. This species builds a large nest from various pieces of plants, located under overhanging roots or among the stems of reeds. This is reminiscent of a bird's nest with the opening pointed downwards. Once spawning has been completed, the male closes the nest opening and then guards the nest until the young leave it. The giant gouramy is a popular food fish in Asia and is also bred in special hatcheries. The breeders let the fish spawn naturally and then remove the nests to raise the young by artificial means.

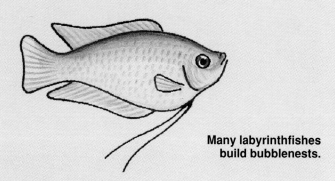

**Many labyrinthfishes build bubblenests.**

### Caring for the young

Those fish which look after their newly hatched larvae as well as juvenile fish already capable of swimming for some time, include mainly the cichlids. Spawning takes place on exposed rocks, in caves or on plant leaves. The clutch, later on also the newly hatched larvae and then (already swimming) young are vigorously defended against intruders. The eggs

are looked after and cleaned by 'chewing' them. When the time for hatching has come, the larvae are practically 'chewed' out of the egg shells and carried to a prepared pit on the bottom, or are 'stuck' to plant leaves with special adhesive glands. During the period between hatching and free-swimming, the parents will frequently move their young and occasionally 'chew' them.

Once the young start to swim the parents communicate with them by means of particular types of behavior and special color patterns. Cichlid parents with young are particularly aggressive. Discus fish give off a skin secretion, on which the young will feed for the first few days of their life.

## MOUTHBROODING

This is a highly specialized form of brood care, which has developed in various fish families. Best known, of course, are the mouth-brooding cichlids from the African lakes. In the most highly developed form of mouthbrooding the eggs are picked up immediately after spawning by the female, who will carry them in her mouth. In fact, the entire development of eggs and larvae takes place in the protecting mouth of the female.

**Eggs on the rock become fry on the loose.**

**Mouthbrooding is a specialized form of brood care.**

Only the free-swimming (already well-advanced) young are released from the mouth to search for food. But they will quickly flee back in the event of danger or until they have become too large for it.

Many groups of fishes exhibit transitional forms between open-brood care and mouth-brooding, for instance, the eggs are normally cared for while attached to a substrate, and only the hatched larvae are taken into the mouth.

Depending upon which one of the parents in brood caring species looks after the clutch and the young, one distinguishes between various forms of 'families', e.g. parent family, maternal family, paternal family, and so on. The reader will appreciate that within the (limited) frame work of this book the entire spectrum of reproduction and brood care behavior cannot be discussed in detail. Anyone who is interested in this exciting area of aquarium keeping is encouraged to review the relevant (aquarium) literature. The most complete book on the subject is Dr. Axelrod's huge book on breeding aquarium fishes.

**T.F.H. Style TS-185, Hard cover, 10x14", 448 pages, over 980 full-color photos.**

*Text continues from page 83*

Now the time has come to feed several times daily with a suitable food. If the young are large enough to handle newly hatched brine shrimp (*Artemia*) nauplii, rearing them becomes an easy task. This type of food can be hatched at home from eggs purchased at any aquarium or pet shop. The procedure is simple and each package contains detailed instructions, so further explanations are largely superfluous.

But the young of many tetras and barbs are, however, so tiny that they need to be fed for the first few days with infusoria (unicellular organisms, usually slipper-shaped). These slipper animals need to be reared by aquarists themselves. Once the newly hatched fish have sufficiently grown, they can be fed on *Artemia* nauplii. Some time later they are gradually 'weaned' onto other types of food (flakes, mosquito larvae, etc.).

It goes without saying, that the rearing tank needs to be cleaned regularly, and as the young fish grow there must also be frequent partial water changes. It is also advisable to install filtration via an air-driven sponge filter. Instead of infusoria or brine shrimp nauplii the young can also be reared with various substitute foods, such as very finely ground flake foods or homogenized liquid food. The (numerical) rearing success, however, is better with live foods during the critical early stage.

**A pair of *Macropodus opercularis* under their bubblenest.**

These so-called "balloon mollies" are a negative example of "breeding efforts."

Some captive-bred strains can no longer reproduce. This swordtail male (upper fish) is hampered by his excessively long gonopodium.

## ALL TO DINNER...!

Being a responsible aquarist includes—apart from providing a species-correct environment—feeding a diet which meets the nutritional requirements of the fish. Since most aquarium fish will rarely ever have an opportunity to find their own food in an aquarium, we, the aquarists, must provide it for them. For details about specific food requirements for individual species please refer to the relevant literature in the next chapter.

We distinguish essentially between three different feeding types: carnivore or meat-eater, herbivore or plant eater and omnivore or one which feeds on both meat and plant matter. Somewhere between the last two are the so-called limnivores—feeders of epiphytic plants and animals. Of course, not every species can be unequivocally placed in one of these three (four) categories. There are many transitional species.

In the course of time, the digestive system of fishes has adapted to the type of food available in their specialized environment. Among other things, this manifests itself in the length of the intestine, which is proportional to the digestibility of the food.

Purely carnivorous fishes, which prey more or less exclusively on fish and other aquatic animals, posses a very short intestine with a large stomach, which serves to digest large prey animals. Since this sort of food is easily digestible a long intestine is not required.

In those fish which feed in a carnivorous manner as well as herbivorous manner the intestine is long, because it has to handle a certain amount of plant matter which is hard to digest.

The intestine of a strictly herbivorous fish is extremely long and is adapted to handle the hard-to-digest plant diet.

This must be taken into consideration when selecting fish food, as well as for the commercial production of fish foods, otherwise there can be serious digestive problems. Also important for a good fish food is the right type and composition of raw materials used. For industrially manufactured food you can assume that these points have been taken into consideration. All you have to do is select the right food from what is an enormously wide commercial offering.

Since despite all this—especially with home-made fish foods –mistakes are still commonly made, here are a few pointers in regard to possible dangers: proteins from warm-blooded animals, especially muscle flesh, should be avoided as an exclusive protein source. Far better suited are proteins from aquatic organisms (especially fish). A one-sided diet of beef heart and other muscle flesh can lead to deficiency syndromes.

Fish oils (fats) can only be used if they remain liquid at an appropriate storage temperature, which means that they contain many so-called unsaturated fatty acids. That alone leaves out fat from warm-blooded animals; invariably, it will be excreted again nearly totally undigested. This pollutes the water and leads to intestinal inflammations.

Since aquarium fishes do not have the same freedom of movement as in the wild and are often fed too much rather than too little, the fat content in aquarium fish foods should not be too high. Three to five % can serve as a reference point.

Carbohydrates (typical representatives are sugar and starch) originate from plants and should be an essential component in conjunction with roughage (cellulose, plant cell walls) in the food for herbivores. Food with too much protein and not enough roughage does not exercise the long intestine of a herbivore sufficiently. Some fish that depend on a herbivorous diet and don't get it will help themselves by nibbling on the plants in the aquarium. Clown loaches, *Botia macracantha*, especially large specimens, simply love to perforate the leaves of large plants.

### Flake foods

Flake foods are, nowadays, manufactured according to complex recipes and are definitely not some low quality substitute food, as is often said. Without professionally manufactured flake foods, aquarium keeping would not be what it is today. Flake foods from reputable manufacturers contain all the required constituents essential for proper fish nutrition. By combining many different raw products with specific vitamin-enrichment, the occurrence

Flake foods, available in a variety of conveniently size packages are among the most commonly offered goldfish foods. Photo courtesy of Wardley.

of nutritional deficiencies is virtually excluded.

Flake foods are available in many different forms and mixtures, prepared to meet specific nutritional requirements of fish. Please consult your aquarium fish dealer for details. What should be mentioned here though is that there are flakes of different sizes suitable for large and small fishes, variable protein contents for those fish which need a more 'meaty' diet or those which are natural herbivores. Also to be mentioned here are the various food tablets for bottom dwelling fishes.

## Live foods

Flake food, in spite of all of its advantages, has one disadvantage: it does not move. There are certain fishes which will persistently and totally refuse to eat flake food; maybe because it does not move or it does not conform in taste and shape to their natural food. Many wild-caught fish are not familiar with flake food and need to be gradually accustomed to it.

Anyone who has ever seen how fish tear after live food would not want to miss this altogether and occasionally give his fish such a treat. There are various ways to get live food. Firstly, you can breed it yourself, using starter colonies available by mail order (refer to *Tropical Fish Hobbyist* magazine for supplier names and addresses) or directly from aquarium shops.

Breeding live foods (especially various worms and flies) is probably only of interest to fish breeders, since this sort of activity is rather time consuming. Catching live food yourself can be an interesting and healthy hobby activity (especially when done by bicycle). But you must be cautious!! Disease pathogens can be transferred from natural waters into the aquarium. Beyond that, nowadays you will rarely find a body of natural water where catching live foods does not conflict with certain proprietary or fisheries (legislative) interests. All the power to those who are members of an aquarium club which has its own food ponds.

That then leaves the walk to the nearest pet or aquarium shop as the main avenue to get live food. Hold it...one thing we almost forgot about: during the summer you can usually collect black mosquito larvae in rainwater and other water containers. If not everything is eaten, however, you will have some unpleasant co-inhabitants in your apartment a few days later.

## Frozen foods

This term refers to deep-frozen food organisms or parts thereof. Apart from the mosquito larvae and small crustaceans, there are a number of other types. For freshwater aquariums we can also use adult *Artemia* (brine shrimp), fish fillets (for large predator type fishes) or fish roe (high in fat content!).

Frozen food needs to be completely thawed out before feeding in order to avoid digestive problems. The same rules for storing deep frozen human foods also apply to frozen fish foods. Frozen foods, if properly stored and not kept for too long in water while thawing out, has the same nutritional content as live food.

Frozen foods offer a wide range of choices to the aquarist. Photo courtesy of Ocean Nutrition.

## Freeze-dried foods

Freeze-dried food is deep-frozen food from which the moisture is removed under vacuum. With this method the full nutritional value is maintained, disease pathogens are killed and the food has the same shelf-life as flake food. In fact, most manufacturers of flake foods also have freeze-dried foods available. Often the term FD-food (freeze-dried) is used. Many of the live-food feeders can gradually be 'weaned' onto flake food by using freeze-dried foods for a transition period. Moreover, it can also be used to add variety to a fish's diet. Freeze-dried fish foods were invented and patented in 1968 by Dr. Herbert R. Axelrod (U.S. patent number 3,361,114).

**A hot battle over a cold buffet!**

*Chironomus*

# LIVE FOODS

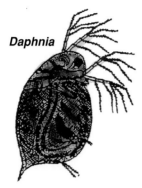
*Daphnia*

### White mosquito larvae
Larvae of *Corethra*. Excellent, uncontaminated livefood which occurs in clean waters only. Because of its transparent appearance also called 'glassworms'. Will last for a month if wrapped in wet newspaper and kept in a refrigerator. Fully developed adults will not bite.

### Red mosquito larvae
Larvae of *Chironomus*. Keenly taken by all fish Originate from polluted waters; should be fed in small amounts only. Storage the same as for white mosquito larvae, however, it has a slightly penetrating odor. Adults do not bite.

**Tubifex**

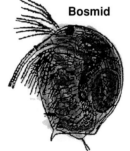
**Bosmid**

## Black mosquito larvae
Only available frozen because of live mosquito danger. Live larvae to be caught at your own risk.

### Mini-crustaceans
Water fleas (*Daphnia*), cyclops and trunk shrimp (Bosmididae) are the types most commonly used by aquarists. Cyclops can be dangerous for very small juvenile fish. In terms of nutritional physiology these small crustaceans are highly beneficial; they contain large amounts of roughage. If they are used exclusively it can lead to deficiencies. They should be stored in a bucket or other large container with cold water; very high oxygen requirements.

*Cyclops*

### Tubifex worms
Usually come from polluted waters. Need to be de-toxified by keeping the worms under running water for several days, but even then feed sparingly only, since tubifex worms have a high fat and protein content. Un-eaten worms will quickly crawl into the tank substrate, will die there and then decay.

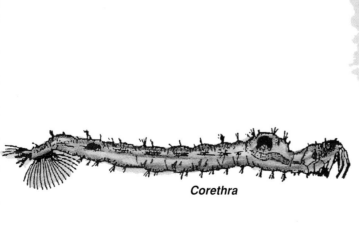
*Corethra*

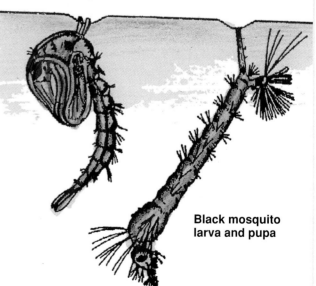
**Black mosquito larva and pupa**

"I wonder what's to eat today?"

## Vegetable foods

Some fish prefer 'fresh greens', even when they are being given flake food containing vegetable matter in sufficient quantities. Many armored catfish, and loaches like some fresh green food as a dietary change. What is really preferred often varies from one species to the next; only experimenting with different types of green food will determine what a particular species prefers. One species may prefer raw cucumber slices, while others go for pieces of boiled potato, peas, spinach (rinsed under boiling water), lettuce or similar items. The buoyancy problem with green food can be overcome by anchoring it to a rock or similar weight.

## How often and how much to feed??

One or two feedings per day are usually sufficient for adult fishes and for those reaching maturity. For sub-adults it may be advisable to add a third feeding. Newly hatched and juvenile fishes need to be fed about 5 to 6 times a day, so that they will grow rapidly. Growth and development missed as a juvenile fish is rarely ever caught up with later on in life!

Give only as much as is eaten completely within two to three minutes. More fish have been 'fed to death' than have died of lack of food! Nocturnal fish, especially bottom-dwellers, should be given an appropriate supplement of food tablets after the lights have been turned off.

Fresh green food (cucumbers, lettuce,etc.) can stay up to two days in the aquarium; if remnant amounts remain, these should be removed.

Flake foods are best not given in a feeding ring. This way the food disperses over the water surface, and small and shy fishes have an opportunity to get sufficient food.

There are also vegetarians among fishes.

**Sub-terminal mouth for bottom feeding.**

**Supra-terminal mouth for surface feeding.**

**Terminal mouth for mid-water feeding.**

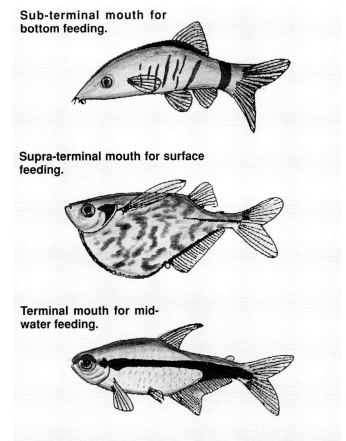

# FEEDING TYPES

The body structure of a fish is usually indicative of the preferred water region by a particular fish. This fact can be used, not only for stocking an aquarium with a balanced assortment of fish, but it also provides clues to the type of feeding practiced by that fish.

There are, for instance, fishes with a straight dorsal profile and a convex abdominal cavity, which live along the surface. The mouth in these fishes is pointed obliquely upward (supra-terminal). Most of these fish look for their food on the surface. They can be fed with flake food, but most prefer freeze-dried insect larvae and the occasional fly.

Fish which remain in the middle water layers, have a more or less equally arched dorsal and abdominal region. The mouth is relatively perpendicular and is located at the end of the body (terminal). These fish usually feed on anything that becomes available (in this region), be it sinking flake-food, live food or frozen foods.

Bottom-dwelling fishes usually have a fairly straight abdominal profile, but inevitably display a more or less strongly arched dorsal region. The mouth is usually pointing downwards (sub-terminal or ventral) and carries barbels, or is modified into a suction mouth. These fish search for food along the bottom, and are most easily fed by means of pellet food. Most benthic fishes are herbivores and tend to nibble on plants unless proper substitute (green) foods are provided.

There are, of course, transitional forms among these three basic types, which are oriented either more towards the surface or more towards the bottom. On the other hand, pure surface or bottom fish will rarely ever leave their domain.

# HEALTHY AS A FISH IN WATER...?

Unfortunately, this little saying is not always true, because in an aquarium fish can be anything but healthy as a fish in water. However, before we deal with possible disease symptoms among aquarium fishes, one point must be clarified right at the beginning: most of the fish diseases occurring in aquariums are a consequence of inadequate husbandry conditions. That mean that the best possible disease prophylaxis can be achieved through species-correct care combined with the appropriate diet. You, as responsible aquarists, therefore have the means to prevent diseases from occurring in the first place. Remember the proverb—'an ounce of prevention is better than a pound of cure!'

Actually, this chapter should finish at this point, because if you maintain your aquarium the way we have tried to convey to you, 'fish diseases' should be an alien concept. Nevertheless, in the event of such problems occurring we would like to give a few appropriate hints on how to deal with them, how to identify some of the more readily recognizable diseases and suggestions on how to treat them effectively.

Never treat fish on pure suspicion of a fish disease being present! Each treatment must be preceded by a clear diagnosis, which must be followed by treatment specifically designed for the disease diagnosed. Please keep in mind, that all medication (including those for human use) are nothing more than specifically effective poisons which at certain concentration levels (doses) will kill or immobilize pathogens without any harmful effects on the infected organism.

**As healthy as a fish in water? ... Today unfortunately not ...**

Frequent, pointless, prophylactic treatments, possibly even with reduced doses, ultimately only weakens the organism (fish) which we intend to protect, and so making it gradually more susceptible to disease pathogens. After all, you are not always taking aspirins as a prophylactic measure simply because next week you might get a headache. Apart from that is the fact that a reduced dose often has no effect on the pathogens, because a very specific amount of medication is required in order to harm the pathogen. In many cases, pathogens may even become resistant to a particular drug due to persistent under-dosing. In an emergency such a drug may then no longer bring the desired relief.

A correct diagnosis requires detailed and regular observations of the fish. One must be familiar with normal behavior and appearance of the fish, so that if any irregularities occur these will become immediately obvious.

## DISEASES

You must also keep in mind that fishes have a certain range of normal behavior and coloration, which also includes courtship and brood behavior. Especially

## BUYING FISH

Before you go out to purchase the fish you need to have a clear picture of what type of fish population your tank is ultimately to contain. When calculating the total number of fish, keep in mind that juvenile fish tend to grow and later—as adults—still have to find sufficient room in the tank. The following scheme can provide realistic reference points:

Fish with a total length of 2 to 3 cm: 2 liters of water per fish (2" of fish per gallon);

Fish with a total length of 3 to 5 cm: 5 to 6 liters of water per fish;

Fish with a total length in excess of 8 cm: more than 10 liters of water per fish.

Purchase only those specimens which are well-fed, appear externally healthy, and exhibit the following characteristics:
- well-rounded (not caved-in) abdomen
- fins intact, without patches or tiny spots
- fins must not be 'pinched'
- specimen must be active and display the characteristic swimming pattern
- specimen must not rub itself against stationary objects or display labored breathing
- tiny whitish spots or nodules must be ABSENT from the skin.

Coloration in juvenile specimens need not be fully developed. The dealer will pack your fish in special (plastic) fish transport bags. Take them home as quickly as possible (during the winter there must be protection against heat loss in transit). Once you arrive home:
- turn off the tank lights
- place the plastic bag with the fish inside on top of the tank surface and let it float there for about 15 minutes
- subsequently open the bag and let small portions of tank water enter until the water volume inside the bag has about doubled
- pour the contents of the plastic bag (water and fish) into a hand net (over a bucket) and then place them in the tank.
- pour transport water down the toilet!
- after a few hours, turn on tank lighting again
- DO NOT FEED until next day!

beginning aquarists tend to be inclined to suspect the presence of a disease every time a fish twitches its fins. In such cases, it is advisable to seek the advice of a more experienced aquarist or aquarium fish dealer.

Only after you have gained experience in assessing disease symptoms and behavioral variations among fishes, should you start going through the relevant literature on fish diseases.

## Poisoning

First of all we must draw your attention to disease symptoms, which are not manifestations of the presence or effects of pathogens, but instead are caused by external (environmental) influences, usually by poisoning. Characteristic of poison symptoms is that without exception all fish in a tank are affected, while an infectious disease commonly affects individual specimens first before the entire tank population shows signs of a disease outbreak.

Typical poisoning symptoms are jerking swimming movements, jumping above the water surface, very rapid respiration (possibly in conjunction with dark, discolored gill filaments) or a dark body coloration.

Appropriate counter-measures must include an immediate, massive water change. But before that about one liter of water is set aside for a subsequent water analysis to determine, if possible, the precise cause.

A common cause of poisoning is a high ammonium or nitrite level, in tanks which have been insufficiently conditioned or which are over-crowded. Also possible is that following a disease treatment bacterial decomposition could have become disturbed leading to increases in ammonium and nitrite accumulations. Nitrite is directly toxic, while ammonium only becomes toxic at high (alkaline) pH values, i.e. the ratio between ammonium and (toxic) ammonia is proportional to the pH value. Both substances compete with oxygen compounds in the blood, in effect causing asphyxiation symptoms.

A strongly elevated or severely depressed pH value can cause acid or alkaline burns. Careless handling of insecticides or herbicides in the living room can also lead to toxic symptoms.

**Severe fungal infection on a female dwarf gourami (*Colisa lalia*).**

## White spot disease

The colloquial name for this disease is **ich** or **white spot**. It is caused by the unicellular organism *Ichthyophthirius multifiliis*. It is generally the most common fish disease. Easily recognizable symptoms include small, granular, whitish dots on the fins and body of the affected fish. This disease can be successfully treated with medications available from pet and aquarium shops. Check water conditions and husbandry practices.

## Fungal infections

Furry, cottonball-like patches on a fish are indicative of a water fungus attack (*Saprolegnia*). Only those fishes which are already injured (traumatic or parasitic) are attacked by fungi. Fungi can easily be cured with medications available from all aquarium and pet shops. Subse-

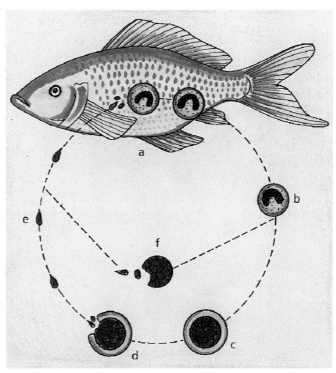

**Developmental cycle of *Ichthyophthirius multifiliis*:**
a) fish with parasites
b) parasite that has fallen off
c) encapsulated parasite on the bottom
d) hatching swarmer
e) unattached swarmers attacking a fish
f) parasites that are prematurely brushed off develop swarmers without encapsulation.

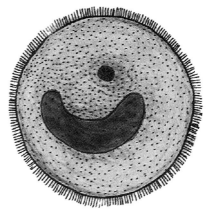

***Ichthyophthirius multifiliis***

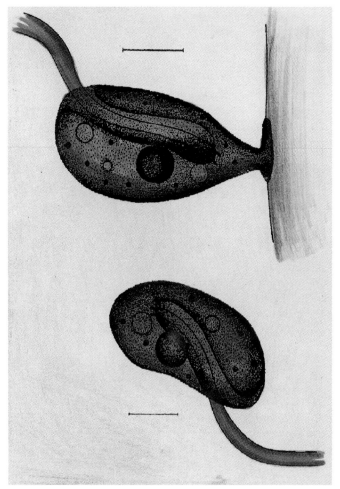

**Small bean-shaped skin cyst (*Costia*, the scale corresponds to 3µm).**

quently the cause for this disease must be determined and eliminated.

## Velvet disease or freshwater Oodinium

Unicellular pathogen of the genus *Oodinium*, which manifest themselves as small, usually yellowish dots on the skin of fishes. These dots are very much smaller than those of *Ichthyophthirius*. They cause a velvet-like appearance, giving rise to the name *velvet disease*. This disease

**Severe attack of freshwater Oodinium (*Piscinoodinium pillularis*) on the dorsal fin of *Aphyosemion gardneri*.**

can be treated with medications available from aquarium and pet shops. Sometimes keeping the tank dark for several days may be sufficient, since the pathogen carries chlorophyll.

## Skin clouding *(Costia)*

Milky, bluish white skin patches are caused by so-called skin-clouding parasites (*Costia, Chilodonella*). The tropical fish trade offers appropriate medications, which are also effective against *Ichthyophthirius*. The treatment may need to be continued for up to 10 days. Temperature increases are often beneficial.

These are the diseases most commonly encountered and easily recognizable. All other fish diseases (and there are a vast number of them) occur relatively rarely under aquarium conditions and inevitably require expert help in diagnosing. Moreover, many of the rarer diseases cannot be treated with over-the-counter medications.

Leave the handling of medications available on prescriptions only to an expert. That is safer, not only for your own health but it saves you trouble with relevant prescription regulations. In any event, you should always have medication for the treatment of white spot (*Ichthyophthirius*) handy at home. You will soon learn that with species-correct care of your fish, you will rarely ever need it!

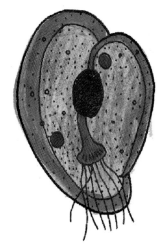

**Large heart-shaped skin cyst (*Chilodonella*).**

**Many different remedies, preventives and tonics are available at pet shops. Photo courtesy of Jungle Laboratories.**

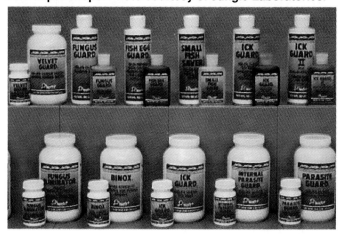

# TORTURE OF TOO MUCH CHOICE...

The fish described here have been placed into groups on the basis of their phylogenetic relationship, that is:
• tetras
• barbs and barb-like fishes
• other carp-like fishes
• loaches and related forms
• catfish
• egg-laying tooth carps (killifishes)
• live-bearing tooth carps (livebearers)
• halfbeaks
• cichlids
• labyrinth fishes
• blue-eyes/hardyheads and rainbow fishes

Within these groups the species have been arranged alphabetically by their scientific name. Each group is preceded by a general description, which contains mutual characteristics and general details on care and maintenance.

In the species descriptions the key word 'distribution' gives the geographical range over which the original wild form of a species occurs. In these times of international trade and captive breeding, this may not necessarily indicate the precise origin of a particular fish kept. The term 'habitat' refers to the region preferentially inhabited by the wild form of a fish. It should be noted here that many tropical and subtropical fish species are highly adaptable and so have explored many different habitats.

The external morphology of fishes is highly variable, and in addition there are variations in body shape, coloration and finnage within certain species, which have been artificially produced through selective breeding techniques. Therefore, the photographs shown in this book cannot cover the entire range of appearances of a species, but have been selected to depict typical representatives.

The sizes given refer to the maximum length of adult specimens. The details listed within brackets in the section on 'Maintenance Plan' refer to captive (aquarium) breeding of a species. These are not patented recipes to guarantee breeding success; the factors involved which interact in an aquarium are far too diverse. Nevertheless, they are based on the collective experiences of many aquarists and tropical fish breeders.

## TETRAS

Within the major group of characoid fishes (in the widest sense) there are several families of tetras and tetra-like fishes. More than 1,000 species are known; most of them occur in South America and the remainder in Africa. Many popular aquarium fishes belong to this group.

These predominantly peaceful, usually highly mobile fishes are agile swimmers, which often form vast schools in their native habitats. They occupy flowing or standing waters, where they prefer the proximity of plant thickets, into which they can withdraw if need be.

Most species possess a small adipose fin (a fin without supporting fin rays, consisting primarily of fatty tissue) between dorsal and caudal fins.

Most tetras prefer soft water, but some species can also tolerate higher water hardness levels. The water must be rich in oxygen.

Tetras must never be kept by themselves; instead small groups of at least 6 to 10 specimens of each species should always be kept together. This induces proper schooling behavior and makes these fishes feel more secure. The vast majority of species do not dig or bury, so that the water remains nicely clear.

*Anostomus anostomus*

**Giant headstander, *Anostomus anostomus***

DISTRIBUTION: Northern South America: Guyana, Colombia, Venezuela; Amazon River.

HABITAT: Shallow river banks, rocky crevices in rapidly flowing waters.

DESCRIPTION: Very elongated, active schooling fish, which swims almost vertically, especially when in search of food. Stays in middle to lower water tank region. Compatible only within a school; individual specimens can be kept together with other fish provided these are equally strong swimmers. Should be given maximum swimming room in an aquarium with ample hiding places (adjacent rocks as sight barriers between individual headstanders). Also roots and long-leafed plants

**Fishes for every taste and to match any wallpaper!**

between rocks. Maximum size about 15 to 18 cm (7"). Some captive breeding, but details not yet standardized.

TEMP: 24-28°C, pH: 5.8 to 7.5., HARDNESS: soft to medium, ideally around 8°DH; powerful filter required to create a strong current, encourage algal growth on rocks with direction lighting.

FOOD & FEEDING: Limnivore (omnivore): small live food and especially frozen foods, dried foods (including tablets), algae, lettuce and other plant matter.

### Arnold's Characin, *Arnoldichthys spilopterus*

DISTRIBUTION: West Africa: southern Nigeria, Niger delta; Lagos.

HABITAT: Flowing waters, also wide rivers.

DESCRIPTION: This active species requires a lot of open swimming space, therefore, sparse perimeter planting with robust plants is sufficient. Long or large and low tanks with dark bottom and a current flow are ideal. If given company of catfishes and other large African tetras, this schooling fish will do well. Prefers to remain in middle or upper water layers. Newly hatched young

*Arnoldichthys spilopterus*

tend to hide in substrate when disturbed. Use soft substrate when breeding this fish. In females the posterior margin of the anal fin is straight, in males it is rounded outwardly. Males are also more colorful and have a red spot or a red-yellow-black striped pattern on the anal fin.

TEMP: 24-28°C, pH: 6 to 7.5 (6 to 6.8), HARDNESS: to 20°DH (softer); peat additive, powerful filtration creating strong current.

FOOD & FEEDING: Omnivore: large live foods, flies, small cockroaches, small earthworms or pieces of them, dry foods (large flakes).

### Marbled hatchetfish, *Carnegiella strigata*

DISTRIBUTION: South America: central and lower Amazon River.

HABITAT: Standing and gently flowing waters.

DESCRIPTION: This is a 4.5 cm long, attractive but somewhat delicate schooling fish with a conspicuous, in-

*Carnegiella strigata*

teresting body shape. Does not have an adipose fin. As a fish of the upper water layer, it prefers to remain among plants and likes to jump. Therefore, must be given a well-covered tank. As rapid swimmer these fish also like to swim against a filter current. Floating plants and bushy plants should leave sufficient open space along the surface. Should only be kept together with bottom dwellers and other delicate species. With a good live food supply and in strongly darkened tanks there have been occasional successful breedings. Only in those rare circumstances when eggs develop will a female's abdomen become roundish, and sometimes transparent eggs become visible. Other than that the sexes are indistinguishable.

TEMP: 24-28°C, pH: 6 to 7.5, HARDNESS: to 10°DH and even up to 20°DH filtration via peat moss or with peat extract additive.

FOOD & FEEDING: Small live foods, miniature flies, dry foods.

### Jumping Characin, *Copella arnoldi*

DISTRIBUTION: South America: Guyana.

HABITAT: Close to banks in small streams.

DESCRIPTION: The males of this interesting schooling fish species reach a size of about 8 cm (3"). They are more colorful, with more elaborately developed fins than the smaller females.

In order to protect the females against continuous courtship pressures from males, this fish should be kept in schools with a clear majority of females (up to three per male). Breeding behavior and brood care of this species are biologically original. Deposit of eggs and fertilization on over-hanging leaves or against the cover glass, above water, on...the jump, so-to-speak. The male is solely responsible for looking after the clutch of eggs (paternal family). It splashes the eggs with water by means of continuous beating with the tail, in order to keep them wet. This species can easily be kept in a community tank, but must have a large, well-covered tank with occasional (direct) sunlight, where the fish like to 'play' close to the surface. Water plants with large leaves which protrude above the surface or a floating plant cover, combined

*Copella arnoldi*

with a couple of peripheral plant thickets resemble closely the natural habitat of this species.

TEMP: 24-28°C, pH: 6.5 to 7.5, HARDNESS: to 12°DH (softer); peat moss, regular water changes.

FOOD & FEEDING: Omnivore: dry foods, small live food, fruit- and vinegar flies (*Drosophila*).

### Silver hatchetfish, *Gasteropelecus sternicla*

DISTRIBUTION: South America: Amazon tributaries, Brazil, Guyana, Peru.

HABITAT: Small to medium-size streams close to plant islands and below over-hanging branches from trees and bushes along the banks.

DESCRIPTION: Silver hatchetfish have an adipose fin; males more slender when viewed from above. Has

*Gasteropelecus sternicla*

not yet been bred in captivity. This fish (6 to 7 cm =3") is initially usually rather shy. Requires swimming space at the surface, but also likes floating plants. The tank needs to be well-covered, since this schooling fish tends to jump. Leave some space between water and

tank cover. Can be kept together with similarly peaceful fish, but also attractive in species tank (low water level) and in paludariums (swamp/rainforest tank with substantial water section). As occupant of flowing waters this species requires a lot of oxygen.

TEMP: 24-28°C, pH: slightly acidic (try around pH 6), HARDNESS: to 10° DH; peat additive.

FOOD & FEEDING: Carnivore: small live foods, dry foods.

### Black widow, *Gymnocorymbus ternetzi*

DISTRIBUTION: South America: Rio Paraguay, southern Brazil, Bolivia.

HABITAT: Shaded, gently flowing waters.

DESCRIPTION: Territorial, but peaceful schooling fish, conspicuous by is shape, with a maximum size of 6 cm. The long, extended anal fin gives this fish an interesting profile. The smaller, more slender males display a more distinct white in the tail fin and usu-

*Gymnocorymbus ternetzi*

ally a more pointed dorsal fin. Unfortunately the black coloration fades with age. This calm, undemanding fish tends to remain predominantly in the middle of the tank. Aquariums which are not too bright and with an open stand of plants and some roots are ideally suited for this species. Can be kept together with other fish up to a length of 12 cm (5"). Captive breeding possible.

TEMP: 24-28°C, pH: 6 to 8, HARDNESS: soft to hard (up to 30°DH).

FOOD & FEEDING: Omnivore: dry food, live food.

### Silver-tipped Tetra, *Hasemania nana*

DISTRIBUTION: South America: southern and southeastern Brazil.

HABITAT: Small and very small, flowing waters with correspondingly high oxygen content.

DESCRIPTION: This active, agile, 5 cm (2") long schooling fish does not possess an adipose fin. It tends to prefer the upper and middle water layers and is an excellent community tank fish. Males form territories.

*Hasemania nana*

The tank should be relatively dark (low light level and dark substrate), with peripheral planting, so that there is lots of swimming space. Coloration of this species is highly variable; males smaller and more colorful than the larger and heavier females. Males virtually radiating with their white fins when kept in a school.

TEMP: 24-28°C, pH: 6 to 7.5, HARDNESS: soft to medium hard; peat moss.

FOOD & FEEDING: Omnivore: small live foods, dry foods.

### Rummy-nose Tetra, *Hemigrammus bleheri*

DISTRIBUTION: South America: lower Amazon, Rio Negro, Rio Vaupes, northern Brazil, Colombia. There are several look-a-likes but all like black, acid waters

HABITAT: Standing and gently flowing, clear black waters.

DESCRIPTION: This fast, attractive schooling fish grows to about 7 cm. (3").The largest and plumper specimens may well be females. The males have tiny

*Hemigrammus bleheri*

hooklets on the anal fin. An adipose fin is present. This active tetra prefers the middle regions of the aquarium. This species does best when the tank is relatively dark, and may well breed there. A community tank fish.

TEMP: 24-28°C, pH: 5 to 6.5, HARDNESS: soft to medium hard (up to 10°DH, carbonate hardness below 4 degrees); frequent water changes or top-up; monitor nitrate level.

FOOD & FEEDING: Omnivore: dry food, small live food, vegetable matter.

### Glowlight tetra, *Hemigrammus erythrozonus*

DISTRIBUTION: Northeastern South America: Guyana.

HABITAT: Small waters with shaded banks.

DESCRIPTION: Territorial, but peaceful schooling fish. Maximum size about 4 cm. Utilizes the middle and lower water zones. Adipose fin present. The somewhat larger (mature) female has a fuller, more rounded abdomen. Should be kept under subdued lighting and together with other, schooling fish. The plant-

*Hemigrammus erythrozonus*

ing scheme must provide lots of open swimming space. Can be bred.

TEMP: 24-28°C, pH: 6 to 7.5, HARDNESS: soft to medium hard (soft, to 10°DH); peat moss additive.

FOOD & FEEDING: Omnivore: dry food, small live food, lettuce.

### Garnet tetra, *Hemigrammus pulcher*

DISTRIBUTION: South America: Peru and Brazil, upper and central Amazon River.

HABITAT: Areas with soft waters.

DESCRIPTION: This 6 cm long schooling fish is most effectively displayed in the middle water zone of tanks with subdued lighting. Densely planted parts of the aquarium have to alternate with open swimming space in order to provide adequate hiding places as well as enough swimming space. The somewhat larger females are of a more compact, stouter appearance. Males have some white in the anal fin region. Territorial but peaceful; suitable only for community tanks with soft water and other delicate species.

*Hemigrammus pulcher*

TEMP: 24-28°C, pH: 5 to 6.5, HARDNESS: soft to medium-hard (soft, to 10°DH), bottom as dark as possible.

FOOD & FEEDING: Omnivore: dry foods, small live foods, vegetable matter.

### Rosy Tetra, *Hyphessobrycon bentosi bentosi*
DISTRIBUTION: South America: Guyana, lower Amazon.

HABITAT: Clear, sunny areas of flowing waters with a sand or gravel bottom.

DESCRIPTION: Red, reddish or nearly transparent, 4 to 5 cm (rarely 6 cm) (2") long fish; best kept in small groups (several pairs). Instead of classic schooling behavior the males tend to form courting territories in the lower water region, where they continuously encircle each other. Females have a plumper appearance and the pennant-shaped dorsal fin extension, common to males, is absent. Needs dense peripheral planting which opens up towards the center of the tank, and the plants change towards the 'bushy' type. A gentle current and a dark bottom are preferred. Suitable for breeding and for community tanks.

*Hyphessobrycon bentosi bentosi*

TEMP: 24-28°C, pH: 6 to 7.5 (5.8 to 7), HARDNESS: up to 20°DH (as soft as possible), color variations, depending upon origin and breeding stock.

FOOD & FEEDING: Omnivore: small live foods, dry foods, vegetable matter.

### Red Tetra, *Hyphessobrycon callistus*
DISTRIBUTION: South America: southern Amazon basin, Paraguay, Mato Grosso.

HABITAT: Black waters; calm, well-planted areas.

DESCRIPTION: This attractive, up to 4 cm long active and not always very peaceful schooling fish, prefers the central region in a tank and there forms small territories. For that reason (and because this species is known to 'nibble' on plants) it is generally suggested to keep this fish in a densely planted tank but with adequate swimming space. Sufficient live food avoids sibling fighting. The female is slightly larger and deeper-bodied than the male.:

TEMP: 24-28°C , pH: 6 to 7.5, HARDNESS: up to 25°DH (soft; up to 10°DH), peat moss and darkened tank required for breeding.

FOOD & FEEDING: Omnivore: small live foods, dry

*Hypessobrycon callistus*

foods, vegetable matter.

### Bleeding Heart or Perez Tetra, *Hyphessobrycon erythrostigma*
DISTRIBUTION: South America: upper Amazon, Peru.

HABITAT: Gently flowing or calm, partially overgrown river section.

DESCRIPTION: A schooling fish of the middle and upper water zones, about 6 cm long (rarely larger); even though territorial, it is considered to be peaceful. Male threat behavior involves spreading the drawn-out dorsal and anal fins, but without actual fighting taking place. Females larger than males and less colorful. Compatible with other quiet species; breeding possible. Must be given open swimming space as well as adequate plant cover.

TEMP: 24-28°C, pH: 6 to 7.2, HARDNESS: up to 12°DH (softer); peat moss supplement.

FOOD & FEEDING: Omnivore: live foods, dry foods,

*Hyphessobrycon erythrostigma*

vegetable food.

### Flame Tetra, *Hyphessobrycon flammeus*
DISTRIBUTION: South America: Eastern Brazil (around Rio de Janeiro).

HABITAT: Shallow waters.

DESCRIPTION: Tough little schooling fish of the middle and lower tank region; about 4 cm total length; peaceful and without special requirements. Coloration of the larger females is paler and more subdued, often pectoral fins with black tips and a light colored anal fin; that of the male is intensely red, ventral and anal fins with a jet black margin. Corners and sides of the aquarium should be densely planted, leaving sufficient swimming space in the middle. Courtship easily visible and breeding in species tank simple. Should be kept together only with other small fish species.

*Hyphessobrycon flammeus*

TEMP: 24-28°C, pH: 6 to 7.5 , HARDNESS: can also be kept in hard water (breeding is easier and more productive in soft water); peat moss supplement, dark bottom and subdued lighting.

FOOD & FEEDING: Omnivore: dry foods, small live foods, vegetable matter.

### Black Neon, *Hyphessobrycon herbertaxelrodi*
DISTRIBUTION: South America: Brazil, Mato Grosso, Rio Taquary.

HABITAT: Shallow water sections of streams and rivers.

DESCRIPTION: Peaceful and very active schooling fish, constantly in motion in the middle and upper water zones of the aquarium; up to 4.5 cm long. Specimens which have been kept on a variable diet will show considerable contrast over the body. This creates a very attractive picture in a school. The school should be as large as the tank dimensions permit. A dark tank bottom and subdued lighting will show off the coloration of this species most effectively. Males rather small and slender. Breed-

*Hyphessobrycon herbertaxelrodi*

ing is most easily done in a separate breeding tank. Should be kept together only with really calm species; fast-swimming fish will visibly disturb black neon tetras.

TEMP: 24-28°C, pH: 5 to 7, HARDNESS: soft to medium hard (soft); likes water current, peat moss filtration.

FOOD & FEEDING: Omnivore: should be given highly variable diet with small live foods, dry foods, vegetable matter.

### Lemon Tetra, *Hyphessobrycon pulchripinnis*
DISTRIBUTION: South America: central Brazil, Amazon.

HABITAT: Small, flowing waters with weed-like plants.

DESCRIPTION: An attractive schooling fish, up to 5 cm long, which tends to prefer tanks with a dense, peripheral plant cover and open swimming space. Individual specimens often take up positions in middle or bottom water zones, from where they make excursions. Always peaceful and active, also suitable for community

Left: *Hyphessobrycon pulchripinnis.* Right: *Inpaichthys kerri.*

tank. The black margin along the anal fin is more intense in males; females appear deeper bodied than males. Breeding is possible.

TEMP: 24-28°C (26-30°F), pH: 5.5 to 8, HARDNESS: up to 25°DH (possibly softer); peat moss additive and frequent partial (small) water changes are beneficial.

FOOD & FEEDING: Omnivore: small live foods, dry foods, vegetable matter.

### King Tetra, *Inpaichthys kerri*

DISTRIBUTION: South America: western Brazil.

HABITAT: Various types of small waters.

DESCRIPTION: Without proper care these maximally 4.5 cm long peaceful schooling fishes are inconspicuous and pale. Most effectively displayed in dark tanks and under subdued lighting and with peripherally open planting, where this species tends to frequent the open swimming space. Females smaller and paler than males, the caudal fin without scales and the lateral line is incomplete. Males tend to de-

### *Megalamphodus megalopterus*

fend their courtship territory even in the presence of smaller and other peaceful fishes. Breeding most likely to succeed in separate, rather dark and small breeding tank.

TEMP: 24-28°C, pH: 6.5 to 7.5, HARDNESS: soft to medium hard (soft, to 10°DH); filtration over peat moss; requires bushy plants for breeding.

FOOD & FEEDING: Omnivores, all types of small foods, variable diet.

### Black Phantom Tetra, *Megalamphodus megalopterus*

DISTRIBUTION: South America: Central Brazil.

HABITAT: In rivers and lakes, underneath floating plants.

DESCRIPTION: Regrettably, breeding of this active, yet peaceful and continuously moving schooling fish is difficult. Males are more slender than females and have enlarged fins (especially the dorsal fin). During threatening behavior these fins are spread, but fighting does not take place. Coloration most intense (black against an intensely grey body) when fish are kept in an undisturbed environment. An open (central) swimming space should be surrounded by dense peripheral planting. From their bottom territories the fish tend to venture intermittently into the middle water region. Lighting should be subdued; can be kept together only with other small fish. Females more reddish.

TEMP: 24-28°C, pH: 6 to 7.5, HARDNESS: up to 18°DH (up to 10°DH); peat moss additive, floating plants.

FOOD & FEEDING: Omnivore: small live foods, dry foods.

### Red Phantom Tetra, *Megalamphodus sweglesi*

DISTRIBUTION: South America: Brazil, Colombia.

HABITAT: Small waters, cool spring regions.

DESCRIPTION: Under optimal care the males of these 4 cm long, quiet schooling fish are intensely brick red. Females sometimes display the color combination red, black and white in the dorsal fin. Very difficult to breed; most likely to succeed in darkened, clean tanks. This species is somewhat more delicate than the black phantom

*Megalamphodus sweglesi*

Break-neck leap.

tetra, but equally durable. Threat behavior similar and also without serious fighting. A lot of swimming space in the lower and middle region of a tank is favorable; can be kept together with other quiet and small species. Avoid very bright lighting.

TEMP: 24-28°C, pH: slightly acidic (5.5 to 6), HARD-NESS: up to 10°DH (1 to 2°DH); good water quality maintenance essential, peat moss additive.

FOOD & FEEDING: Omnivore: small live foods, dry foods, given often and in small portions.

### Red-eyed Moenkhausia, *Moenkhausia sanctaefilomenae*

DISTRIBUTION: Central South America: Paraguay, eastern Bolivia, eastern Peru, western Brazil.

HABITAT: Gently flowing waters.

DESCRIPTION: Undemanding, active and yet peaceful schooling fish, which is considered to do well in an aquarium; maximum length up to 7 cm. This species tends to prefer the middle to upper water zones, ideally where this a slight water current. In a community tank this species should not be kept together with quiet surface fish. Partially dense stands of tough water plants must leave sufficient swimming space. Breeding is possible.

*Moenkhausia sanctaefilomenae*

TEMP: 24-28°C, pH: 5.5. to 8.5, HARDNESS: soft to hard (soft); peat moss additive.

FOOD & FEEDING: Omnivore, dry foods, small live foods, very small flies (*Drosophila*).

### Golden Pencilfish, *Nannostomus beckfordi*

DISTRIBUTION: South America: Gayana, Parana, lower Rio Negro, central and lower Amazon.

HABITAT: Shallow water vegetation thickets along river and stream banks and among submerged branches in flowing waters.

DESCRIPTION: Maximum length 4.5 to 6.5 cm, very active schooling fish especially at dusk; unfortunately with short longevity. Males establish mini-territories

*Nannostomus beckfordi*

in the middle and upper water layers, with threat displays and in optimum coloration. Will accept the company of other active fish in relatively dark community tanks. Breeding is possible. In males the lower ventral fin tips and the anal fin are red; females with a more rounded abdomen. Coloration in this species tends to be highly variable. An adipose fin is absent.

TEMP: 24-28°C, pH: 6 to 7.5, HARDNESS: up to 10°DH, can be cautiously acclimated up to 20°DH (extremely soft); clear water with peat moss additive.

FOOD & FEEDING: Omnivore: small live foods, fruit and vinegar flies (*Drosophila*), dry foods.

### Emperor Tetra, *Nematobrycon palmeri*

DISTRIBUTION: South America: western Colombia.

HABITAT: Delta region of river systems.

DESCRIPTION: Maximum length about 6 cm; peaceful schooling fish, periodically very active; tends to maintain territories in lower water regions from where it ventures up to the middle water region. In males, fins more pointed than in females; they establish courtship territories with threat displays, without actually engaging in direct fighting. Older females have a relatively arched dorsal profile; breeding with them is usually successful. In a densely planted tank with adequate swimming space, the emperor tetras can also be kept together with other fish which are not too active.

*Paracheirodon axelrodi*

tempts should be made under substantially darkened conditions.

TEMP: 24-28°C, pH: 5 to 7, HARDNESS: up to 10°DH (very soft, only 1 to 2°DH); peat moss, subdued lighting.

FOOD & FEEDING: Omnivore: small live foods, dry foods.

### Neon Tetra, *Paracheirodon innesi*

DISTRIBUTION: South America: Upper Amazon, eastern Peru.

HABITAT: Various river systems of variable width.

DESCRIPTION: The color emphasis of this schooling fish species is on the beautiful metallic blue-turquoise lateral band. Maximum optical effect can only be

*Paracheirodon innesi*

*Nematobrycon palmeri*

TEMP: 24-28°C, pH: slightly acidic, HARDNESS: up to 10°DH (softer, if possible); likes peat moss, monitor water quality while changing water.

FOOD & FEEDING: Omnivore: small live foods, dry foods.

### Cardinal Tetra, *Paracheirodon axelrodi*

DISTRIBUTION: South America: Venezuela, northwestern Brazil, western Colombia.

HABITAT: Shaded section of clear water streams.

DESCRIPTION: Active schooling fish, characterized by conspicuously red coloration; rarely longer than 4 to 5 cm. For many aquarists, this fish is the most beautiful of all aquarium fishes. It is also the most popular. About 12,000,000 are collected in the waters of the Rio Negro every year. Tends to stay preferentially in middle and lower water regions. Plant thickets together with adequate swimming space in between and the company of small to middle-size fishes assure species-correct conditions. Most specimens available are wild-caught. Breeding is not easy, but quite possible under the conditions described. Females with a more rounded abdomen; breeding at-

A school of cardinal tetras (*Paracheirodon axelrodi*) is a magnificent sight in a fully planted aquarium. Photo Aqua Press Piednoir.

achieved with a large school of this 4 cm long fish. Should not be kept together with large species. Sexual differences not easy to determine, but specimens that are heavier-set and where the lateral band is pale and with a bend, are usually females. This species prefers a dense plant cover as well as sufficient open swimming space; breeding is difficult; requires bushy plants. A dark bottom and very subdued lighting promote the longevity of neon tetras. They can live as long as 10 years.

TEMP: 24-28°C, pH: 5 to 7, HARDNESS: soft to hard after proper conditioning (very soft, up to 2°DH); peat moss, regular water changes; breeding tank with very subdued lighting.

FOOD & FEEDING: Omnivore (limnivore): small live foods, dry foods, especially food tablets, vegetable matter.

Petitella georgiae

### Black-finned Rummynose Tetra, *Petitella georgiae*

DISTRIBUTION: South America: upper Amazon, Colombia, Brazil.

HABITAT: Small blackwater streams.

DESCRIPTION: Active, peaceful schooling fish; with adipose fin; reminiscent of other fishes also called "Rummynose Tetras." Sexes hard to determine. Males often with greater contrasting coloration in the striped pattern of the tail. Has apparently not yet been bred in captivity. Can also be kept together with larger fish, provided these are peaceful. In tanks with dense plant cover but ample swimming space, this species tends to use mainly the middle and lower zones.

TEMP: 24-28°C, pH: 5.5 to 7, HARDNESS: up to about 12°DH; peat moss filtration; use only well-conditioned water for partial water changes.

FOOD & FEEDING: Omnivore: small live foods, dry

Phenacogrammus interruptus

foods, vegetable matter.

### (Blue) Congo Tetra, *Phenacogrammus interruptus*

DISTRIBUTION: West Africa.

HABITAT: River systems in Zaire (formerly Congo).

DESCRIPTION: A beautiful species, with finnage which is very much dependent upon excellent water conditions for proper development. In large tanks with a dark bottom and sparse peripheral planting these 8.5 to 12 cms long very active fishes will find adequate swimming space. Apart from a pronounced water current, these fishes also like floating plants. Breeding can be triggered by direct sunlight or increased lighting level. In males the dorsal, tail and anal fins are extended.

TEMP: 24-28°C, pH: 6 to 7, HARDNESS: up to 10°DH (very soft); peat moss additive, water can be allowed to turn brownish; dark bottom; nitrate and hardness levels need to be closely monitored (occasional hardness levels of up to 18°DH can be tolerated, provided all other water parameters are acceptable).

FOOD & FEEDING: Omnivore: live foods, large and small flies, dry foods, lettuce. If not enough vegetable matter included in the diet, aquarium plants will be chewed on!

### Red-finned Glass Tetra, *Prionobrama filigera*

DISTRIBUTION: South America: Amazon and various tributaries, Argentina, southern Brazil.

HABITAT: Small streams, tributaries to large flowing waters, sometimes in lake-like (river) extensions.

DESCRIPTION: Very peaceful and durable (6 to 6.5 cm long) schooling fish of the middle to lower aquarium region. The fins of the male are conspicuously thread-like. Parallel to and above the white area of the anal fin margin there is a black line. Highly suitable for community tanks with open stands of plants along the inside perimeter of the tank. The open swimming space should also afford protection from above with the surface leaves of water plants, supplemented (during breeding) with a few floating plants.

*Prionobrama filigera*

TEMP: 24-28°C, pH: 6 to 7.8, HARDNESS: up to 30°DH (soft), this species likes to swim against the discharge current of a powerful filter.

FOOD & FEEDING: Omnivore: dry foods, small live foods.

### Star-spot Tetra, *Pristella maxillaris*

DISTRIBUTION: South America: Venezuela, Guyana, lower Amazon.

HABITAT: Small bodies of water.

DESCRIPTION: This about 5 cm (2") long fish should

*Pristella maxillaris*

be viewed in back-light in order to recognize the sex. In males the abdominal organs in the area of the swim bladder appear to be pointed; the same region in females is rounded off. Females are also larger and plumper than males. An active and durable schooling fish which prefers a peripherally planted tank with a dark bottom and subdued lighting. Easy to breed. Suitable for community tanks.

TEMP: 24-28°C, pH: 6 to 8, HARDNESS: to 35°DH. Displays full coloration only in soft water.

FOOD & FEEDING: Omnivore: dry foods, small live foods.

### Penguin Fish, *Thayeria boehlkei*

DISTRIBUTION: South America: Amazon region, Rio Araguaia, Peru.

HABITAT: In areas of calm water, among plants.

DESCRIPTION: About 7 cm (2³/₄") long, active school-

*Thayeria boehlkei*

ing fish. Often not as quiet and peaceful as described, but poses hardly any serious problems in the middle and upper regions of an aquarium. Swimming position is obliquely upward; adipose fin present; female somewhat more plump. Tank should be planted widely dispersed but with some dense stands; there must be sufficient swimming room.

TEMP: 24-28°C, pH: 6 to 7.5, HARDNESS: 19 to 20°DH (softer).

FOOD & FEEDING: Omnivore: dry foods, small live foods, also fruit flies, some vegetable matter.

## BARBS AND BARB-LIKE FISHES

These fishes belong to the so-called carp-like fishes. They form the largest group of freshwater fishes. All species described here are member of the family Cyprinidae (carp-like fishes), which contains more than 1,400 species. Those kept in warm water aquariums originate in Asia and Africa. By the way, most fish in central European rivers and lakes also belong to this group. North America also has a few (coldwater) cyprinids. On the other hand, this group is found neither in South America nor in Australia (apart from artificially introduced forms).

It appears intuitively obvious that such a vast group of (related) fishes has developed biologically different species inhabiting very diverse habitats. The individual species descriptions below reflect these facts.

The barbs discussed in this chapter are generally undemanding and hardy, but some of the related forms can be a bit more delicate. A characteristic of most of these fish is cycloid (round) scales. The head is not covered by scales. Most of these fish are schooling fish which, just like tetras, should always be kept in groups of at least 10 or more fish per tank.

One of the common feeding characteristics of most members of this group is digging through bottom debris for food; consequently, powerful filtration is essential.

*Puntius nigrofasciatus*

TEMP: 24-28°C, pH: 6 to 8 (6 to 6.5), HARDNESS: soft to hard (8 to 15°DH), frequent small water changes with well-conditioned water.

FOOD & FEEDING: Omnivore: dry foods, live foods, lettuce and other vegetable matter.

### Black Ruby Barb, *Puntius nigrofasciatus*
DISTRIBUTION: Sri Lanka (southern regions).

HABITAT: Slow-flowing forest streams with substantial plant growth.

DESCRIPTION: Durable, active and peaceful fish with a maximum length of 6.5 cm; barbels absent. Schooling fish which tends to frequent the middle region of an aquarium, but also spends considerable time along the bottom in search of food. The bottom substrate should be soft and covered by organic debris. The tank should have some dense water plant stands around its perimeter and a few solitary, robust plants throughout. Floating plants assure subdued lighting; this, and lots of swimming space, are essential for this species to display its full coloration. Close monitoring of water values will guarantee breeding success. Mature males can be recognized by a black dorsal fin and generally more intense colors than those of females.

TEMP: 24-28°C, pH: 5.5 to 6.5 (only up to 6), HARDNESS: soft to medium hard (up to 12°DH); frequent small water changes with well-conditioned water.

FOOD & FEEDING: Omnivore: dry foods, live foods, vegetable supplements.

### Island or Chequered Barb, *Capoeta oligolepis*
DISTRIBUTION: Southeast Asia: Indonesia, Sumatra.

HABITAT: Standing and flowing waters at higher elevations (highlands).

DESCRIPTION: Up to 5 cm long; one pair of barbels present; hardy schooling fish in the lower and middle regions of the aquarium. Peaceful species although males (dorsal and anal fin with a dark border) tend to 'threat display'. Requires soft bottom substrate, with dense peripheral planting with robust plants, some solitary plants and lots of swimming space. Lighting in-

*Puntius conchonius*

### Rosy Barb, *Puntius conchonius*
DISTRIBUTION: Northern India: Assam, Bengal.

HABITAT: Rivers, ponds and small pools. Prefers somewhat cooler water than other barbs.

DESCRIPTION: Reaches sexual maturity at size of about 6 cm, but can attain a maximum length of about 15 cm. Barbels absent. Schooling fish, predominantly of the lower and middle tank region; often jointly scouring along the bottom in search of food. Ideal companions for other fish requiring moderate temperatures and preferring upper- to surface regions of a tank. Large swimming space in a tank with a soft bottom substrate, some debris and a few robust plants essential for the well-being of this species. Easy to breed. Males more colorful than females; females with a fuller abdomen.

*Capoeta oligolepis*

tensity appears to be irrelevant, and is essentially dependent only upon the plants used. Community tank fish, including other active species. Breeding easy, but requires more light.

TEMP: 24-28°C, pH: 6 to 7.5 (up to 7), HARDNESS: soft to hard (up to 10°DH); frequent, small water changes with well-conditioned water.

FOOD & FEEDING: Omnivore: dry foods, live foods,

*Barbodes pentazona*

lettuce and algae.

### Five-banded Barb, *Barbodes pentazona*

DISTRIBUTION: Southeast Asia: Singapore, Malay Peninsula, Borneo.

HABITAT: Close to the banks in lowland waters; black waters.

DESCRIPTION: This 5 cm (2") long, attractively marked fish tends to be quiet, almost shy and is not a

very active swimmer, which sets this species apart from most other barbs. It should be kept in a tank with a gravel bottom covered with a layer of leaves or peat moss, and only in the presence of similarly quiet fishes. It displays its best coloration in a relatively dark tank with scattered planting and with root and plant thickets (along the sides and back of the tank) to hide in. This is a fish of the lower to middle tank regions, where the smaller, more streamline-shaped males can be seen courting the paler female. But breeding is not simple.

TEMP: 24-28°C, pH: 5.5. to 7 (to 6.5), HARDNESS: soft to medium hard (up to 10°DH); orange coloration only intense when water filtered over peat moss; weekly partial water changes of $^1/_5$ to $^1/_4$ of total tank

*Puntius semifasciolatus schuberti*

volume ideal.

FOOD & FEEDING: Carnivore: demanding mainly live foods, try quality dry foods; when breeding, adults should get white worm supplements (essential for many barb species).

### Half-banded Barb, *Puntius semifasciolatus schuberti*

DISTRIBUTION: The original form of this variant is assumed to be *P. semifasciolatus* from southeastern China.

HABITAT: This variant does not occur in the wild.

DESCRIPTION: The original form reaches a maximum length of 10 cm (4"), also attained by some strains of the 'Schuberti' variety, although most will not exceed 7 cm. Two pairs of barbels present. This is an active, peaceful schooling fish which stays mostly in middle to lower regions of an aquarium. This needs to be taken into consideration when the tank is set up. Apart from a few solitary plants, most plants should be confined to the tank perimeter, where dense stands can occur.

At least some of the bottom should be made up of soft substrate. This species likes bright, sunny tanks; this is important when breeding is to take place. The larger females have dark patches along the sides of the body.

*Capoeta tetrazona*

TEMP: 24-28°C, pH: 6 to 7.5 (up to 6.5), HARDNESS: soft to hard (up to 10°DH); frequent, small water changes with well-conditioned water.

FOOD & FEEDING: Omnivore: dry foods, live foods, lettuce and vegetable matter.

### Tiger Barb, *Capoeta tetrazona*
DISTRIBUTION: Southeast Asia: Sumatra, Borneo, possibly also Thailand.

HABITAT: Bottom regions of standing or gently flowing waters.

DESCRIPTION: Maximum length 5 to 7 cm; barbels absent. Clearly visible hierarchy within an established school. Preference given to the middle region of a tank; often the entire school moves along the bottom in search of food. Substrate should be soft (fine) sand. Some solitary, robust plants along the sides of the tank. The tiger barb, of which there are many artificially produced color variants, needs a lot of swimming space. Restricted use for community tank; will pester most other fish, except large and very fast ones. Tends to 'nibble' on all elongated finnage (e.g. *Pterophyllum*). Mature females slightly larger than males. Males of the typical (wild) form display a lot of red (rather than orange).

*Capoeta titteya*

TEMP: 24-28°C, pH: 6 to 7.5, HARDNESS: soft to hard (up to 10°DH); frequent small water changes with well-conditioned water.

FOOD & FEEDING: Omnivore: dry foods, live foods, lettuce or similar vegetable matter.

### Cherry Barb, *Capoeta titteya*
DISTRIBUTION: Sri Lanka.

HABITAT: Dark areas of stream and river bottoms.

DESCRIPTION: 4 to 5 cm (2") long; one pair of barbels present; an active yet quiet and peaceful fish. No distinct schooling tendencies; males argumentative. Soft, dark bottom preferred in a relatively dark tank. If need be, provide additional shading with overhanging or floating plants. Apart from lots of swimming room, adequate hiding places are also required. Females with paler coloration and a plumper body. Breeding and community tank keeping possible. The eggs are suspended from plants by means of a tiny thread.

TEMP: 24-28°C, pH: 6 to 7.5 (below 6.5), HARDNESS: soft to hard (up to 12°DH).

*Brachydanio albolineatus*

FOOD & FEEDING: Omnivore: dry foods, live foods, vegetable supplements.

### Pearl Danio, *Brachydanio albolineatus*
DISTRIBUTION: Southeast Asia: India, Burma, Thailand, Malay Peninsula, Sumatra.

HABITAT: Streams and rivers.

DESCRIPTION: A very active, about 6 cm long, schooling fish with two pairs of barbels. Quietly and peacefully the school frequents predominantly the middle and upper water region in the aquarium. Consequently, there needs to be ample swimming space. Long tanks with gravel and rocks and a few plants along the sides are ideal for this species. The tank needs to be tightly covered (excellent jumpers!). Can be kept together with similar fish; breeding is easy. There is a degree of pair bonding; the smaller, more slender males have more intense colors than females.

TEMP: 24-28°C, pH: 6.5 to 7.5 (to 7 ), HARDNESS: soft to hard (5 to 12°DH); coloration particularly spectacular under sunlight, ideally from above. Separate, small

*Brachydanio frankei*

(20 cm (8") high) breeding tank, fresh (conditioned) water and small-leafed, bushy plants required for maximum success.

FOOD & FEEDING: Omnivore: small live foods, dry foods, vegetable supplements.

### Leopard Danio, *Brachydanio frankei*
DISTRIBUTION: Southeast Asia: India.
HABITAT: Fast-flowing, small streams.
DESCRIPTION: Conspicuously spotted, 5 to 6 cm long, very active but peaceful schooling fish; two pairs of barbels present. Considered to be either naturally occurring color form or a variety of *B. rerio* (zebra danio). So far systematic position uncertain. Requires tightly covered tank, normal planting with open swimming spaces (in the middle or upper regions) or a community tank; direct sunlight beneficial.
TEMP: 24-28°C, pH: 6 to 8, HARDNESS: soft to hard; spawning after water change.
FOOD & FEEDING: Omnivore: all small live foods and dry foods, sometimes also water plants.

### Zebra Danio, *Brachydanio rerio*
DISTRIBUTION: East coast of India.
HABITAT: Clear, rapidly flowing water.
DESCRIPTION: This fish tends to frequent mainly the middle of the tank upwards to the surface. It is a very active, peaceful species. Maximum size is 6 cm; two pairs

*Brachydanio rerio*

of barbels are present. A very bright tank with a strong current from a filter discharge is most suitable. Similarly, relative shallow (but long) tanks, well-covered with normal plant growth and lots of swimming space are also recommended. The zebra danio can easily be kept together with other small to medium-size fish, which are also active. The females are somewhat heavier and larger than males, but their colors are paler than those of males. Breeding is easy at low water, following a partial water change with conditioned water.
TEMP: 24-28°C, pH: 6 to 8, HARDNESS: soft to hard; sunlight very beneficial.
FOOD & FEEDING: Omnivore: small dry and live foods, frequent vegetable supplements.

### Malabar Danio, *Danio aequipinnatus*
DISTRIBUTION: Asia: Sri Lanka, west coast of India.
HABITAT: Usually in flowing waters, but can also occur in standing waters.
DESCRIPTION: Usually 8 to 10 cm long, but can grow up to 15 cm (6") long. Very active schooling fish but always peaceful. When kept as a surface school very suit-

*Danio aequipinnatus*

able for keeping together with bottom-dwelling fish, or even larger ones which utilize the lower half of the aquarium. Sandy bottom and lots of swimming room are essential. Plants should be robust, otherwise these fish might nibble on them. The blue lateral band in the caudal fin in the (heavier) females bends upward, while that in males continues straight. Breeding most successful in a large spawning tank. There are various local color varieties.
TEMP: 24-28°C, pH: 6.5 to 8 (to 7), HARDNESS: soft to hard (5 to 12°DH); breeding after a substantial water change; sunny location.
FOOD & FEEDING: Omnivore: live foods, also *Drosophila* and other flies, dry foods, vegetable matter.

### Hengel's Rasbora, *Rasbora hengeli*
DISTRIBUTION: Southeast Asia: Central Sumatra, Thailand.

*Rasbora hengeli*

HABITAT: Small black waters.

DESCRIPTION: Maximum size about 3.5 cm. Males with a bright, rusty-violet red and a larger wedge-shaped mark than females. An aquarium fish oriented towards the middle and upward. A schooling fish which likes lots of shade. Tank set up should be with little light and dense peripheral planting. A small *Cryptocoryne* can serve as a spawning substrate for breeding. Breeding as such is not easy; can be kept together with other small fish.

TEMP: 24-28°C, pH: 6 to 6.5, HARDNESS: soft to medium hard, up to about 12°DH, peat moss filtration.

FOOD & FEEDING: Omnivore: all small dry and live foods.

### Harlequin Rasbora, *Rasbora heteromorpha*

DISTRIBUTION: Southeast Asia: southeastern Thailand, western Malaysia, Sumatra, Java, Borneo.

HABITAT: Close to embankments of clear, standing waters with dense vegetation below and above water.

DESCRIPTION: This is an active but peaceful (4.5 cm long) schooling fish which frequents the upper and middle regions of an aquarium. There may be some threat behavior among males, but without actual fighting. The most suitable aquarium decor consists of a dark bottom, roots as decor together with dense stands of bushy plants.

*Rasbora heteromorpha*

Between the plants there must be sufficient swimming space, also for courtship and spawning (breeding not exactly easy), using a single, small *Cryptocoryne* as the spawning medium. In males the wedge-shaped spot extends to the edge of the abdomen and is rounded off at its anterior margin. Females are somewhat plumper and their 'wedge' has a straight anterior margin. Optimum breeding results by pairs, using a young (newly mature) female and a large (2 year old) male. Can be kept together with other fish of equal size range.

TEMP: 24-28°C, HARDNESS: up to 12°DH; peat moss filtration.

FOOD & FEEDING: Omnivore: small dry foods and live foods.

### Dwarf Rasbora, *Boraras maculata*

DISTRIBUTION: Southeast Asia: southwestern Malaysia, Singapore, western Sumatra.

HABITAT: Within dense plant cover close to embankments in standing or very gently flowing waters, swamps.

*Boraras maculata*

DESCRIPTION: With 2.5 cm (1") body length a real mini-schooling fish, which appears very fragile. Yet, it can be considered as hardy provided the water parameters are closely monitored. Among dense, bushy, plant thickets the open swimming space in the middle of the tank is generally preferred. The well-being of these fish is further enhanced with subdued lighting and a dark bottom. Should only be kept together with other miniature fish. Females are yellower, with a fuller abdomen. Breeding is possible.

TEMP: 24-28°C, pH: slightly acidic, around 6.5, HARDNESS: to 10°DH; peat moss filtration.

FOOD & FEEDING: Omnivore: very small dry foods and live foods.

### Scissortail Rasbora, *Rasbora trilineata*

DISTRIBUTION: Southeast Asia: Sumatra and Borneo, western Malaysia.

HABITAT: Cloudy areas in standing and gently flowing waters.

DESCRIPTION: In spite of its size (up to 15 cm) (6") this is a relatively quiet and peaceful schooling fish. Tends

*Rasbora trilineata*

to favor the middle of a tank and upward towards the surface. Requires considerable open swimming space. Aquariums which are large and long are ideal for this *Rasbora*. In addition, a dark bottom and open peripheral planting are also beneficial. In the back of the tank should be a few dense plant thickets to offer appropriate hiding places. Can be kept together with other active fish which inhabit the middle to lower regions of the aquarium. Breeding is possible.

TEMP: 24-28°C, pH: 6 to 7 (to 6.5), HARDNESS: soft to medium hard (5 to 8°DH); peat moss filtration.

FOOD & FEEDING: Omnivore: dry foods and live foods.

## Other carp-like fishes

Here we find four species which are also cyprinids, but do not belong to the barbs, danios or related forms. They have also little in common with the loaches, discussed later. Therefore, they are discussed here separately.

### Siamese Flying Fox, Siamese Algae Eater, *Crossocheilus siamensis*

DISTRIBUTION: Southeast Asia: Thailand, Malay Peninsula.

HABITAT: Medium to large rivers at moderate elevations (hill country).

DESCRIPTION: Has not yet been bred in captivity. One pair of barbels present on the upper jaw; maximum size 15 cm (6"). External sex characteristics unknown. Very effective algae eater! In carefully manicured tanks they must be given supplementary algae. Somewhat aggressive toward each other; normally po-

**Some fishes should be kept in schools. One of them is *Rasbora heteromorpha*. Not only is this esthetically pleasing to the eye but the fish are less stressed. Aqua Press Piednoir.**

*Crossocheilus siamensis*

*Epalzeorhynchos bicolor*

sitioned on the bottom or perched on a water plant leaf. In a tank with a soft bottom and dense water plant growth this species tends to be hardy and an excellent inhabitant for a community tank, but they also like some water current and are alleged to be sensitive to low oxygen levels.

TEMP: 24-28°C (26-30°F), pH: 6 to 7.5, HARDNESS: soft to medium hard; after gradual, cautious acclimatization at the dealer, this fish can be kept at home at a pH of 8 and a hardness of 20°DH.

FOOD & FEEDING: Omnivore: dry foods, particularly tablets, lettuce, also live foods.

### Red-tailed Black Shark, *Epalzeorhynchos bicolor*

DISTRIBUTION: Southeast Asia: Malaysia, Thailand.

HABITAT: Flowing waters with rock and wood accumulations along the bottom.

DESCRIPTION: An imposing fish (15 to 20 cm (8")long) of the lower aquarium region. Essentially solitary and tends to establish territories, which are strongly defended even against siblings. These interactions can be quite physical, and so adequate hiding places are required if more than one specimen is kept in the same tank. Must be arranged with sight barriers! The females are somewhat larger but with paler coloration. The lower posterior edge of the dorsal fin of males is drawn out to a point. Captive breeding is rare (= accidental!); the eggs are deposited in an egg case.

TEMP: 24-28°C (26-30°F), pH: 6 to 7.5, HARDNESS: up to 15°DH (soft); if properly acclimated will also tolerate harder water; peat supplement in the filter.

FOOD & FEEDING: Omnivore: dry foods, live foods, algae, various vegetable matter (lettuce, dandelion, spinach and others).

### Red-finned Shark, *Epalzeorhynchos frenatus*

DISTRIBUTION: Southeast Asia: northern Thailand.

HABITAT: Flowing waters.

DESCRIPTION: Depending on precise origin, the maximum size can vary from 8 to 12 cm (5") length; some specimens may even be larger. This active, occasionally aggressive species is largely nocturnal and carries two pairs of barbels. A territory is usually estab-

lished and guarded from within some hiding place; intruders are vigorously pursued, but rarely causing injuries. Less aggressive than *E. bicolor,* especially in large tanks. Hiding places made up of roots and rocks and sight barriers using plant thickets are strongly advisable. Has been bred on rare occasions, but these are viewed as non-repeatable random events. The male has a black margin along the anal fin and the females are heavier. Can be used in a community tank under the conditions discussed above.

TEMP: 24-28°C, pH: 6 to 7.5, HARDNESS: up to 10°DH; peat moss filtration.

FOOD & FEEDING: Omnivore: dry foods, live foods, algae, dandelions, lettuce.

### White Cloud Mountain Minnow, *Tanichthys albonubes*

DISTRIBUTION: East Asia: southern China, especially around Canton.

HABITAT: Clear mountain streams.

*Epalzeorhynchos frenatus*

DESCRIPTION: In the early days of the aquarium hobby, this peaceful and highly active schooling fish (4 to 5 cm (2") long) used to be referred to as the 'poor man's neon tetra,' presumedly because in those days it was much cheaper than the real neon tetra. Over the years a number of different color varieties of white clouds have been produced, as well as some veiltail forms. The rather colorful males (smaller and more slender than females) will enhance their appearance even more during color-intensive threat behavior. Schools of this species tend to frequent the middle regions as well as the surface of an aquarium. This hardy fish needs a lot of swimming space! Dense planting along the sides and back of the tank or dispersed plant thickets forming a more or less closed backdrop planting provide the right environment for this fish. An excellent fish for a community tank and easy to breed.

*Tanichthys albonubes*

TEMP: 24-28°C, pH: 6 to 8, HARDNESS: soft to hard; frequent partial water changes.

FOOD & FEEDING: Omnivore: dry foods, small live foods.

# LOACHES, SPINY EELS

The family Cobitidae is a rather small fish family of only about 100 species, all native to freshwaters of Asia. They are characterized by the presence of barbels, which have sensory functions and are equipped with taste receptors for gathering food. All species have very small scales or are essentially naked. They are bottom-dwellers with a sub-ventral mouth, toothless jaws, some with a movable spine below the eye, and some have the ability to produce clicking sounds.

Many loaches use intestinal respiration, i.e. atmospheric air is swallowed at the surface and the oxygen taken in is absorbed in richly vascularized intestinal segments.

To the research-minded aquarist, the reproductive biology of this fish group opens up a wide field, because there are still many unknown aspects. Most breeding in the past has consisted of little more than totally unplanned random events.

### Coolie Loaches, *Pangio* spp.

DISTRIBUTION: Various species from different countries in Southeast Asia.

HABITAT: Usually found in little streams where vast schools of the young hide amongst dense stands of underwater plants; later in life these fish become largely solitary.

DESCRIPTION: Precise species identification of coolie loaches can only be done by systematic specialists. They are reminiscent of small eels, but are equipped with three pairs of barbels. A lateral line is absent and they stay mainly on the bottom.

There have been a few accidental breedings in aquariums, when the female became cylindrically rotund due to the development of eggs. These fish are nocturnal (should be fed in the evening) with a substantial longevity. They frighten easily and tend to jump out of the tank. In dark aquariums with a soft bottom and lots of plants these fish appear quite comfortable. They should only be kept together with fish of the upper water regions.

TEMP: 24-28°C, pH: 5.5. to 6.5, HARDNESS: up to 10°DH; peat moss filtration.

FOOD & FEEDING: Omnivore: sinking live foods, vegetable matter, dry foods (adapt to tablet foods).

### Clown Loach, *Botia macracantha*

DISTRIBUTION: Southeast Asia: Indo-Australian Archipelago, Sumatra, Borneo.

HABITAT: Lakes, flooded rivers.

DESCRIPTION: Clown loaches are very active schooling fish, which rarely achieve lengths in excess of 16 cm (6") in captivity, but specimens in the wild have been measured up to 30 cm (12"). This species has four

"Tank mates?"

115

*Pangio myersi*

## Hora's Loach, *Botia morleti (Botia horae)*
DISTRIBUTION: Southeast Asia: Thailand.

HABITAT: Streams and small rivers.

DESCRIPTION: Most specimens 7 to 10 cm (4") long; one of the smaller loaches, which is an active swimmer and usually very peaceful. Occasional aggression is not serious, since this species is not very agile. Largely nocturnal and most daylight hours are spent in hiding close to the bottom. There must be at least one hiding place per specimen. The tank bottom should be soft (fine sand), some rocks and roots. The plants should be tough, and the light level must be subdued (floating plants!). Can be kept to-

*Botia macracantha*

pairs of barbels and it is able to produce clicking noises. Active swimmer which is not quite as shy as other loaches. Most active at dusk and dawn. This slow-growing species is sensitive to chemicals and prone to be infected by *Ichthyophthirius*. In its native environment it is considered to be a delicious food fish.

A tank to hold clown loaches should have a soft bottom with lots of hiding places and caves made of driftwood, roots, rocks and bamboo sticks. Apart from incidental breeding little is known about captive reproduction; when viewed from above older females tend to look heavier (i.e. wider abdominal region). Old males develop an arched dorsal profile and remain more compact, but these are considered to be highly unreliable characteristics. In nature this species presumedly undergoes considerable spawning migrations towards the fast-flowing spring regions of streams and rivers. Such a triggering mechanism to induce spawning is hard to duplicate under captive conditions.

TEMP: 24-28°C, pH: 5 to 7, HARDNESS: not above 10°DH, if anything, lower than that; should not be kept in small tanks; required tank size in excess of 1.2 (48") meters; frequent partial water changes.

FOOD & FEEDING: Omnivore: dry foods (including tablets), live foods with worms, small snails, algae and other vegetable matter.

gether with larger fish, e.g. barbs or armored catfish. External sex characteristics and captive breeding unknown.

TEMP: 24-28°C, pH: 6 to 7, HARDNESS: to 5°DH, frequent partial water changes, about 20% per week.

FOOD & FEEDING: Omnivore: live foods, dry foods, algae.

## Checkerboard- or Dwarf Loach, *Botia sidthimunki*
DISTRIBUTION: Southeast Asia: northern Thailand.

HABITAT: Small, muddy, standing or gently flowing waters.

DESCRIPTION: Delightful loach with three pairs of barbels, day-active, peaceful schooling fish. Now bred on a commercial scale in Thailand. Maximum length 7 to 9 cm; should be kept in a school only. Adequate hiding places (caves) need to be provided along with a soft bottom. Partially dense planting, but leave sufficient open swimming space. Small, non-territorial or calm larger species are suitable partners for this loach in a well-kept community tank. Breeding should be confined to a species tank, approaching courtship indicated by visibly paler coloration.

TEMP: 24-28°C (26-30°F), PH: 6 to 7.5, HARDNESS: soft to hard; frequent water changes.

FOOD & FEEDING: Omnivore: small dry and live foods, algae.

*Botia morleti*

*Botia sidthimunki*

# CATFISHES

From among this very diverse group of (principally in freshwater occurring ) catfishes (Siluroidei), we are going to present here only a selection of those which are of significance as aquarium fishes. Of the (at least) 2,000 species in 33 families we are going to discuss here only 13 species from 4 families.

In the foreground we have the various in terms of maintenance rather similar armored catfish, which belong to the family Callichthyidae. Of the mailed catfishes (Loricariidae) we have 4 species and one representative each of the antenna catfish (Pimelodidae) and the true catfish (Siluridae). The latter also includes the native European catfish that grows to a size in excess of two meters (6$^{1}/_{2}$") (a South American catfish species gets one meter longer!), which in stark contrast to the 2.5 cm (1") long dwarf catfish, depicts quite impressively the variability within this group.

Some catfish can utilize atmospheric oxygen: like loaches, they gulp air at the surface, from which oxygen is then absorbed, usually in the swim bladder.

Catfish do not have scales. Unless the body remains naked (in many species) it is protected by an armored casing made up of bony plates.

Barbels, also found in other families, are often substantially elongated (whisker-like) in catfish, and function as highly sensitive tactile and taste mechanisms, used mainly in the search for food.

Anyone keeping catfish does not need to worry about left-over food scattered along the bottom; but it is certainly wrong to keep catfish purely as waste-disposal animals, and so many catfish may well end up being under-fed. Those species which are active mostly after dark should get their own feed ration in the evening, so that they maintain their condition.

Breeding is done best in a separate species tank. In non-brood caring species the parents are removed after spawning has been completed, or the clutch of eggs is transferred to a separate hatching tank.

## Blue Antenna Catfish, *Ancistrus dolichopterus*

DISTRIBUTION: South America: Amazon tributaries.

HABITAT: In flowing waters, around submerged trees, branches, etc., in clear streams.

DESCRIPTION: These 13 to 14 (5$^{1}/_{2}$") cm long, bizarre catfish do best in a large, clear tank with a substantial current from the filter discharge. They tend to frequent the lower tank regions, especially around roots, etc. The males carry several antenna-like structures on their head. In females they are short and thin. These catfish spend a lot of the day in hiding among roots, submerged branches and in caves. It is a peaceful species that can be kept together even with smaller fishes. Spawning takes place in caves, thereafter the territorial males will guard the brood.

TEMP: 24-28°C, pH: 6 to 8 (up to 7), HARDNESS: soft to hard (4 to 10°DH), in oxygen-rich water.

FOOD & FEEDING: Herbivore: algae, vegetable matter, also boiled carrots and frozen (thawed out) peas, dry foods, live foods, requires submerged wood for rasping.

## Green Catfish, *Brochis splendens*

DISTRIBUTION: South America: Amazon Basin, Peru, Brazil, Ecuador.

HABITAT: Slow-flowing waters in densely overgrown, shallow water regions close to river banks.

DESCRIPTION: As in many other armored catfish, the small adipose fin is supported by a spine; the genus *Brochis* has 10 or more rays in the dorsal fin, *Corydoras* only 6 to 8. This species has 3 pairs of barbels; it grows to a maximum length of 8 cm (3") and is a day-active schooling fish in the lower tank region. The tank needs to be well-planted and have a fine-grained gravel or coarse sand (dark!) bottom. There should also be adequate hiding places such as rocks, roots and large leaves. Areas of small debris next to clean bottom patches are beneficial. Should be kept together only with other peaceful species (large cichlids are not good company!). Can be bred. although external sex characteristics (apart from heavier females) are not distinguishable. Partial water changes with initially slightly cooler water often triggers spawning.

TEMP: 24-28°C, pH: 5.8 to 7.5 (up to 6.5), HARDNESS: soft to hard (up to 4°DH); frequent, partial (small) water changes.

FOOD & FEEDING: Omnivore: dry foods (tablets), live

**Dwellers of the underworld!**

foods, occasional vegetable supplements.

**Skunk Cory,** *Corydoras arcuatus*
DISTRIBUTION: South America: central Amazon.
HABITAT: Streams and small rivers.
DESCRIPTION: An attractive bottom-dwelling fish which grows up to 5 cm (2") long and has 2 pairs of barbels. Should be kept in a school over soft, dark substrates (fine sand). Normal planting and a few large, roundish pebbles complete the tank set-up for this species, which can also be kept in a community tank. Has already been bred in captivity.

*Ancistrus dolichopterus*

TEMP: 24-28°C, pH: 6 to 8 (to 7), HARDNESS: 2 to 25°DH (about 6°DH).
FOOD & FEEDING: Omnivore: live foods, dry foods, including vegetable supplement.

**Spotlight Mini-Cory,** *Corydoras hastatus*
DISTRIBUTION: South America: Brazil (Amazon, Mato Grosso).
HABITAT: Open water, close to the banks of small streams and rivers.
DESCRIPTION: Maximum size 3 to 3.5 cm. Very active swimmer; peaceful, day-active schooling fish which will also frequent the middle region of the tank. Females are larger and heavier than males (only about 2.5 cm (1") long). Has already been bred in captivity, apparently triggered by partial water changes with

cooler water. Should be kept in a tank with soft substrate and plant thickets, to be kept company only with other small fishes.
TEMP: 24-28°C, pH: 6 to 7.5 ( up to 7), HARDNESS: soft to hard (up to 6°DH); frequent, small water changes.
FOOD & FEEDING: Omnivore: small live and dry foods, with occasional vegetable supplements.

*Brochis splendens*

**Peppered Cory,** *Corydoras paleatus*
DISTRIBUTION: South America: southeastern Brazil.
HABITAT: Small flowing waters.
DESCRIPTION: Because this peaceful and undemanding little catfish is a very hardy fish, it was one of the first pioneers in the tropical fish trade in Europe. It possesses two pairs of barbels and is a schooling fish which tends to favor the bottom of the aquarium, which should consist of soft sand, so that the fish cannot injure themselves as they scurry along the bottom. In a tank planted with large, leafy plants a small school of this (7 to 8 cm (3") long) species makes excellent community tank fish. Captive breeding has already produced an albino form.

*Corydoras hastatus*

TEMP: 24-28°C, pH: 6.5 to 8 (up to 7), HARDNESS: soft to hard (up to 6°DH); frequent, small water changes.
FOOD & FEEDING: Omnivore: small dry foods and live food, food tablets.

**Panda Cory,** *Corydoras panda*
DISTRIBUTION: South America: Peru.
HABITAT: Clear, flowing waters, over sandy bottom.
DESCRIPTION: The cute face markings of this (5 cm (2") long) fish, reminiscent of that of a panda bear, have

*Corydoras arcuatus*

*Corydoras paleatus*

given this species its common name. Plants should be arranged in little groups, along a sandy bottom; peaceful, day-active species. This fish likes a gentle current (filter discharge!) and well-filtered, oxygen-rich water. Can be kept in a community tank with other peaceful fish which are not too large; has already been bred. No external sex characteristics; a cool water change appears to induce spawning. Should be kept in small groups, which conforms to the behavior of this fish in the wild.

TEMP: 24-28°C, pH: 6.5 to 7.5, HARDNESS: soft to hard; regular water changes about every two to three weeks.

FOOD & FEEDING: Limnivore, omnivore: live and dry foods (including tablets).

### Reticulated Cory, *Corydoras reticulatus*
DISTRIBUTION: South America: Peru, Amazon.
HABITAT: Various types of small waters.
DESCRIPTION: Peaceful and durable schooling fish with two pairs of barbels, actively moving along the bottom but also sometimes venturing into the middle and even upper water regions in an aquarium. The bottom substrate should consist of very fine sand combined with

*Corydoras panda.*

some larger rocks, often used by this species as resting places. Can be kept in a community tank when sufficient plants are present. Has been bred in captivity (females are heavier). Maximum size is about 7 cm.

TEMP: 24-28°C, pH: 6 to 8 ( up to 7), HARDNESS: 2 to 26°DH (about 6°DH); frequent but small water changes.

FOOD & FEEDING: Omnivore: dry foods, live foods,

occasionally vegetable matter.

### Three-line Cory, *Corydoras trilineatus*
DISTRIBUTION: South America: Peru.
HABITAT: Soft-bottom rivers and lakes.
DESCRIPTION: When kept in groups in tanks with a soft bottom substrate, this 6 cm long catfish does well. Also day-active; tends to remain in the lower regions,

*Corydoras reticulatus*

among roots and plant thickets; does well in a community tank with adequate plant cover along the bottom. Can be bred by using cooler water as spawning stimulant. In general, this species requires slightly higher water temperatures than many other *Corydoras* species.

TEMP: 24-28°, pH: 6 to 7.5 (up to 7), HARDNESS: soft to hard (6°DH), frequent, small water changes.

FOOD & FEEDING: Omnivore: dry foods, live food.

### Spotted Pleco, *Hypostomus punctatus*
DISTRIBUTION: South America: southern and southeastern Brazil
HABITAT: Juveniles in rapidly flowing waters; adults in slow flowing waters.
DESCRIPTION: Maximum length about 30 cm (12") ; adipose fin present; a slow-growing species. Solitary bottom dweller which is shy and nocturnal. Tends to dig quite severely after dark, therefore plants must be potted and protected with rocks. In nature this species apparently spawns in caves; no further details are known; external sex characteristics unknown. Floating plants should produce subdued lighting, and roots, rocks, etc. must be present to provide adequate hiding places. Soft and slightly acid water is preferred; can be kept in a community tank with fishes of equal size.

119

*Corydoras trilineatus*

TEMP: 24-28°C, pH: 5 to 8, HARDNESS: soft to hard; only suitable for large tanks from 1.2 m length.

FOOD & FEEDING: Herbivore: algae, lettuce, water-soaked oats, spinach, dry foods, live foods.

## Indian Glass Catfish, *Kryptopterus bicirrhis*

DISTRIBUTION: Southeast Asia: Malaysia, Thailand, Java, Sumatra, Borneo.

HABITAT: In open, sunny areas of gently flowing streams and rivers.

DESCRIPTION: In this 10 cm (4") long catfish, equipped with two long, thin barbels, the dorsal fin has only small supporting rays, and the anal fin extends close to the caudal fin. Because of the transparent body this somewhat delicate species makes an interesting aquarium fish. It is a day-active schooling fish, which likes to stay among open stands of water plants, which can be denser towards the sides and back. Other requirements are a partial cover of floating plants, a slight current and sufficient swimming room. Can be kept together with other peaceful fish, as well as with other catfish and schooling fish. Instances of captive breeding have been rare, and the glass catfish is alleged to be an open spawner over water plants after simulation of the rainy season.

TEMP: 24-28°C, pH: 6 to 7.6, HARDNESS: soft to hard; good water quality is important.

*Hypostomus punctatus*

*Kryptopterus bicirrhis*

FOOD & FEEDING: Omnivore: live foods, dry foods.

## Dwarf sucking catfish, *Otocinclus affinis*

DISTRIBUTION: South America: southeastern Brazil.

HABITAT: Clear, rapidly flowing water with extensive water plant growth.

DESCRIPTION: Maximum length about 4 cm; adipose fin is absent; this catfish likes to remain in hiding during the day; it is active during the night, grazing over various substrates. It requires clear water with a distinct current and needs algae-covered rocks and roots in its tank. If the tank has a dense plant cover, this species can easily be kept together with medium-sized fishes (but not preda-

*Otocinclus affinis*

tors!). Females appear periodically fatter, probably due to the formation of eggs; otherwise there are no external sex characteristics. Has occasionally been bred; no brood care.

TEMP: 24-28°C, pH: 6 to 7.5, HARDNESS: soft to hard; requires more oxygen than many other catfishes.

FOOD & FEEDING: Limnivore, herbivore: dry foods (tablets), algae, live foods, vegetable matter.

**Pretty Peckoltia,** *Peckoltia pulcher*

DISTRIBUTION: South America: Rio Negro and tributaries.

HABITAT: Rivers and streams.

DESCRIPTION: Peaceful community tank fish; 6 to 8 cm long and quite hardy. Usually found along the bottom among wood, roots, etc. This has to be taken into acount in the aquarium. Moreover, this species must have algae in the tank; without it the fish will waste away. Rocks and roots should be provided as hiding places. Has not yet been bred in captivity. Periodically there are hard, bristly skin regions on head and tail; these occur presumedly in males.

TEMP: 24-28°C, pH: 5.5 to 7.8, HARDNESS: soft to hard; only up to 10°DH.

FOOD & FEEDING: Limnivore (herbivore): wood for 'rasping,' vegetable matter, live foods.

# AQUARIUM CLUB EXHIBITIONS

For outsiders this may not exactly be THE EVENT of the year, but for the membership of an aquarium club it is a welcome change and a highlight in their club activities: *the aquarium exhibition.*

Sometimes there is a special occasion, such as a club anniversary, but more often than not together with all the hard work involved, it is simply part of the regular activities of an aquarium club.

Such an exhibition must be properly planned, well-thought out and be properly organized. This is not an easy task! Unless one is to settle for bare tanks and only a few fish species, the financial and technical requirements are substantial.

Weeks earlier, usually when the brave words of the club leadership has to be gradually translated into appropriate action, tensions mount and adrenaline begins to flow. The last few touches must be added after an intensive period of hammering, setting-up tanks, planting, transferring fish, laying electrical cables, installing lighting and all the last minute cleaning up and polishing.

Aquarists are only human and many are not that good in detailed pre-planning, so work commences sometimes aimlessly. But somehow everything gets done on time, even though it may be at the very last minute.

Finally the moment has arrived and masses of people flow into the exhibit hall. The owners of individual tanks mingle with visitors or quietly move into the proximity of their tanks in order to catch words of praise.

Soon the crowd splits up into marine aquarium fans and those interested in freshwater animals, provided both of these categories are on display. Some visitors stand excited in front of a tank with live corals and sea anemones, while others become engrossed in tanks with imaginative planting schemes and magnificent stands of water plants (garnished with a few fish) or absorb the beauty of a tank full of cichlids from the lakes of East Africa.

Fishes, with names everyone knows, are magical attractions, although most of them may have retreated into plant thickets and there is little more to see than the odd tail fin. Certain expectations of being able to experience 'blood-thirsty' piranhas close up are often not fulfilled.

The fish tend to adapt fairly quickly to their new surroundings and show little adverse reactions. Soon even the imprints of children's dirty hands on the aquarium glass are no longer any reason for concern.

Behind the scenes, of course, work goes on for the club members. The fish need to be fed and the water quality must be maintained at optimum levels.

It becomes real work if such an exhibition lasts longer than one or two weeks, and extends for several months. Then the full-time aquarists among club members—the pensioners and retirees—are urgently required. They are entrusted with getting all sorts of fish foods, especially live foods, and they have to maintain an ongoing monitoring program of all show tanks.

But even the part-time aquarist will abandon those members of his family who do not share his enthusiasm for his finned friends.

When the last day of the exhibition has come and gone, one can usually look back on an interersting and stimulating time. But wait a minute...there is still the topic of dismantling the exhibition and transferring and transporting the fish back to their original homes. The party can finally begin at some later meeting with the other club members. Then is also the time to admire all the photographs and videos of the 'big event'!

In spite of all the strenuous efforts that everyone had to put up with before, during and after the exhibition, soon new plans are made for the next exhibition...and next time it will most certainly be bigger and better!

**Upside down world!**

**Angel Antenna Catfish,** *Pimelodus pictus*

DISTRIBUTION: South America: Peru, Amazon River.

HABITAT: Cloudy, shallow waters in the Amazon drainage region.

DESCRIPTION: Maximum (aquarium) size about 12 cm (5"); in the wild this fish may get larger. Pectoral fins with small hooks, difficult to remove from nets; should be caught in transparent containers. Tends to swim in small groups, usually quite peaceful, in the lower to middle region in an aquarium; very small fish are pursued. Tank decor must consist of floating plants, roots,

*Peckoltia pulcher*

rocky caves and similar hiding places, but there must be sufficient swimming space since these are very energetic fish. Large capacity filtration with a slight current is beneficial. Breeding and sexual details are unknown. Can be kept together with other fish which are sufficiently large to not be considered as prey.

TEMP: 24-28°C, pH: 6 to 7, HARDNESS: soft water preferred, although will adjust to greater hardness; peat moss filtration.

FOOD & FEEDING: Omnivore: dry foods (tablets), live foods.

# KILLIFISHES
# (EGG-LAYING TOOTHCARPS)

There are more than 450 species in the family Cyprinodontidae, arranged within 5 subgroups. Egg-laying toothcarps are generally referred to as 'killifishes'. They occur in fresh water on all continents, except Australia. In this chapter we are going to talk only about some African and Asian representatives. The size variance of killifish in general ranges from 2 to 30 cm(12"). The lateral line organ usually occurs only along the head, and the mouth is equipped with sharp,

*Pimelodus pictus*

bent teeth.

Depending upon the type of spawning medium used, one distinguishes between attachment spawners (deposit their eggs on plants) and bottom spawners. In those species which live in waters which dry up seasonally, the adults will die after they have spawned. The embryos will then survive the drought period inside the egg shell. One refers to these fish as being 'annual fishes', when the eggs require such a rest period (diapause), independent of where they have been laid.

**Gardner's Killifish,** *Aphyosemion gardneri*

DISTRIBUTION: Africa: Nigeria, western Cameroon.

HABITAT: Small and very small bodies of water in savanna and jungles.

DESCRIPTION: Very beautiful, but somewhat aggressive (especially among males) annual fish which reaches a size of 6 to 8 cm (3"). Several subspecies as well as geographical color varieties make this species rather variable in appearance. The small females have more subdued coloration. A species tank with dark bottom and dense planting (including floating plants) is ideal, possibly together with some *Aphyosemion* species which frequents the surface. *A. gardneri* has a preference for the middle to lower water layers. Likes to hide among roots. The eggs of this species need to dry out in peat moss for a 4 week rest period. Create subdued lighting with floating plants.

TEMP: 24-28°C, pH: 6 to 7 (up to 6.5), HARDNESS: to 10°DH (5 to 8°DH); peat moss filtration, DO NOT ADD salt.

FOOD & FEEDING: Carnivore: live food, worms; dry foods are rarely eaten.

**Striped Panchax,** *Aplocheilus lineatus*

DISTRIBUTION: Asia: India (Malabar, Madras); Sri Lanka.

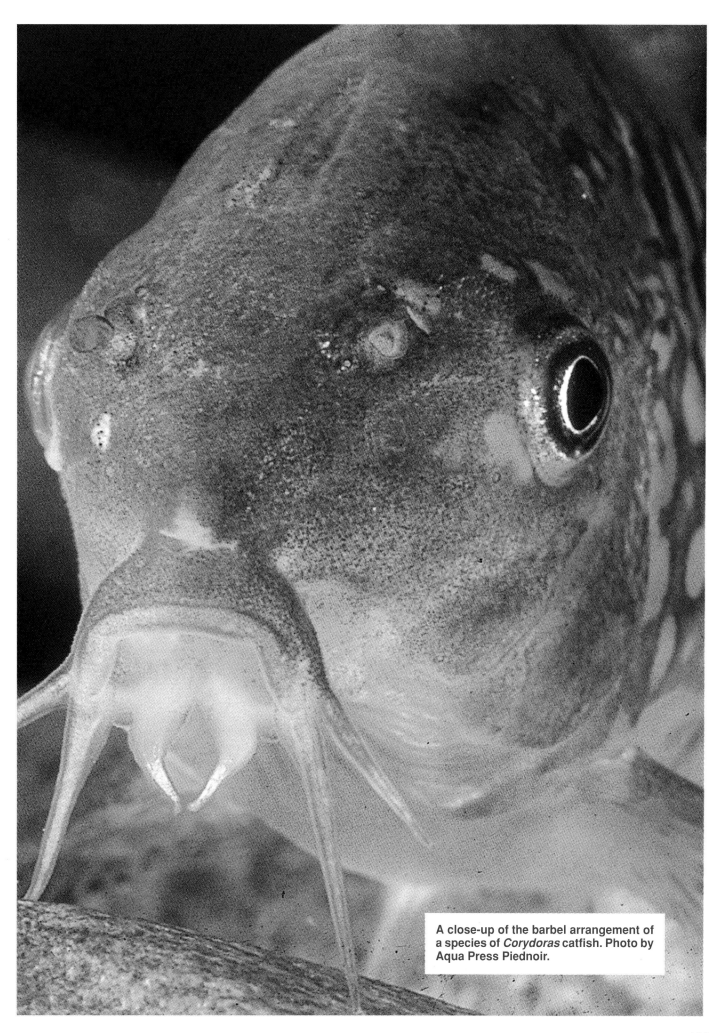

**A close-up of the barbel arrangement of a species of *Corydoras* catfish. Photo by Aqua Press Piednoir.**

**Aphyosemion gardneri**

HABITAT: Small standing waters.

DESCRIPTION: Durable and robust surface fish, but tends to extend its territories down to the middle water layers. Maximum length 10 to 12 cm (5"). Intraspecific aggression and towards fish of similar shape; tends to jump so tank must be well-covered. Suitable for a community tank with larger fish, which also prefer dense, bushy plants but must also have adequate swimming space. Tank decor should include roots and floating plants. The smaller, paler females attach their eggs to plant leaves or in artificial spawning mops, provided the water level is lowered to about 20 cm (8"). The eggs are removed and incubated separately in shallow containers.

TEMP: 24-28°C, pH: 6 to 7.5 (6 to 6.8), HARDNESS: not too hard (up to 12°DH); sand or gravel bottom.

FOOD & FEEDING: Carnivore: Live foods, include also *Drosophila* and larger flies, earthworms, small fishes, as well as dry foods.

### Common Panchax, *Aplocheilus panchax*

DISTRIBUTION: Asia: India, Burma, Thailand, Malay Peninsula and Indo-Australian Archipelago, as well as Sunda Islands.

**Aplocheilus lineatus**

HABITAT: Rice paddies; swamps, silted, overgrown areas.

DESCRIPTION: Undemanding killifish, with a length of 7 to 8 cm (3"). Prefers surface waters; geographically related color variations. Jumper! Tank needs to be tightly covered; dense planting but adequate swimming space; tank decor should include floating plants and some roots as hiding places. Can be kept together with larger fishes; external sex characteristics hard to distinguish. Fins of the somewhat larger females are smaller and colors paler. Not difficult to breed (for details refer to *A. lineatus*).

TEMP: 24-28°C, pH: 6 to 7.5 (6 to 6.8), HARDNESS: soft to medium hard (up to 12°DH); use artificial spawning mops as spawning substrate.

FOOD & FEEDING: Carnivore: live foods, including *Drosophila*, other flies and small insects, small fishes, as well as dry foods.

### Daget's Panchax, *Epiplatys dageti*

DISTRIBUTION: Africa: Sierra Leone, Liberia, Ivory Coast, Ghana.

HABITAT: Small, flowing waters.

DESCRIPTION: 6 to 7 cm long (females smaller with

**Aplocheilus panchax**

less well-developed fins). Juveniles and subadults are peaceful, adults increasingly aggressive and predatory. Can only be kept together with other fish of equal size (e.g. schooling fish of the middle water layer, catfish or small cichlids). Dense planting along the sides and back and lots of floating plants to provide subdued lighting and dark sand on the bottom are all part of species-correct maintenance. The eggs are attached to plants and should be removed as soon as spawning has been completed. The anal fin of the male is extended and drawn out.

TEMP: 24-28°C, pH: 6 to 7 (up to 6.5), HARDNESS: to 10°DH; peat supplement.

FOOD & FEEDING: Omnivore: life foods plus *Drosophila*, later also small fishes, dry foods.

### Rice Fish, *Oryzias* spec.

DISTRIBUTION: East Asia: Indonesia.

HABITAT: Small bodies of water like rice paddies.

DESCRIPTION: There are various species of rice fish, with a maximum length of 4 to 5.5 (2") cm. Dorsal and anal fins in males are larger than those of females. As one of the few groups of egglaying toothcarps the *Oryzias* species are schooling fishes throughout their entire life. They prefer to remain close to the water surface, where a few floating plants should leave sufficient swimming space. Also required for the well-being of rice fish are a gentle current, bushy plants and a sunny location. These will readily spawn, but raising the young is not easy. Can be kept together with fishes of similar size which frequent the lower and middle water layers.

*Oryzias* sp.

*Epiplatys dageti*

TEMP: 24-28°C, pH: 7 to 8.5, HARDNESS: 10 to 15°DH; do NOT ADD salt!

FOOD & FEEDING: Omnivore: small live foods, including *Drosophila*, dry foods.

# LIVEBEARERS (LIVEBEARING TOOTHCARPS)

About 30 to 40 million years ago, nature developed a reproductive system in fishes whereby the eggs, which are always under threat of being eaten or damaged, are kept away from the outside world and are protected against egg predators. Female live-bearing toothcarps give birth to fully developed fish which can immediately swim and eat.

Litter sizes are dependent upon the species but also on the individual condition of a fish, ranging from 20 to more than 100 young, which will quickly hide in plant thickets or other places soon after birth. In fact, while they are young they will never be far from the nearest cover where they tend to hide as soon as they detect an approaching danger.

Opposed to egg-laying fishes (with thousands to hundreds of thousands of eggs) live-bearers with relatively few young achieve the same reproductive success.

Characteristic for all male live-bearing toothcarps is the copulatory organ (gonopodium), which developed from a modification of the anal fin. Distinctly visible, this external feature makes it easy to sex the

fish. In fact, a specialist can determine the sex of even small species at an age of three weeks! A single transfer of sperm to the female can affect several fertilizations, that is, once females have been fertilized they can store sperm packages and so produce several litters without males being present.

Livebearers are adaptable and easy to breed, which has made them very popular aquarium fish. The livebearer tank (identical for all species) should be set up with a sand or gravel bottom and some robust plants which can easily handle the water conditions (*Sagittaria, Vallisneria,* as well as Java Moss and Java Fern).

Breeding livebearers (in a species or community tank) requires dense planting for the young to hide in. They can be reared with *Artemia salina* (brine shrimp) and quality, very fine-grained dry foods.

### Least Killifish, *Heterandria formosa*

DISTRIBUTION: Southern United States: Florida, South Carolina.

HABITAT: Small and very small waters with a dense waterplant cover.

DESCRIPTION: This is one of the smallest aquarium fishes; males to only about 2 cm; females to 4.5 cm. An active fish which tends to favor the middle water region in even the smallest of aquariums. Males will fight but without inflicting any injuries; this can be mitigated with a dense plant cover, also with floating plants. Should only be kept together with small peaceful fish. Will breed readily.

TEMP: 24-28°C, pH: 7 to 8, HARDNESS: medium; hard water after acclimatization.

FOOD & FEEDING: Omnivore: live foods, *Artemia*, small dry foods, algae.

### Guppy, *Poecilia reticulata*

DISTRIBUTION: Originally probably from northern South America; wild populations also in Central America and the Carribbean. Other natural populations in many tropical and subtropical countries, derived from escapees, accidental and/or deliberate releases from local aquaculture activities.

HABITAT: Standing gently flowing waters.

**Top left:** *Heterandria formosa*. **Top right:** Guppy female with "normal" anal fin in contrast to the gonopodium of the male. **Bottom:** Guppy variety with a fantail (males).

DESCRIPTION: Undemanding, hardy and in an abundance of varieties kept and bred by aquarists around the world. Due to its prolific breeding it is also being referred to as the *'millions fish.'* The optimum breeding potential is realized not so much through the number of young per litter, but indeed due to the rapid sequence of litters. In a well-planted tank with sufficient swimming space some of the young will always survive the predatory efforts of their parents. However, quality line-breeding of guppies is virtually a science

of its own. Guppies are excellent community tank fish, but the various veiltail varieties are best kept by themselves. They are not very agile swimmers and their elaborate finnage is often nibbled on by other fishes.

TEMP: 24-28°C, pH: 7 to 8.5, HARDNESS: not too soft, medium hard to hard water (20 to 30°DH); good water quality is rewarded with high fertility.

FOOD & FEEDING: Omnivore: dry foods, live food, algae, vegetable supplements.

### Black Molly, *Poecilia sphenops*

DISTRIBUTION: Central and South America: Mexico to Venezuela.

HABITAT: The wild form is found mainly in flowing waters and may even venture into brackish water.

DESCRIPTION: Black specimens occur occasionally in 'wild' populations, but the genuine black mollies are a short-lived and delicate artificially produced variety (through selective breeding of 'black' mutants). The wild form reaches a maximum size of only 6 cm, while captive-bred black mollies may get to be 8 to 12 cm (5") long. They require warmer water than the natural stock, which can get by on 20 degrees C (68°F).

In tanks with hardy plants, some roots and rocks, together with sufficient swimming room, black mollies occupy the middle and upper areas of the tank. Floating plants provide suitable protection for the young, even in a community tank. Black mollies are excellent algae eaters. The wild form should be given a sea salt additive (up to .1%); for captive-bred forms it depends

Upper photo: *Poecilia sphenops*
(Black molly)

Right: *Poecilia velifera*
(Sailfin molly)

on the breeding and rearing conditions. Salt supplements can have a detrimental effect on plant growth.

TEMP: 24-28°C, pH: 7.5 to 8.5; HARDNESS: medium to hard; frequent partial water changes.

FOOD & FEEDING: Omnivore (but mostly herbivore): dry foods, vegetable supplements, algae, small soaked oats, live foods.

## Sailfin Molly, *Poecilia velifera*

DISTRIBUTION: Central America: Mexico.

HABITAT: Coastal (sometimes brackish) waters.

DESCRIPTION: Impressive 15 cm (6") long fish, but prime quality (with a high 'sail fin') specimens are not too common. Males can be recognized by their very high dorsal fin (18 to 19 rays), without having to look at the gonopodium. The males' threat displays, by raising the dorsal fin, are amazing, especially since the males tend to be aggressive towards one another. For a school of these fish the tank decor should consist of hardy plants, with roots and some rocks, as well as lots of swimming space. Not very easy to breed; inquiries need to be made in regard to the salt requirements in the water (often 2 to 3 g/l are added). Those brackish water fishes are not easy to find tankmates for.

TEMP: 24-28°C, pH: 7.5 to 8.5, HARDNESS: hard (25 to 35°DH).

FOOD & FEEDING: Herbivore: dry foods, algae, soaked oats and other vegetable supplements, live foods.

## Swordtail, *Xiphophorus helleri*

DISTRIBUTION: Central America: Mexico, Guatemala.

HABITAT: Rivers and streams.

DESCRIPTION: 12 to 15 cm (6") maximum length; occurs in many varieties and colors, most obtained through selective breeding of particular genetic mutants.

Very active schooling fish; some males are aggressive towards each other. Swordtails do particularly well in a tank with dense planting, but leaving sufficient swimming room; they make excellent community tank fish, with a preference for the middle water zone. Breeding is easy.

TEMP: 24-28°C, pH: 7 to 8.3, HARDNESS: medium to hard (12 to 30°DH); salt supplements to be avoided.

FOOD & FEEDING: Omnivore: live foods, dry foods, algae, vegetable supplements.

## Platy, *Xiphophorus maculatus*

DISTRIBUTION: Eastern Central America.

HABITAT: Lowland rivers and streams.

DESCRIPTION: The males of this highly variable species reach a maximum size of only about 3.5 cm; females grow to 6 cm. A peaceful and hardy fish which tends to frequent the middle water layers, preferably underneath floating plants (= hiding places for the young) and among solitary plants as well as plant thickets. There must be sufficient swimming room for these active fish. A good community tank fish; the red color varieties provide for a beautiful contrast to other fish species.

Right: "Tuxedo" swordtail, a variety of *Xiphophorus helleri.*

Below: Red variety of the swordtail, Xiphophorus helleri (female above, male below).

Left: A male so-called "green" swordtail, Xiphophorus helleri (natural form).

TEMP: 24-28°C, pH: 7 to 8.2, HARDNESS: medium to hard (10 to 25°DH); must not be kept in soft water or with salt supplement.

FOOD & FEEDING: Omnivore: dry foods, live foods, algae, vegetable supplements.

**Variatus Platy, *Xiphophorus variatus***

DISTRIBUTION: Central America, southern Mexico.

HABITAT: Shallow water; standing water regions in streams and rivers.

DESCRIPTION: This is another peaceful, hardy and active livebearer which also has been commercially bred in different color varieties. Maximum size 6 to 7 cm. A very active fish needs sufficient swimming room in a tank with dense plant growth. Breeding is easy.

Above: Wagtail platys.

Above: Tuxedo platys.

Below: Parrot platy with
Simpson dorsal fin.

*Right:*
Marigold
platys.

This species is an excellent algae eater and a good community tank fish. It tends to prefer the middle to upper regions in an aquarium.

TEMP: 24-28°C, pH: 7 to 8.3, HARDNESS: medium to hard (15 to 30°DH); can be kept at lower temperature provided the fish are slowly acclimated to the unheated tank.

FOOD & FEEDING: Omnivore: algae, dry foods, live foods.

## HALFBEAKS

The members of the family Hemirhamphidae, commonly called halfbeaks, are also livebearers, but are not related to the live-bearing tooth carps.

Halfbeaks occur only in Southeast Asia, where they live in small waters, usually just below the surface. They are characterized by a "half beak," a shape of the mouth where the lower jaw extends far beyond the short upper jaw. Moreover, the mouth is superior in location and facilitates catching mosquito larvae and flying insects.

In this group the anal fin of the male has also been transformed into a copulatory organ, which permits internal fertilization. In halfbeaks this organ is called an *andropodium*.

A species-correct diet and successful breeding requires the maintenance of a fruit fly (*Drosophila*) food culture, since only such small food insects are sufficiently nutrient-rich to assure proper growth of the young.

129

# OTHER AQUARIUM INHABITANTS

Snails are generally uninvited, annoying guests in our aquariums, but there is one species which, due to its size and interesting mode of reproduction, is actually recommended for an aquarium. Here we are talking about the Apple Snail (*Ampullaria* spec.). It reaches the size of an apple, and so is easily seen in the tank should the population get too large.

Apple snails are excellent for eating leftover food, but when this is not available it may occasionally attack the plants. As air breathers they possess an approximately 5 cm (2") long respiratory tube, that is extended above the surface for breathing air. They deposit a grape-cluster-like clutch of eggs outside the water (tank cover glass). After a development period of a few weeks the fully developed young simply fall into the water and can then easily be raised with flake food. Surplus snails can be given away to aquarist acquaintances or pet shops.

In recent times freshwater shrimp have been available from aquarium and pet shops. They, too, are easy to keep and are useful for eating leftover food. The actual feeding mechanism of *Atyopsis* spec. is particularly interesting. With an extended fan-shaped "hand" it sifts food particles out of the water. Cichlids and very active fishes should not be kept together with apple snails and freshwater shrimp.

## Halfbeak, *Dermogenys* spec.

DISTRIBUTION: Southeast Asia: Malay Peninsula, Thailand, Singapore, Indonesia.

HABITAT: Shallow, flowing waters close to the coast, sometimes in brackish water.

DESCRIPTION: Generally rather aggressive toward

*Dermogenys pusillus.* Photo by Mark Smith.

siblings; males often fight with severe consequences; maximum size about 7 cm (3"). This fish is best kept in a large tank with floating plants and large underwater plants reaching the surface; also in shallow 20 cm (8") high tanks with a gravel or sand bottom. Newly introduced specimens tend to frighten easily,

Marigold platys.

Apple snail with extended breathing tube.

and with panic flights through the tank there is great danger that the 'beak' gets damaged. Therefore, during the acclimatization stage all sides of the tank are covered with cloth in a curtain-type fashion, or the inside glass is permitted to get covered in algal growth. Very capable jumpers, and so the tank must be tightly covered, unless the water level is severely reduced. Breeding is not easy. It would be desirable if aquarists would devote more time to breeding this species, irrespective of the efforts involved in getting the right live foods. This is an interesting species, which can also be kept in a community tank.

Glass shrimp are ideal leftover eaters for aquaria with peaceful fishes.

TEMP: 24-28°C, pH: 7 to 8, HARDNESS: up to 10°DH; at least during acclimatization 2 to 3 teaspoons of sea salt per 10 liters (2½ gallons) of water can be added.

FOOD & FEEDING: Carnivore: live foods plus *Drosophila* and other small flies as well as other small insects, also dry foods. Occasionally food animals should be covered with vitamin preparations in an oily solution or plant oils with multiple unsaturated fatty acids.

# CICHLIDS

With more than 160 genera containing more than 1500 species the family Cichlidae is one of the largest and at the same time one of the most diverse of fish families. In many genera there is only a single species, which means that the genus is monotypic. Asia has only a single cichlid genus, the focal points of distribution being located in Africa, as well as Central and South America.

The body shapes are highly variable but generally from elongated to deep, thin bodies. By far the majority of species can be considered as having the typical fish shape. The dorsal fin consists of two parts; the anterior one is supported by spines and the posterior one by soft rays.

This, in terms of biological development, highly adaptable fish group, has invaded the most diverse habitats. Cichlids can be even be found in extreme habitats. For details about this, please refer to the most complete cichlid book: *TS-190 Lexicon of Cichlids* by Dr. Herbert R. Axelrod.

Maximum sizes among cichlids in the wild vary from 5 to 80 cm. Cichlids have also developed vastly different feeding methods; this, together with behavioral diversities has made these fish popular with aquarists around the world. Species identification, particularly at higher (genus and family) level is often confusing, and the systematics of cichlid fishes is constantly being revised.

In order to understand the individual descriptions following below, first a brief explanation about the reproductive strategies of cichlids. One distinguishes the following types of brood care: *OPEN BROODER*, which attach their large numbers of small, oval-shaped eggs at one of the long ends, to various substrates. *SECRETIVE BROODERS*, on the other hand, hide their eggs either in caves (*cave brooders*) or in their own mouth *(mouthbrooders)*. Cave brooders with medium-sized eggs produce clutches which have fewer eggs than open brooders. Mouthbrooders have even larger, but fewer, eggs than cave brooders. Obviously nature reduces the number of progeny commensurate with the greater protection given to the eggs.

Beyond that, the following five types of "families" are recognized among cichlids:

In the *PARENT FAMILY* both male and female share the brood caring tasks, and both parents will herd their young once they are free swimming.

In the *PATERNAL-MATERNAL FAMILY* (father-mother family), the female takes on the brood care, while the male defends the territory and is only indirectly involved in looking after his progeny. In polygamous species, that is, where a male always has several females with progeny, one can further distinguish the *'man-mother'* family. In this situation the male has to defend a sort of super territory, which is made up of the individual brood territories of the females.

The *MATERNAL FAMILY* ( mother family) occurs only among mouthbrooding cichlids. Here the male has no role as a defender of a territory, nor does he get involved in any aspect of the brood care.

Finally, there is (presumedly only in one cichlid species NOT listed here) the extreme of a *PATERNAL FAMILY* (father family), where solely the male takes on the role of a mouthbrooder. Mouthbrooding is found in many fishes.

### African Butterfly Cichlid, *Anomalochromis thomasi*
DISTRIBUTION: Africa: Sierra Leone.

HABITAT: Clear streams and smaller, clear rivers.

DESCRIPTION: This small and peaceful cichlid grows to maximum size of 8 to 10 (4") cm; it tends to frequent the middle to lower regions of the aquarium. The ideal set-up is a relatively dark tank with open areas of gravel bottom as well as dense stands of water plants and some caves made up of rocks and roots. But there must also be sufficient open swimming space, and then breeding is quite possible. Reproduction is as a mouthbrooder within a typical parent family setting. Can be kept together with surface fishes.

TEMP: 24-28°C, pH: 6 to 7.5 (up to 6.5), HARDNESS: soft to medium hard (soft).

FOOD & FEEDING: Omnivore: live foods, dry foods.

### Agassiz's Dwarf Cichlid, *Apistogramma agassizii*
DISTRIBUTION: South America: Paraguay, Parana, Amazon.

HABITAT: Shallow water regions with barely perceptible flow, where the bottom is covered with dead leaves and small branches.

**Above:** *Anomalochromis thomasi*
**Below:** *Apistogramma agassizi*

Apistogramma cacatuoides

Cichlasoma meeki

Biotodoma cupido

Cichlasoma nigrofasciatum

DESCRIPTION: An attractive, peaceful cichlid, with a maximum length of 8 to 10 cm (4"), which is considered to be somewhat sensitive, especially to chemicals. This species establishes a territory close to the bottom not far from open swimming space, in tanks which are densely planted and have adequate hiding places (wood, rocks, etc.). In males, the tail is drawn out lancet-like; in females it is rounded off. Three color strains are recognized; blue-white, yellow, and red. This is a typical cave brooder, which needs a dark tank for successful breeding. The young are not easy to rear and are looked after in a man-mother family setting. Can easily be kept together with schooling surface fishes.

TEMP: 24-28°C, pH: 5 to 6.8 (up to 6), HARDNESS: up to 10°DH (very soft); frequent partial water changes, PEAT MOSS FILTRATION.

FOOD & FEEDING: Omnivore: live foods, dry foods.

Cockatoo Dwarf Cichlid, *Apistogramma cacatuoides*

DISTRIBUTION: South America: Peru, Amazon Basin.

HABITAT: Shallow, clear and white water in small side arms of rivers.

DESCRIPTION: An attractive dwarf cichlid, with males reaching a maximum size of 8 to 9 cm, and females up to about 5 cm (2") body length. Males with an extended, drawn-out dorsal fin, a feature absent in females. Has been bred in various color varieties, so that the spots in the dorsal and tail fin of some males, for instance, may be fire red with black margins. Should be kept in tank with dispersed plant thickets and a dark bottom of small gravel or sand; adequate hiding places (rocks, roots) must also be provided. Progeny are virtually guaranteed when one male is kept together with several females; will deposit its eggs in a cave (cave brooder) within parent family setting; female engages in brood care.

TEMP: 24-28°C (26-30°F), pH: about 7 (depending on origin of specimens: neutral to slightly alkaline), HARDNESS: soft to medium hard (to 10°DH); optimum water quality must be maintained.

FOOD & FEEDING: Carnivore: live foods.

## Dwarf Cupid Cichlid, *Biotodoma cupido*

DISTRIBUTION: South America: western Guyana, central Amazon.

HABITAT: Flowing waters.

DESCRIPTION: Maximum length about 13 cm (5"); aggressive and actively digging, tends to frequent lower and middle tank regions. External sex characteristics are vague; the more colorful males display a shiny band underneath the eye. The tank (species or community tank with larger catfishes or other medium size fishes) should consist of rocky background with caves and crevices, soft sand, some pebbles, a few rocks and roots toward the front of the tank; some robust plants along the sides. Open spawner, with the eggs being deposited in a depression. The young, when free-swimming, will be led through the tank within a parent family setting.

TEMP: 24-28°C, pH: 6 to 7.5 (about 7), HARDNESS: soft to hard (about 10°DH); hardy with proper care.

FOOD & FEEDING: Carnivore: live foods, also worms and dry food supplements.

## Firemouth Cichlid, *Cichlasoma (Thorichthys) meeki*

DISTRIBUTION: Central America: Mexico (Yucatan), Guatemala.

HABITAT: Along river banks in shallow water areas, among submerged wood and rocks.

DESCRIPTION: Maximum length about 14 to 15 cm (6"); should be kept in pairs only. The (usually smaller) female has less intense coloration. A hardy fish, which is probably among the most attractive of American cichlids. It remains mostly in the lower tank region. Breeding is considered to be easy (open spawner, parent family). The tank must have a thick layer of clean sand, hiding places consisting of rocks and roots, as well as plants along the sides and back (roots to be protected by rocks against the burrowing activities of this species). The territorial firemouth cichlid can be kept together with other robust fishes in a large tank. Really dangerous attacks on other tank occupants are rare, but smaller sibling specimens will be pursued.

TEMP: 24-28°C, pH: 6.5 to 8.5 (about 7), HARDNESS: soft to very hard (to 10°DH); sufficient swimming space must be provided.

FOOD & FEEDING: Omnivore: live foods, worms,

**A fish with a house of its own!**

**Top:**
*Julidochromis marlieri*
**Left:**
*Julidochromis ornatus.*

dry foods.

## Zebra Cichlid, *Cichlasoma nigrofasciatum*

DISTRIBUTION: Central America: Panama to Mexico.

HABITAT: Different habitats.

DESCRIPTION: An aggressive, incompatible, plant-eating cichlid of 10 to 15 cm (6") length; should be kept in pairs in a species tank. In a large tank this fish must have caves and hiding places made of heavy rocks and roots to provide suitable spawning sites (cave brooder!). Normally the young are raised in a father-mother family setting, but this behavior is prone to problems. Color deviations and size disparities are common. The larger, but less colorful males have more extended median fins and a steeper sloping forehead.

TEMP: 24-28°C, pH: 7 to 8.5, HARDNESS: medium to very hard; undemanding species.

FOOD & FEEDING: Omnivore: dry foods, live foods plus worms, small fishes, lettuce and oats.

## Checkerboard Cichlid, *Julidochromis marlieri*

DISTRIBUTION: Africa: Lake Tanganyika.

HABITAT: Rocky shoreline.

DESCRIPTION: A slender cichlid, reaching a maximum length of about 15 cm. Marked with an attrac-

Laetacara dorsigera

Melanochromis auratus

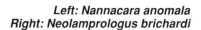
Left: Nannacara anomala
Right: Neolamprologus brichardi

tive checkerboard pattern, this species tends to be aggressive toward sibling specimens. In small tanks should be kept in pairs only; a number of specimens can be kept in large tanks with suitable hiding places. Incompatible pairs must be separated, otherwise serious injuries and mortalities may occur. This species is difficult to sex on the basis of external characteristics, since genital papillae are visible only in (usually larger) females ready to spawn. Possible hybridization between this species and the related *J. ornatus* should be avoided. This is a cave brooder with a parent family situation, and so the tank must have appropriate hiding places (rock structures with caves and other recesses).

TEMP: 24-28°C, pH: 7.5 to 9, HARDNESS: medium hard (about 12°DH); aquarium can have plants.

FOOD & FEEDING: Omnivore: live foods, dry foods.

**Banded or Yellow Slender Cichlid, *Julidochromis ornatus***

DISTRIBUTION: Africa: Lake Tanganyika.

HABITAT: Gently sloping rocky shore areas.

DISTRIBUTION: Territorial, often incompatible with siblings, tends to prefer the lower and middle tank region. When kept in pairs in a rocky (theme) tank other fish can be added. Optimal tank set-up includes adequate swimming spaces among partially dense plant thickets of hardy plants, rocky caves, roots and other hiding places. Cave brooder with parental family behavior; prolonged brood care of the young, supported by strong territorial behavior.

TEMP: 24-28°C, pH: 7.5 to 9 (8 to 9), HARDNESS: medium to hard (11 to 20°DH); roots do not occur in the natural habitat of this species; planting possible.

FOOD & FEEDING: Omnivore: live foods, worms, dry foods, lettuce.

**Red-breasted Cichlid, *Laetacara dorsigera***

DISTRIBUTION: South America: border region between Bolivia and Brazil.

HABITAT: Gently flowing water in bays and along river banks in the Amazon region.

DESCRIPTION: Not only peaceful, but almost retiring and somewhat shy cichlid species with a maximum length of 8 cm (3") for males and only 6 cm for females. This species can undergo dramatic color changes to an intense red-black. The dark dorsal spot, often considered to be characteristic for males, sometimes occurs in both sexes, but the male has longer pelvic fins. Tank set-up to include a dark mixture of fine-grained gravel and sand, supplemented by rock, roots and plant hiding places, but leaving sufficient swimming room. Can be kept together with other small cichlids (e.g. *Apistogramma* species), some large tetras or livebearers. The water quality parameters given below, together with a flat spawning substrate provide the correct breeding prerequisites (open spawner with parental family behavior). The newly hatched progeny are frequently moved around.

TEMP: 24-28°C, pH: about 7 (6.5), HARDNESS: to 20°DH (softer); regular water changes.

FOOD & FEEDING: Omnivore: live foods, dry foods.

### Golden Cichlid, *Melanochromis auratus*
DISTRIBUTION: Africa: Lake Malawi.

HABITAT: Rocky coastline, along bottom sediments.

DESCRIPTION: The males of this impressive looking species reach a maximum length of 12 cm (5"), while the females grow only to 9 cm. Males are also characterized by a black abdomen, while the female's abdomen is yellow-white. This is an active, somewhat incompatible cichlid, which is best kept at a ratio of one male with several females, together with other species from the same habitat in a species-tank. It should be set up as a rocky tank, with some rock caves and stone structures behind a few robust plants, and so have as many hiding places as possible. Mouthbrooder with maternal family structure; the young are led through the tank for another week or so after release from the female's mouth.

TEMP: 24-28°C, pH: 7 to 8.5 ( 7.5 to 8.5), HARDNESS: medium to hard (10 to 15°DH); not a community tank fish.

FOOD & FEEDING: Limnivore (omnivore): live foods, worms, algae (including blue-green algae), lettuce, dry foods for captive-bred specimens after having become accustomed to it.

### Banded or Shiny Dwarf Cichlid, *Nannacara anomala*
DISTRIBUTION: South America: western Guyana.

HABITAT: Small streams or residual bodies of water from large rivers or swamp regions.

DESCRIPTION: Maximum length 8 to 9 cm for males and only up to 5 cm (2") for females; subject to intense color changes with changes in prevailing mood to an extreme pattern of contrasting vertical and horizontal bands. Peaceful cichlid of the lower and middle tank region. In an adequately planted tank this hardy species can be kept together with other fish which are not too large and aggressive. Eggs are often deposited in inaccessible locations (cave

brooder); female will provide brood care and guard territory (maternal family).

TEMP: 24-28°C, pH: 6 to 7.5 (to 6.8), HARDNESS: soft to hard (to 10°DH); does not dig.

FOOD & FEEDING: Carnivore: live foods, reluctant to take dry foods.

### Princess of Burundi, *Neolamprologus brichardi*
DISTRIBUTION: Africa: Lake Tanganyika.

HABITAT: Rocky bottom areas with sediments with 2 to 3 m open water above it.

DESCRIPTION: The group of fork-tailed cichlids contains many similar-looking species. This 8 cm long 'Princess of Burundi' and the related 10 cm (4") long 'Prince of Burundi' are best kept in pairs only in a rocky theme tank with lots of hiding places. Caves and other rocky structures should be placed toward the back of the tank so that there is sufficient swimming room in the front half of the tank. Sexes are difficult to distinguish; often the dorsal fin of the male is more drawn out into a point. This cave brooder deposits its eggs in crevices between rocks (parent family). When the parents spawn again the previous, growing young will be left in peace.

TEMP: 24-28°C, pH: 7.5 to 9, HARDNESS: medium to hard (10 to 12°DH); tank can be planted.

FOOD & FEEDING: Omnivore: live foods, dry foods.

### Butterfly Cichlid, *Microgeophagus ramirezi*
DISTRIBUTION: South America: Venezuela, Colombia.

HABITAT: Small, clear streams with lake-like expansions, in 'oases' of the savanna country (llanos).

DESCRIPTION: In the wild this species seems to reach a maximum length of about 5 to 6 cm (2"); captive (selective) breeding in Asiatic aquaculture facilities has raised the maximum length. Those facilities have also produced many colorful varieties, but unfortunately brood care in those specimens has been severely disrupted or is lost altogether. It is not easy to distinguish the sexes, although in males the first dorsal fin ray tends to be somewhat longer and fin membranes are overall larger than in the slightly smaller females. The females

*Microgeophagus ramirezi*

*Pelvicachromis pulcher*

*Pelvicachromis taeniatus*

**Above: *Pseudotropheus lombardoi* (female)**
**Above: *Pseudotropheus lombardoi* (male)**

have a red abdominal region when sexually mature. This species is best kept in pairs in a densely planted, shaded aquarium, with rocky caves and similar hiding places. This should structure the tank layout into rest and protection zones with swimming space between them. Sensitive to chemicals, sudden transfers and to any stress in general (poor tank layout). Unfortunately, the longevity of this species is rather short. Open brooder with a parental family.

TEMP: 24-28°C, pH: acidic (6 to 6.5), HARDNESS: to 10°DH (very soft, in the wild below 1°DH and 1°KH); frequent, large water changes; peat moss filtration.

FOOD & FEEDING: Omnivore: small live foods, dry foods.

### Krib, *Pelvicachromis pulcher*

DISTRIBUTION: Africa: southern Nigeria.

HABITAT: Shallow areas in slow-flowing waters; also ventures into brackish water.

DESCRIPTION: Rather compatible, quite attractive cichlid with a maximum length of 10 cm (4"). Should be kept in pairs; tends to frequent more the bottom than the middle water regions of a tank. The smaller, often more colorful females (during courtship) have dorsal and anal fins that are not drawn out into points, as those in males. Cave brooder with a father-mother family courtship behavior. This species likes to dig in coarse gravel, but without damaging the dense planting adjacent to the open swimming space. This cichlid needs hiding places and caves made up of rocks and roots; can be kept together with schooling fishes of the upper tank regions. The dorsal fin of the female often has a magnificent, metallic sheen.

TEMP: 24-28°C, pH: 6 to 7 (to 6.5), HARDNESS: soft to hard (8 to 12°DH); usually spawns on the roof of a cave.

FOOD & FEEDING: Omnivore: live foods, dry foods.

### Striped Kribensis, *Pelvicachromis taeniatus*

DISTRIBUTION: Africa: southeastern Nigeria, Cameroon.

HABITAT: Along the banks of clear rivers; tends to venture into brackish water.

DESCRIPTION: Maximum length of the more attractive female is about 7 cm (3"). The males with a more angular tail and dorsal and anal fins drawn out and terminating in a point, reach a maximum length of about 9 cm. Although peaceful even towards siblings, this fish is best kept in pairs only. It forms a territory in the lower and middle aquarium regions, and becomes somewhat more aggressive during the breeding season. In a relatively dark tank with dense planting, caves and various other hiding places made up out of rocks and roots, there should also be sufficient open swimming space above fine sand as a bottom substrate. This species likes to dig, but without damaging the plants. Can easily be kept together with a school of surface fish. This is a cave brooder with a father - mother family set up. There are different color varieties, some natural as well as some due to selective (captive) breeding.

TEMP: 24-28°C, pH: 6.2 to 6.8, HARDNESS: 5 to 10°DH; slight current should be provided.

FOOD & FEEDING: Omnivore: live foods, dry foods.

### Sky-blue Malawi Cichlid, *Pseudotropheus lombardoi*

DISTRIBUTION: Africa: Lake Malawi.

HABITAT: Rubble, rocky areas.

DESCRIPTION: Bright yellow males with egg spots

*Pterophyllum scalare*

**Above: Royal blue (right) and brown discus**

**Below: Royal blue X turquoise discus**

on the anal fin and sky-blue females with six black vertical bands; maximum length about 15 cm (6"). Intra-specifically rather aggressive (even the females) and territorial in all tank regions. Can be kept together with other species in very large tanks where there is sufficient flight space and enough hiding places for the companion species. This tends to divert the intra-specific aggression. The desired tank decor should consist of a rocky back wall with many crevices as hiding places; rock structure in front of that should provide additional caves, which this mouthbrooder (mother family) likes to use. This species sometimes nibbles on plants, so that only hardy, tough plants should be used in such a tank. Always keep one male together with several females.

TEMP: 24-28°C, pH: about 8, HARDNESS: medium to hard (10 to 20°DH); tank decor without plants is species-correct.

FOOD & FEEDING: Limnivore (omnivore): dry foods, live foods, fish and crustacean meats.

**Angelfish, *Pterophyllum scalare***

DISTRIBUTION: South America: Amazon River.

HABITAT: Deep, standing or gently flowing river sections.

DESCRIPTION: Peaceful schooling fish, which forms territories during the breeding season. This attractive fish occurs in various color and veiltail varieties. Outside the breeding season there are no reliable external sex differences. Many of the captive-bred varieties have degenerated and no longer display the species-specific brood care of the parent family. Can be kept together with other quiet fish which are not too small (neon tetras will be eaten!) provided tanks in

excess of 50 cm (20") height are used. When given lots of swimming space, surrounded by *Vallisneria* and large-leafed plants, together with submerged drift wood (roots) and subdued lighting, this 15 cm (6") long open brooder will readily spawn.

TEMP: 24-28°C, pH: 5.5 to 7.5 (to 6.5), HARDNESS: soft to medium hard (about 5°DH); will not do well when kept too cold.

FOOD & FEEDING: Omnivore: live foods, dry foods, some vegetable supplement such as lettuce; tends to over-feed!

**Brown Discus, *Symphysodon aequifasciatus axelrodi***

DISTRIBUTION: South America: clear and white waters throughout Amazonia.

HABITAT: Calm, deep clear and white waters.

DESCRIPTION: A majestic cichlid, which is conspicuous, especially when kept in a school, because of its shape. It is durable, but because of its requirements, it is not a fish for beginners. With a maximum size of 15 to 20 cm (8") it requires a minimum tank height of 50 cm (20") and dense peripheral planting with large leafy plants, lots of swimming space, submerged drift

*Tropheus duboisi*

wood and free-standing solitary plants, in order to facilitate species-correct maintenance. A species tank is the correct accommodation for this fish, where this open spawner (usually on flat, vertical substrates) breeds in a parent family. The discus feeds its young with a skin secretion formed along the dorsal region and which is 'grazed off' by the young for at least 10 days after hatching.

TEMP: 24-28°C, pH: 5 to 7.5 (5.5 to 6.5), HARDNESS: to 10°DH (very soft, 1 to 3°DH); peat moss filtration, frequent partial water changes.

FOOD & FEEDING: Carnivore: must be given a variable diet; live foods, special dry foods.

### Duboisi, *Tropheus duboisi*
DISTRIBUTION: Africa: Lake Tanganyika, coastal strip in the northwest, as well as along the central coast of the lake.

HABITAT: Sediment-free rocky zones in 3 to 15 m (50')depth.

DESCRIPTION: In this 12 cm (5") long cichlid there are hardly any external sex characteristics; the males are slightly larger and have longer pelvic fins than the females. Adult females often have white spots along their back. Must be kept in a (thematic) rocky species aquarium without plants but with lots of transit caves (two exits!). This species should be kept in pairs in tanks with a medium coarse sand bottom, where they are likely to breed (mouthbrooder, mother family). It is interesting to note here that this species undergoes an age-related color change: only juveniles have white spots on a dark background color, which later disappear. At that time a vertical band develops over the body. This species is closely related to *T. moorii*.

TEMP: 24-28°C, pH: 7.5 to 9 (8.5 to 9), HARDNESS: medium to hard (10 to 12°DH).

FOOD & FEEDING: Limnivore (omnivore): live foods and rich foods, such as algae, lettuce, spinach, soaked oats, are important; tubifex should only be given on occasion, essentially as a choice tidbit.

**One of Gan's high quality turquoise discus varieties. Photo courtesy Gan Aquarium Fish Farm.**

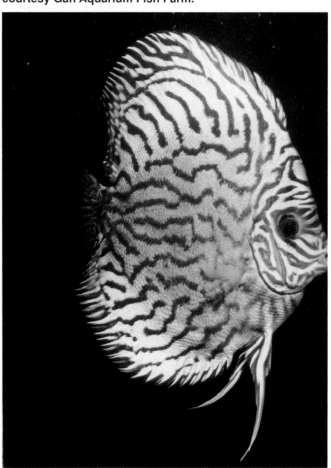

**A vertically striped Gan turquoise discus variety. Photo courtesy Gan Aquarium Fish Farm.**

Brown discus, *Symphysodon aequifasciatus axelrodi.*

# LABYRINTHFISHES

In terms of biogenesis the labyrinthfishes and climbing perches are a relatively young group, which originated only about 50 million years ago. In the wider sense they are included in the perch-like fishes and systematists recognize four different families. The Anabantoidei occur in Africa and Asia. Here we deal only with Asian representatives.

These fishes are characterized by the presence of a biologically very interesting respiratory organ (in addition to having conventional gills), which has given the entire group its name: the *labyrinth*.

Basically it consists of richly vascularized, heavily folded layers of skin and lamellae. This apparatus is located above the gills, inside the head. The labyrinth is supplied with atmospheric air through an active intake at the water surface, which then enables these fishes to utilize atmospheric oxygen.

This then made it possible to invade aquatic habitats which contain hardly any dissolved oxygen. In fact, the labyrinth enabled those fishes which had it, actually to leave the aquatic environment provided they were kept moist. This way extreme habitats such as tiny bodies of water, swampy ponds and flooded rice paddies, even in the very shallow parts, could be conquered by these fishes.

The adaptation of 'air breathing' has proceeded to such an extent that these fishes MUST have access to the water surface. If they had to rely only on gill respiration they would probably suffocate (drown). And there is yet another, inherent danger in this way of respiration, which aquarists must be aware of. If the air above the aquarium's water surface is not the same as that of the water, labyrinthfishes can easily catch a severe cold! Consequently, it is important that the tank is well covered, and then the air will warm up quickly and this danger is eliminated. So that the air is not too humid, there should be a few ventilation slots in the tank cover.

Most labyrinthfishes engage in intense brood care. Most of them build a bubblenest, made of mucus-coated air bubbles which float at the surface. Once the mucus dries up, a rather stable structure remains, which often has additional rigidity due to (partially) built-in floating plants. The eggs are taken to this nest and are guarded there until the larvae hatch.

Other types of brood care or even total absence of care for the young are also represented within this group of fishes.

For instance, the 70 cm giant goramy (widely used as a food fish in Southeast Asia) does not build a bub-

**Above:** Wild form of the Siamese fighting fish.

**Below:** Male long-finned fighting fish variety at his nest.

**Above:** *Colisa labiosa.*

**Below:** *Colisa lalia.*

A dwarf gourami (*Colisa lalia*) strain called the "peacock dwarf gourami." Photo by Aqua Press Piednoir.

blenest at all, but instead constructs from plant parts a large, concave structure at the surface, which resembles a giant, upside-down bird's nest. Inside floating eggs develop into larvae.

### Siamese Fighting Fish, *Betta splendens*

DISTRIBUTION: Asia: widely distributed in central and western Thailand (veiltail forms of the short-finned wild fighting fish).

HABITAT: Rice paddies, ditches, swamps.

DESCRIPTION: Only ONE male (recognizable by its beautiful coloration and well-developed finnage) per tank! Otherwise males tend to fight severely and often with fatal consequences, after some interesting threat behavior. The initial threat phase, with spread gill covers and maximum fin display, is followed by lashing with body and fins and proceeds into direct, close combat with biting and tearing until complete exhaustion and severe injuries take their toll.

The inconspicuous female develops a white genital papillae when ready to spawn. A typical fighting fish aquarium is characterized by several dense groups of underwater plants and floating plants at the surface. Keeping in mind the above prerequisites, the fighting fish is a good community tank fish in the company of peaceful species which do not nibble on fins. This species is easy to breed (bubblenest with father family). Keeping males in tiny containers of less than 1 liter volume is animal cruelty!

TEMP: 24-28°C, pH: 6 to 7.5, Hardness: soft to hard (to 25°DH); water movements must be avoided during breeding since the bubble nest is rather fragile!

FOOD & FEEDING: Omnivore: live foods, dry foods.

### Thick-lipped Gourami, *Colisa labiosa*

DISTRIBUTION: Asia: Burma, Bangladesh

HABITAT: Small and very small bodies of water.

DESCRIPTION: This peaceful labyrinthfish grows to a maximum length of 9 to 10 cm (4"), and is ideally suited for a community tank. Breeding of this bubblenest builder (father family) is best done in a species tank. In both instances, there should be floating plants, a dark bottom and generally subdued lighting with stands of low-growing underwater plants. This species prefers the upper and middle regions. Males have a drawn-out (to a point) dorsal fin.

TEMP: 24-28°C, pH: 6 to 7.5 (slightly acidic), HARDNESS: 4 to 10°DH.

The normal male dwarf gourami (*Colisa lalia*) is very colorful in its own right. Photo by Aqua Press Piednoir.

A female dwarf gourami of the peacock strain. She has developed some very bright colors herself, which is very unusual in females. Photo by Aqua Press Piednoir.

Compare this male with the "normal" male on the opposite page and you can see what some selective breeding has accomplished. Photo by Aqua Press Piednoir.

*Helostoma temmincki*

FOOD & FEEDING: Omnivore: dry foods, live foods.

**Dwarf Gourami, *Colisa lalia***
DISTRIBUTION: Asia: northern India, Bangladesh.
HABITAT: Rivers, also in river deltas and flood plains; canals with plants.
DESCRIPTION: A very attractive and peaceful fish which reaches a maximum length of 6 cm. The colorful males have extended dorsal and anal fins which terminate in a point. The females are silvery gray. This fish tends to prefer the middle or upper water layers, among plants and below floating plants. Submerged driftwood can be used in tank decor. This fish can easily be kept together with bottom-dwellers or peaceful schooling fish. The brood-caring father fish is considered to be a meticulous bubblenest builder; plant parts are often integrated in the nest structure. With

*Colisa chuna*

good water quality controls easy to breed.
TEMP: 24-28°C, pH: 6 to 7.5, HARDNESS: soft to medium; sensitive to disturbances, but regular partial water changes are absolutely essential.

FOOD & FEEDING: Omnivore: all small live foods and dry foods.

**Honey Gourami, *Colisa chuna***
DISTRIBUTION: Asia: northeastern India, Bangladesh.
HABITAT: Rivers, including river delta regions.
DESCRIPTION: Suppressed males and females have a brownish-gray coloration, periodically with a brown longitudinal band. On the other hand, a dominant male is conspicuous because of his magnificent color contrast. This is basically a shy, reserved fish, but it does establish a territory during the breeding season. Honey gouramies can be kept together with small bottom-dwelling fish. The tank for this species should include many bushy as well as regular plants, floating plants or submersed plants that grow up to the surface. Bubblenest builder (father family), but not easy to breed.
TEMP: 24-28°C, pH: 6 to 7.5, HARDNESS: not too hard (to 15°DH); should be kept relatively dark.
FOOD & FEEDING: Omnivore: small live and dry foods.

**Kissing Gourami, *Helostoma temminckii***
DISTRIBUTION: Asia: Sumatra, Borneo, Thailand, Malaysia.
HABITAT: Swamps and rivers, also found in small lakes.
DESCRIPTION: In its native countries a popular food fish (maximum length 30 cm(12")); captive specimens rarely get larger than 15 to 20 cm(8"). The wild form is green-silvery, but the pink-flesh colored variety is better known. The ideal set-up for this fish includes a large tank (not less than 1 m (40") length for adult specimens) with diverse decor of hardy, strong plants, including floating plants and submerged plants with floating surface leaves. Can be kept together with other labyrinthfishes; kissing gouramies tend to prefer the middle tank regions. Breeding of this open spawner (without a bubblenest and parental brood care) is not easy but can be done in large tanks, provided the fish have reached a size of about 14 cm.
TEMP: 24-28°C, pH: 6 TO 7.5, HARDNESS: soft to hard (soft); requires good filtration.
FOOD & FEEDING: Omnivore: live foods, dry foods, vegetable matter.

**Paradise Fish, *Macropodus opercularis***
DISTRIBUTION: Asia: southern China, Korea, Vietnam, Taiwan.
HABITAT: Ditches, swamps, small and very small streams, rice paddies.
DESCRIPTION: A robust, hardy species which must be considered the Asian pioneer fish for aquarists. Maximum length 10 to 12 cm (5"); can easily be kept in larger tanks. The more colorful male has longer fins. Bright tanks, partially with dense plant cover and floating plants, are ideal for the paradise fish. Tank appearance can be further enhanced with submerged driftwood and growth of *Microsorium*. Should not be

Blue gourami, female on the right

kept together with small, peaceful fishes; only robust species are suitable for that. Breeding is most successful when pairs are kept by themselves; male takes over brood care (father family). Large specimens can be somewhat aggressive.

TEMP: 24-28°C, pH: 6 to 8, HARDNESS: soft to hard.

FOOD & FEEDING: Omnivore: dry foods, live foods.

### Pearl Gourami, *Trichogaster leeri*

DISTRIBUTION: Asia: Malaysia, Sumatra, Borneo

HABITAT: Soft, acid, slow-flowing, often semi-dark, shallow waters.

DESCRIPTION: This labyrinthfish reaches a maximum length of about 12 to 15 cm (6"); external sex characteristics become visible once the fish has reached a size of about 8 cm. Males are colored red on the gill, chest and abdominal regions; the dorsal fin is drawn out into a point. This species is very peaceful, almost shy, and seems to do best in a large tank. Prerequisites for successful breeding are subdued lighting (floating plants) and a well-planted tank (include

"Cosby" gourami, the marbled variety of the blue gourami (male).

*Macropodus opercularis*, pair.

*Trichogaster leeri*

bushy plants), so that there are sufficient hiding places. Bubblenest builder; father family. Can be kept together with bottom-dwelling fish of similar, retiring nature.

TEMP: 24-28°C, pH: 5.5 to 7.5 (to 6.5), HARDNESS: 5 to 30°DH (to 4°DH); peat moss filtration until water turns tea-colored.

FOOD & FEEDING: Omnivore: dry foods, live foods.

### Blue Gourami, *Trichogaster trichopterus*

DISTRIBUTION: Asia: Sumatra

HABITAT: Different flowing waters with a weak current and calm bays.

DESCRIPTION: Maximum length 12 cm (5"). *Trichogaster trichopterus sumatranus* is a subspecies of *T. t. trichopterus* from Indonesia and Malaysia (= max.length 15 cm(6")). This fish tends to remain among dense stands of plants and among floating

Fry of *Macropodus ocellatus*
55 hours after spawning. Photo
by Aqua Press Piednoir.

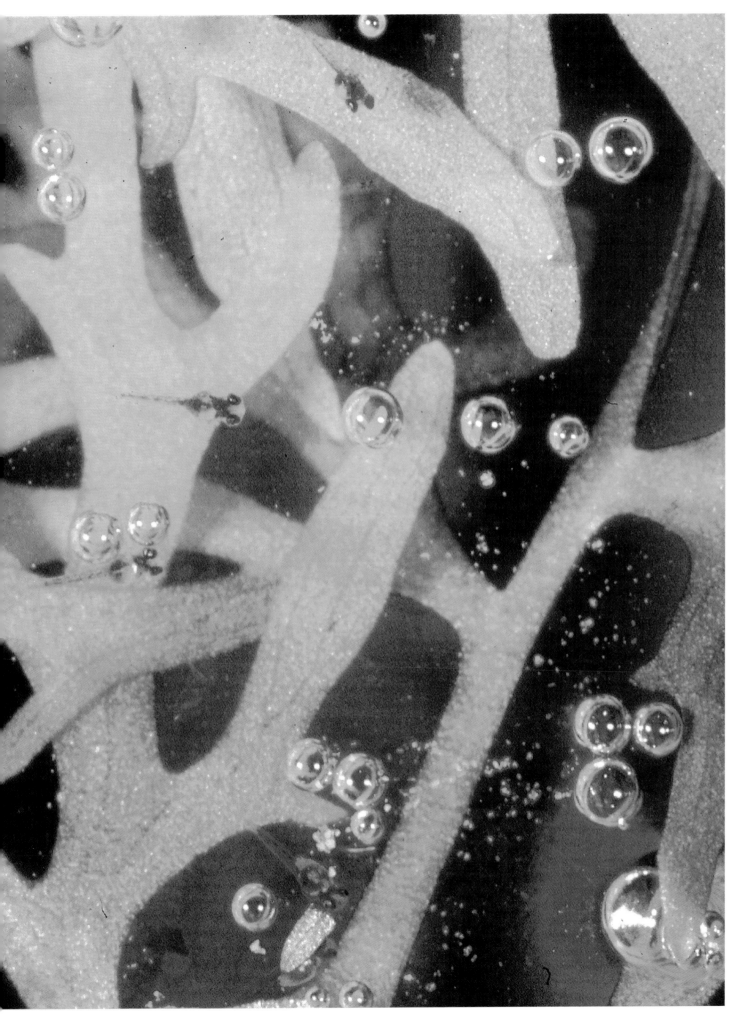

A pair of *Macropodus ocellatus* in breeding colors. Photo by Aqua Press Piednoir.

One of the favorite color varieties of the blue gourami is this gold gourami. Photo by Aqua Press Piednoir.

This individual is closer to the normal colors of the blue gourami, *Trichogaster trichopterus*. Photo by Aqua Press Piednoir.

*Bedotia geayi*

*Glossolepis incisus*

plants in the middle to upper water layers in an aquarium. Males have extended dorsal fins (terminating in a point). Marbled and albino varieties are unfortunately not as vital and prolific as the wild form. Breeding is easy; should not be kept together with rough, robust species. It is important to maintain good water quality for optimum breeding results.

TEMP: 24-28°C, pH: 6 to 8 (slightly acidic), HARDNESS: 5 to 35°DH (very soft); older specimens sensitive to transfers.

FOOD & FEEDING: Omnivore: dry foods, live foods, vegetable matter.

## SILVERSIDES (HARDYHEADS) AND RAINBOW FISHES

Although these are two distinctly different families, we would like to discus the Atherinidae (silversides) and the Melanotaeniidae (rainbow fishes) together here. The principal reasons for this are uniformity in body shape,

schooling behavior and basic requirements for a species-correct maintenance.

The vast majority of silversides live (worldwide) in shallow coastal regions of the sea, and there are only a few freshwater representatives. Characteristic for this family are two dorsal fins, which are widely separated from each other.

On the other hand, the distribution of rainbow fishes is rather limited, being confined to Australia, Papua-New Guinea and some of the adjacent island groups, as well as to a lake region in Indonesia. These fishes also have two dorsal fins, but these are closer to each other.

Members of both families usually have an elongated, oval-shaped and laterally compressed body. Full coloration is reached only at full maturity. As typical schooling fish they are happiest when kept in groups. Optimum water quality is essential for the fish not to lose their coloration prematurely.

In terms of breeding, both types of fishes are so-called continuous spawners, i.e. each day of the breeding season a few eggs are laid. Java Moss, bundles of wool threads or artificial fibers are suitable spawning substrates. The spawning substrate or the eggs (removed by hand) should be transferred to a rearing tank (same water quality values as the main tank!). The newly hatched young will take food immediately, but growth is rather slow and rearing the young is not easy.

### Madagascar Rainbow Fish, *Bedotia geayi*

DISTRIBUTION: Madagascar.

HABITAT: Clear mountain streams.

DESCRIPTION: This somewhat delicate species reaches a maximum length of about 15 cm (6"), but it is easy to breed provided the correct water quality conditions are provided. Males are stouter and have a red margin along the dorsal and tail fins. After spawning the eggs are suspended by a tiny thread among plants (arrange small-leafed plants along the sides and back of the tank). Long tanks, to provide good swimming exercise, with a slight current and clear water, conform to the prevailing conditions in the natural habitat of this species. Can be kept together with other peaceful schooling fish which also like a water current.

TEMP: 24-28°C, pH: 7 to 8, HARDNESS: medium to hard (from 10°DH), weekly water change up to 1/3 of total tank volume.

FOOD & FEEDING: Omnivore: live foods, dry foods, vegetable matter.

### Red Rainbow Fish, *Glossolepis incisus*

DISTRIBUTION: Asia: Indonesia.

Boeseman's rainbowfish, *Melanotaenia boesemani*.

HABITAT: Lake Sentani, close to underwater plant thickets.

DESCRIPTION: Males are intensely red and develop an arched back at full maturity (color dependent upon mood and hierachial status). Females are golden yellow-olive; maximum length is about 15 cm (6"). This species displays a distinct sexual dichromatism, similar to cichlids. Somewhat shy and peaceful schooling fish, which tends to frighten easily. Normal coloration commences early, from a length of about 5 cm onward. Breeding is not difficult in a tank with open stands of underwater plants and lots of swimming space.

TEMP: 24-28°C, pH: 7 to 8 ( to 7.5), HARDNESS: medium to hard (18 to 25°DH); Java moss as spawn-

*Iriatherina werneri*

ing substrate.

FOOD & FEEDING: Carnivore: live foods, some dry foods.

### Werner's Rainbow Fish, *Iriatherina werneri*

DISTRIBUTION: Northern Australia, southern Papua-New Guinea.

HABITAT: Small standing or gently flowing waters with plants.

DESCRIPTION: Distinctly elongated fin rays are visible sex characteristics of the males. Maximum size about 5 cm (2"); peaceful schooling fish of the middle aquarium regions. The aquarium for this species is characterized by fine sand as a substrate, lots of swimming space, with peripheral planting, possibly with partial cover by floating plants. Breeding is not easy. This species should be kept in either a species or a community tank with other small fishes or other rainbow fish species, respectively.

TEMP: 24-28°C, pH: 6 to 7.5 (about 7), HARDNESS: soft to medium hard (from about 10°DH), $1/4$ partial water change per week.

FOOD & FEEDING: Omnivore: small live foods, dry foods.

### Boeseman's Rainbow Fish, *Melanotaenia boesemani*

DISTRIBUTION: Indonesia: Lake Ajamaru (Irian Jaya).

HABITAT: Shallow lake regions with plants.

DESCRIPTION: Maximum length about 10 to 14 cm. Males more intensely colored, somewhat larger and with a more arched profile than females. Schooling fish which tends to prefer the middle and upper tank

*Melanotaenia trifasciata*

*Telmatherina ladigesi*

regions. A peaceful species which requires a lot of swimming space. Therefore, only an open, peripheral planting required, which can become denser toward the back of the tank. An excellent community tank fish which likes to jump. Tank with a sandy bottom. Although in nature this species lives in soft and alkaline water of pH 9 to 9.5, the values listed within brackets have proven effective for easy breeding.

TEMP: 24-28°C, pH: 7 to 8.5 (7), HARDNESS: medium to hard (8 to 15°DH); continuous spawner.

FOOD & FEEDING: Omnivore: mainly live foods, dry foods.

### Jewel Rainbow Fish, *Melanotaenia trifasciata*

DISTRIBUTION: Northern Australia.

HABITAT: Diverse river systems.

DESCRIPTION: Depending on original location there are differently colored varieties of this 12 cm (5") long fish, which also may have slightly different requirements in regard to water quality parameters. Ask about this at the time of purchase. A peaceful, active schooling fish, this species tends to frequent the middle of the tank. This should have a dark bottom and peripheral planting, leaving enough swimming room. Breeding this continuous spawner is easy. Should be kept in a species tank or in the company of other rainbow fishes.

TEMP: 24-28°C, pH: 7 to 8, HARDNESS: medium to hard, regular partial water changes required, which also tends to trigger breeding readiness.

FOOD & FEEDING: Omnivore: live foods, dry foods.

### Celebes Rainbow Fish, *Telmatherina ladigesi*

DISTRIBUTION: Southeast Asia: Sulawesi (Celebes).

HABITAT: Streams in the hill country.

DESCRIPTION: Maximum length 7 to 8 cm (3"); males with extended fin rays; peaceful fish of middle water regions of the aquarium. Schooling fish that likes the morning sun, actively courting in the sunshine penetrating the tank surface. The tank should

have dense peripheral planting as well as floating plants. Lots of swimming room in the direction of the longest tank dimension required. A good community tank fish; breeding is relatively easy.

TEMP: 24-28°C, pH: 7 to 8 (7), HARDNESS: medium to hard (from 12°DH); frequent partial water changes and very clear (and clean) water essential.

FOOD & FEEDING: Omnivore: live foods, dry foods.

"It's show time!"

# Suggested Reading

**AQUARIUM FISH**
By U. Erich Friese
**KW-026**
ISBN 0-86622-766-0
UPC 018214-27660-9
Presents sensible, easy-to-follow recommendations about selecting and caring for aquarium fish.
*HC, 5 1/2 x 8", 96 pages, over 50 full color photos.*

**ALL ABOUT AQUARIUMS**
By Earl Schneider
**PS-601**
ISBN 0-86622-805-5
UPC 018214-28055-2
This very practical and useful book makes a splendid first aquisition for any aquarist who would like to learn more about aquariums.
*HC, 5 1/2 x 8", 128 pages, 70 full color photos.*

**YOUR FIRST AQUARIUM**
By Sylvan Cohen
**YF-100**
ISBN 0-86622-057-7
UPC 018214-20577-7
Colorful and easy-to-read, concentrates on providing just the right information.
*SC, 6 x 7 1/4", 32 pages.*

**OUR FIRST AQUARIUM STEP -BY-STEP**
By Anmarie Barrie
**SK-003**
ISBN 0-86622-454-8
UPC 018214-24548-3
Magnificently colorful books feature a completely new design format combining humorous drawings with TFH's use of full color photos.
*SC, 5 1/2 x 8 1/2", 64 pages, over 50 full color photos.*

**THE BIOTOPE AQUARIUM**
By Rainer Stawikowski
**TT-026**
ISBN 0-86622-519-6
UPC 018214-25196-5
This book describes what a biotope aquarium is and why you would want a biotope aquarium. It is a unique wonderfully informative and colorfully illustrated book.
*HC, 7 x 10", 208 pages, over 200 full color photos.*

**AQUARIUMS (Pbk)**
By Wolfgang Ostermuller
**PB-101**
ISBN 0-86622-845-4
UPC 018214-28454-3
The 64 pages of easy-to-read text provide expert practical advice for both beginners and those more advanced.
*SC, 6 1/4 x 8 1/2", 80 pages, 16 full color photos.*

**SETTING UP AN AQUARIUM, COMPLETE INTRO.**
By Jim Kelly
**CO-003S**
ISBN 0-86622-291-X
UPC 018214-80018-7
Highly informative, perfect for beginners and experienced owners.
*SC, 5 1/2 x 8 1/2", 128 pages, 52 full color photos.*

**COMPLETE INTRO TO A COMMUNITY AQUARIUM**
By Dr. Herbert R. Axelrod
**CO-013S**
ISBN 0-86622-283-9
UPC 018214-22839-4
This is a good reading and good looking book which is highly informative for beginners and experienced owners.
*SC, 5 1/2 x 8 1/2", 128 pages, 113 full color photos.*

**AQUARIUMS FOR THOSE WHO CARE**
By Dr. Herbert R. Axelrod
**B-101**
ISBN 0-7938-1375-1
UPC 018214-11375-1
This book contains enjoyable easy-to-read text that serves as a perfect step-by-step guide to aquariums by concentrating on the basics.
*SC, 7 x 8 1/2", 32 pages, over 100 full color photos.*

**STEP-BY-STEP SETTING UP AN AQUARIUM**
By DR. C.W. Emmens
**SK-033**
ISBN 0-86622-961-2
UPC 018214-29612-6
Magnificently colorful books with humorous drawings, color photos and practical easy-to-read text.
*SC, 5 1/2 x 8 1/2", 64 pages, over 50 full color photos.*

**AQUARIUMS FOR YOUR NEW PET**
By Mary Sweeney
**TU-016**
ISBN 0-86622-624-9
UPC 018214-26249-7
This book was scientifically designed to provide the information new hobbyists need and want.
*SC, 7 x 8 1/2", 64 pages.*

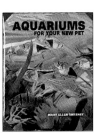

**DR. AXELROD'S ATLAS OF TROPICAL FRESHWATER AQUARIUM FISHES, 8TH ED.**
By Dr. Herbert R. Axelrod
**H-1077**
ISBN 0-7938-0194-X
UPC 018214-21360-4
This is a comprehensive identification guide to aquarium fishes that find their way into world markets.
*HC, 8 1/2 x 11", 1150 pages, 7500 full color photos.*

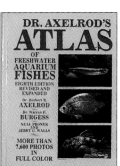

**DR. AXELROD'S MINI ATLAS OF TROPICAL FRESHWATER AQUARIUM FISHES**
By Drs. Herbert R. Axelrod, Warren E. Burgess, and Cliff W. Emmens
**H-1090**
ISBN 0-86622-385-1
UPC 018214-23851-5
The most complete book on aquarium fishes ever published. Includes a full-length section treating up-to-date methods of aquarium fishes and plant care.
*HC, 5 1/2 x 8 1/2", 992 pages, over 2200 full color photos.*

**HANDBOOK OF TROPICAL FISH (REV ED)**
By Drs. Herbert R. Axelrod and Leonard P. Schultz
**PS-663**
ISBN 0-86622-138-7
UPC 018214-21387-1
This catalog of fishes contains ichthyology, the aquarium and its management and plants in the home aquarium.
*HC, 5 1/2 x 8 1/2", 718 pages, 30 full color photos.*

**EXOTIC TROPICAL FISH**
By Axelrod, Vorderwinkler, Emmens, Sculthorpe, Pronek and Burgess
**H-907**
ISBN 0-87666-051-0
UPC 018214-60510-2
This immense work covers not only exotic tropical fishes but exotic aquarium plants, raising tropical fish commercially and aquarium management.
*HC, 5 1/2 x 8 1/2", 868 pages, 704 full color photos.*

**LOOK AND LEARN, BASIC BOOK OF AQUARIUMS, SOFT COVER**
By Dr. Herbert R. Axelrod
**KD-017S**
ISBN 0-7938-0169-9
UPC 018214-10169-7
This delightful book tells you all you need to know about starting and maintaining a freshwater aquarium. Photos of fishes, plants and equipment were selected with beginners needs in mind.
*SC, 7 x 10", 64 pages, 229 full color photos.*

**INNES EXOTIC AQUARIUM 21ST ED.**
By W.T. Innes
**TS-226**
ISBN 0-7938-0098-6
UPC 018214-10098-0
Here is the most recent edition of a true aquarium classic. The book provides a family-by-family treatment of popular aquarium fish species.
*HC, 5 1/2 x 8 1/2", 288 pages, 325 full color photos*

**HOW TO HAVE A SUCCESSFUL AQUARIUM**
By Stephan Dreyer & Rainer Keppler
**TS-225**
ISBN 0-86622-2090-1
UPC 0-18214-12090-2
Book presents in great detail all of the information a new aquarist needs to be able to choose and use the variety of aquarium equipment available to tropical fish hobbyists and also gives sensible, practical advice about selecting and breeding the tank's inhabitants.
*HC, 7 x 10", 192 pages, over 150 full color photos.*

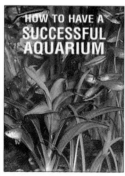

**LOOK AND LEARN BASIC BOOK OF TROPICAL FISH**
By Mary E. Sweeney
**KD-002**
ISBN 0-7938-0071-4
UPC 018214-10071-3
This authoritative book describes the habits, proper care, and interesting facts about fishes that we love to watch, keep and breed as a hobby.
*HC, 7 x 10", 64 pages, 229 full color photos.*

**JURASSIC FISHES**
By Haruto Kodera
**TS-207**
ISBN 0-7938-0086-2
UPC 018214-10086-7
The fishes discussed and shown in this book keep their viewers entertained for hours on end and can't be ignored. This fascinating book covers their ancient lineage and their primitive anatomy and behavior
*HC, 9 1/4 x 12 1/4", 144 pages, 221 full color photos.*

**LOOK AND LEARN BASIC BOOK OF TROPICAL FISH SOFT COVER**
By Mary E. Sweeney
**KD-002S**
ISBN 0-7938-0170-2
UPC 018214-10170-3
This authoritative book describes the habits, proper care, and interesting facts about fishes that we love to watch, keep and breed as a hobby.
*SC, 7 x 10", 64 pages, 236 full color photos.*

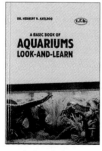

**LOOK AND LEARN, BASIC BOOK OF AQUARIUMS**
By Dr. Herbert R. Axelrod
**KD-017**
ISBN 0-7938-0070-6
UPC 018214-10070-6
This delightful book tells you all you need to know about maintaining a freshwater aquarium. Photos of fishes, plants and equipment are selected with beginners needs in mind.
*HC, 7 x 10", 64 pages, 229 full color photos.*

**THE NATURAL AQUARIUM**
By Satoshi Yoshino and Doshin Kobayashi
**TS-195**
ISBN 0-86622-629-X
UPC 018214-80071-2
Shows and explains how to set up the tank, select the plants and fish to make a natural aquarium.
*HC, 7 x 10", 128 pages over 200 full color photos.*

## t.f.h.

### ESTABLISHED 1952

**TFH PUBLICATIONS, INC.**
One TFH Plaza
Neptune, NJ 07753 • USA

# INDEX

# INDEX

# INDEX